D1716060

The Legacy
Teachings for Life from
the Great Lithuanian Rabbis

MAGGID

Berel Wein
Warren Goldstein

The Legacy

Teachings for Life from
the Great Lithuanian Rabbis

Maggid Books

The Legacy
Teachings for Life from the Great Lithuanian Rabbis

First Edition, 2012

Maggid Books
An imprint of Koren Publishers Jerusalem Ltd.

Gila Fine, Editor in Chief

POB 8531, New Milford, CT 06776-8531, USA
& POB 4044, Jerusalem 91040, Israel
www.korenpub.com

© Berel Wein, Warren Goldstein 2012

The publication of this book was made possible through
the generous support of *Torah Education in Israel*.

ISBN 978 159 264 3622, *hardcover*

A CIP catalogue record for this title is
available from the British Library.

Printed and bound in the United States

In memory of my parents

Yosef Zvi ben Mordecai Halevi Weiss
who passed away on 12 Tishrei, 5754

and Miriam bas Elchanan (Liff) Weiss
who passed away on 29 Adar, 5745

from Antwerp, Belgium

Dedicated by their son Elchanan Weiss,
a graduate of Yeshivas Sha'arei Torah
Suffern, New York

In memory of

Captain Leo V. Berger
Shem Tov ben Yosef

Dedicated by the Leo V. Berger Fund
Harvey Schwartz, President
Sigmund Kassap, Vice President

Dedicated to my Rebbi and Rosh Yeshiva

Rabbi Azriel Chaim Goldfein
of blessed memory

who bequeathed to me and all his students
the inspiring legacy of the great Lithuanian rabbis

Warren Goldstein

שמואל קמנצקי
Rabbi S. Kamenetsky

2018 Upland Way
Philadelphia, PA 19131

Home: 215-473-2798
Study: 215-473-1212

TRANSLATION: RABBI SHMUEL KAMENETSKY'S LETTER

August 29, 2012

To Rabbi Berel Wein שליט"א
and Rabbi Warren Goldstein שליט"א

I have gone over the manuscript of your book *The Legacy* and it finds favor in my eyes; I am Lithuanian and everything in it is true. I had already heard what is brought in the book in the name of the great Gaon Rosh Yeshiva of Ponivezh of blessed memory; also when I visited the city of Johannesburg I found the truth of these words and therefore I have seen the *ba'alei teshuvah* that are there, that they are *bnei aliyah*, people who are raising themselves spiritually and their source and all of their origins that they are the children of those who have come out of Lithuania.

Your hands should be strengthened to express the paths of Hashem, may He be blessed, and I pray that your words will enter the hearts of the Jewish people and they will know and recognize the origins of their families, how far back they reach, that they are the children of Avraham, Yitzchak, and Yaakov.

May this book find favor in the eyes of all who read it. With blessings from the depth of the heart that you will continue to be counted amongst those who bring merit to the multitudes whose righteousness stands forever.

Contents

Introduction

The Gemara describes numerous instances of a rabbi imparting his unique wisdom to his students toward the end of his life.[1] These sages could have simply told their disciples to do all the *mitzvos* and live a full Torah life, but instead they chose to pinpoint just a few concepts.[2] Following this approach, in every era, sages have taught us that we need to focus, in particular, on only a few central Torah values and principles and live by them with sincerity.

Many Torah sages achieved this through ethical wills – letters of guidance, inspiration, and instruction to their children and students. The letter of the Ramban to his son, one of the most famous in Jewish history, is a classic example of emphasis on specific Torah values. The letter could have been just an instruction to his son to do his best to keep all of the 613 *mitzvos*. Yet the Ramban didn't do that: instead, he chose to focus on key values, including humility, equality of all people before God, and fear of Heaven.

---

1. Megillah 27b and 28a.
2. For example, Rabbi Zeira answered his students, "In all my days I did not become angry [at the people] in my home; I did not walk in front of someone greater than me; I did not think [thoughts of Torah] in dirty alleyways; I did not walk four cubits without [learning] Torah and *tefillin*; I did not sleep in the *beis midrash*, neither a substantial sleep nor a nap; I did not rejoice in the downfall of my fellow; I did not call my fellow by a nick name." Ibid., 28a.

The Vilna Gaon wrote to his wife and children when he was about to embark upon a long, arduous, and challenging journey to the Land of Israel. While his objective was to later bring his family and students to join him, he did not know how long he would be away. So he wrote a letter setting out the values that should permeate his home until the family would be reunited. That is what makes it such a fascinating document. In writing a letter of only a few pages, the Vilna Gaon had to evaluate which principles, ideas, thoughts, and moral instructions he would emphasize. He was not forced to do this. He, too, could have instructed that all of the *mitzvos* and values of the Torah were to be carefully observed, because that would have included everything. But like many of our sages, he knew that his disciples and children needed more direction. Among other values, the Vilna Gaon chose to focus on purity of speech, the importance of Torah study, and of pursuing peace in all interactions with others.

Obviously, in the message of focus, our sages were not advocating neglect of even one iota of the myriad details that comprise *halachah*. And they were certainly not advocating indifference to any *mitzvah*, as the Mishnah states, "Be careful with a light *mitzvah* as with a severe one, for you do not know the reward that is given for the *mitzvos*."[3] This is a blunt warning against prioritizing and treating with greater attention the *mitzvos* that appear to be stricter and carry more serious punishments than the *mitzvos* that seem to be less important. Torah is a holistic system that integrates all of its various parts into a whole: no one part can be separated from the system and elevated above the rest.

And yet, our great leaders over the generations have found it appropriate and helpful – indeed necessary – to give instruction, and even rebuke, by spotlighting certain central values and principles, while unequivocally committing to the integrity and binding nature of the entire system of *mitzvos* and *halachah*. In fact, every one of the *sifrei Mussar* is an exercise in focus and emphasis. No book can contain the entirety of all the important principles of philosophy and personal character development necessary to live as a Torah Jew.

One of the great challenges of coming to grips with Torah is that

---

3. Pirkei Avos 2:1.

it is the wisdom of Hashem and therefore unlimited in its breadth and depth. As mere mortals, we are confronted with how to understand it, where to channel our efforts, and how to view specifics in the context of the entire system. Through understanding what *Gedolei Yisrael* (the great sages of Israel) over the ages chose to emphasize, we get a better understanding of Torah itself. We are able to gain perspective and a context for understanding Torah Judaism, as well as a broad map for the direction of our lives. Limitations of the mental and emotional capacity of students, not to mention limitations of space and time, may have led our Torah sages to emphasize certain principles.

On a practical and strategic level, focusing on a few key objectives helps people to achieve success because the objectives are clear. This clarity prevents distraction and confusion and provides a clear framework of eternal principles in a changing world, to inspire strength and commitment.

And that is what this book is about. It is a presentation of a few key values of Torah thought and action, which we believe are crucial for this generation to explore and live by. Especially during times of confusion such as ours, we need to follow the advice of our sages and focus, as individuals and as *Klal Yisrael* (the Jewish people as a whole), on certain key Torah principles and develop them to the full extent that our minds, hearts, and energies will allow.

It is impossible, and it would be arrogant and a breach of basic integrity, for us to put forward our own choices of which central Torah values *Klal Yisrael* should focus upon in this generation. Therefore, we have dared to embark upon such a project based only on the *mesorah* (tradition) that we ourselves received.

In this book, we have sought to construct a virtual "letter" to this generation according to the teachings and worldview of the remarkable Torah sages of Lithuanian Jewry, as we received these teachings from our own *rebbeim* and mentors, *zt"l*, who were the disciples of these sages. Rabbi Berel Wein was a student of Rabbi Chaim Zvi Rubenstein, a student of Volozhin; Rabbi Zev Wein, a student of Rav Shimon Shkop; Rabbi Yisrael Mendel Kaplan, a student of Yeshivos Mir and Baranovitch; Rabbi Mordechai Rogow, a student of Mir; and Rabbi Chaim Kreisworth, a student of Slabodka. Rabbi Warren Goldstein was a student of his late

Rosh Yeshiva and *rebbi*, Rabbi Azriel Chaim Goldfein, who was a student of Rabbi Mordechai Gifter (late *Rosh Yeshiva* of Telz), who himself had learned from Rav Avraham Yitzchak Bloch, who was a student of Rav Yosef Yehudah Lev Bloch, a student of Rabbi Eliezer Gordon, the founder of Telz (from Telshe, Lithuania), who, in turn, was a student of Rav Yisrael Salanter, a student of Rav Zundel Salant, who was a student of Rav Chaim Volozhiner, who was a student of the great Vilna Gaon himself.

We attempted to identify some key Torah principles based on the teachings of these and other distinguished *Roshei Yeshiva* (heads of yeshivas) and rabbis of Lithuanian Jewry from the Vilna Gaon until the destruction of European Jewry in the Holocaust, and the first generation of survivors of that terrible catastrophe. So much of the modern Jewish world has the imprint of their vision and work. The names of the legendary Lithuanian yeshivas – Mir, Ponivezh, Telz, Slabodka, Brisk, and many others – sparkle across the landscape of the Jewish world, with their students teaching and providing leadership to Jews across many continents.

Of course, most of the material is comprised of classic Torah sources from all generations and places. But from our *mesorah*, we have learned to give certain values and mores special emphasis. We have tried to write this book in the spirit of the great *Mussar* Movement, which so permeated the philosophy, strategic vision, and way of life of so many scholars who form the foundation of our *mesorah*. The spirit of the *Mussar* writings is an unlikely combination of the philosophical, practical, psychological, and spiritual. More than anything, the *Mussar* Movement strived to change people, and thereby, change the world, in a profound and exciting way, bringing together thought, emotion, and action. In this spirit, this is a book of ideas and deeds, a book of values and action and of a strategic moral vision for the Jewish People.

It is also a book of history. It provides a glimpse of a society – Lithuanian Jewry – where the *Mussar* Movement was born and which was so deeply influenced by its values. The history is important because it demonstrates how these values were lived and practiced – albeit with human imperfections and vulnerabilities, which are dealt with openly. It also demonstrates that the values and principles highlighted in this book are not merely in the realm of theory and philosophy, but were the actual way of life of a real society and real people.

Of course, *Klal Yisrael* has been blessed with many noble and illustrious Torah traditions and communities, all expressing different facets of the "seventy faces" of the Torah. We encourage others to write and present to the Jewish world their own "letter" to the generation so that the entire *Klal Yisrael* can be strengthened and uplifted by the depth and beauty of their *mesorah*, and in so doing, bring out as much of the light of Hashem's Torah as possible.

It goes without saying that what we present here is a mere fragment of what we received from our mentors. There were other values transmitted by our teachers, and we present but the few that stand out for us. As much as we tried to be completely faithful to our *mesorah*, the responsibility for what we have written must be shouldered by us alone.

The eternal values and principles we have crystallized in this book are aspects of the legacy from the great Lithuanian rabbis, and are vital to strengthening and uplifting *Klal Yisrael* in today's times. It is our earnest hope that renewed understanding of and commitment to these central Torah values will inspire us all with a revitalized sense of mission, purpose, and responsibility for our God-given personal and collective Jewish destiny. May Hashem bring our destiny speedily to complete fruition with the Final Redemption.

Rabbi Berel Wein
Jerusalem, Israel

Rabbi Warren Goldstein
Johannesburg, South Africa

Kislev 5772/November 2012

Rabbi Mordechai Katz, Rabbi Aharon Kotler and Rabbi Yitzchak Ruderman at the opening of new Telz building in Wickliffe Ohio, 1955, accompanied by then-Telz yeshiva students, Rabbi Avraham Tanzer and Rabbi Azriel Chaim Goldfein

A Word about Language

This book is written with numerous Hebrew words, as many of its readers are likely to appreciate this familiar terminology. A glossary of Hebrew terms and basic Jewish concepts, as well as a glossary of personalities, can be found after the last chapter. Please avail yourself of it liberally.

Chapter One

Seeking Paths of Pleasantness

Rabbi Berel Wein

T he Torah's goal, emphasized by many of the leading Lithuanian rabbis, is to create a deeply sensitive, caring, modest, introspective, and pleasant person. Pleasantness is not a surface characteristic, for it is cultivated within the inner recesses of each person.

It is generally accepted that concern for others is the key to being a good person. To the Jew, however, true concern is not expressed in random and sporadic acts of good – no matter how individually noble those acts may be – but in cultivating the governing characteristic and attitude of pleasantness. Good habits and good actions can become habitual, but the platform upon which all of this goodness is built is the individual's inner pleasantness and serenity of soul.

Is pleasantness inborn or the product of environmental or societal training? To answer that question, we must differentiate between politeness and pleasantness. There are many societies in our world that are very polite, but at the same time quite unpleasant. Politeness is only a social norm, not necessarily a true character trait. Pleasantness, on the other hand, involves a deep caring and tolerance for others. Of course, politeness is stressed throughout Jewish and Talmudic works as a necessary and worthy attribute.[1] But to engender a climate of pleasantness, both the society and the individual have to develop a culture that fosters a pleasant outlook on life.

This value was not unique to Lithuanian Jews, of course, for it is deeply rooted in Torah sources. A verse in Proverbs states that the Torah's paths are paths of pleasantness and all of its ways lead to peace.[2] This is not to be understood merely as a pious platitude or an optimistic hope: it is a fundamental value of Judaism. In fact, Judaism can be described as a set of values that govern human behavior in personal, social, monetary, and ritual matters. Each of these values – in the abstract and isolated – is holy and true and governing. Yet, sometimes they can conflict with one another when applied in the real world of human and social life.

The primary example of this type of conflict is the one of peace versus truth. The Talmud in Kesubos[3] raises the question of praise for a bride on her wedding day. The opinion of the House of Shammai was that the truth will out: words of praise must be accurate and specific to that particular bride. The House of Hillel was of the opinion that the praise should be lavish and standard for all brides, for the idea of peace and harmony should overcome that of absolute truth in such a circumstance. As in most instances, we rule according to the House of Hillel, and discretion wins over what could be hurtful truths.

A resolution of the conflict between these two values can be found in the Torah itself. When an angel told Sarah that she would give birth to a child, she laughed to herself saying, "Now that I am old and withered, will I again become fresh and young? And my master is very old!"[4] But when communicating Sarah's wonder to Avraham, the Lord omits the comment that Sarah made about Avraham being old. The value of

---

1. See, for example, Berachos 43b; Niddah 16b; Yerushalmi Kesubos 11:3; and many other such statements scattered throughout Talmudic and rabbinic writings.
2. Proverbs 3:17.
3. Kesubos 16b–17a.
4. Genesis 18:12.

absolute truth and accuracy is compromised in favor of domestic harmony and household peace. It is a powerful teaching – an example of the Torah helping us understand its basic values and guiding us in determining which values are paramount when they conflict with each other.

Far from being a vague mandate for cordiality, the "paths of pleasantness" represent an absolute value in Jewish law and thought. We find its presence in halachic issues. When discussing the Four Species specified by the Torah to be taken on Sukkos, the Talmud determines that certain types of plants of those species may not be used because they are dangerous due to their thorns, or because they are poisonous – and therefore inconsistent with the value of pleasantness.[5] One does not use threatening or offensive utensils when performing a *mitzvah*.

Moreover, the Torah does not ordain acts that are inconsistent with pleasantness. The concept of levirate marriage is tempered by dedication to this value.[6] In his seminal work *Meshech Chochmah*, the great Lithuanian sage, Rabbi Meir Simchah of Dvinsk, states that the reason women are not included in the commandment to be fruitful and multiply is the danger and pain involved in childbirth.[7] Though maternal instinct urges them to want to have children, the Torah does not command them to do so – for such a mandate would be a violation of the supreme value of pleasantness that underpins all Torah understanding and law.

Though the English term "pleasantness" has a benign tone, the concept is robust in Jewish life, and paramount in Torah law and behavior. In its broadest sense, it is the basis for many of the particular *mitzvos* and laws of the Torah. The Torah prohibits actions – stealing, murdering, slandering others, for example – that violate the essential principle of pleasantness, while positive commandments – such as hospitality, charity, caring for the sick, and comforting the bereaved – exemplify pleasantness in human affairs. The seven Noahide laws,[8] which Judaism

---

5. Sukkah 32a.
6. Yevamos 87b. Also see Tosafos Yevamos 17b, the top Tosafos on the page.
7. Genesis 9:7.
8. As enumerated in Sanhedrin 56a, they are: prohibitions against paganism, blasphemy, stealing, murdering, sexual immorality, the mandate to establish a lawful and just society, and the prohibition against eating from an animal while it is still alive.

holds to be universal for all humankind, are basically laws of pleasantness that lead to a dignified and just society.

Because of this emphasis, a concept arose in Judaism that took on societal importance, though it was not codified in absolute law: one is prohibited from doing things that are not nice. Public opinion of the probity of a person's behavior was always to be taken into account.[9] A good Jew was usually defined in Jewish life in terms of pleasantness and goodness toward others and not exclusively in terms of observance and piety. The common response of Lithuanian Jews regarding the *frumkeit* of a person was *"frum iz a galach,"*[10] i.e., that superficial religiosity – exclusively concentrating on personal spirituality and punctilious observances of the law – is not the measure of a good Jew; it belongs to monks. A good Jew lives by the overall values of the Torah, including consideration and pleasantness in human affairs.

In the introduction to his monumental commentary to Torah, *Haamek Davar*, Rabbi Naftali Tzvi Yehudah Berlin (known by the acronym, Netziv) describes our ancestors in Genesis as *yesharim*: pleasant, straight, unbiased, righteous people. In a veiled criticism of attitudes that were already apparent in his time in Eastern European Jewish life, he points out that in Second Temple times, even though there was widespread observance of Torah laws, and there were many great *talmidei chachamim* (Torah scholars) within Jewish society, the Temple was destroyed because of unwarranted hatred, intolerance, and false condemnations of one another by different groupings within Jewish society.[11] Anyone who had different ideas or who deviated from what one group thought to be Jewishly correct, politically or socially, was immediately branded as an *apikores* (a non-believer and heretic). In that context, the Netziv points out that God is, so to speak, *Yashar* and therefore cannot abide "righteous" people who are not pleasant, straight, and tolerant in their dealings with other humans.[12] He concludes that the require-

---

9. See Avos 2:1, 2:13–14, and numerous other places in the Talmud.
10. My Lithuanian-born teachers in the yeshiva of my youth drummed this phrase into my mind.
11. Introduction to Genesis, *Haamek Davar*, Jerusalem, 1959, p. XIII.
12. Ibid.

ment of pleasantness, as set forth in the Torah, covers one's relationship with others, even those with whom one may disagree on the methods of serving God. Our father Avraham even attempted to convince God to save Sodom!

Rabbi Berlin's attitude was typical of the rabbinic leadership of Lithuania, where the sharp divisions within nineteenth- and twentieth-century Eastern European Jewish life were clearly present, but without the venom and violence that often marked these disputes in other places. It was not that the leaders of Lithuanian Orthodoxy were more compromising in their opposition to secularism, Marxism, nationalism, and the other panaceas that swept through the streets of Eastern European Jewry. On the contrary, they were the leading opponents, both intellectually and practically, of these false gods. But even in the midst of their struggle to stem the tide of assimilation, they never lost sight of the value of respect and pleasantness in dealing with other people. Observing how they reacted to this challenge, we see continual striving for pleasantness in their personal and communal lives.

Pleasantness is one of the central values of the *Mussar* Movement,[13] founded in Lithuania by Rabbi Yisrael Lipkin of Salant. (The unique and far-reaching *Mussar* phenomenon will be discussed in Chapter Four.) Rabbi Salant once described an encounter he experienced on his way to the synagogue on Yom Kippur eve: A well-known, God-fearing man passed near him on the street. The man was weeping and trembling in anticipation of the holy Day of Judgment. Rabbi Yisrael stopped and asked him for some information that he needed. The man completely ignored Rabbi Yisrael and made no response to his request; he simply walked away. Although Rabbi Yisrael forgave the man his rudeness, he nevertheless remarked to his disciple, Rabbi Yitzchak Blazer, "When he hurried away I thought to myself: Why should I be victimized by that person's fervor to prepare himself for Yom Kippur? What does his con-

---

13. For a thorough review of the *Mussar* Movement, its philosophies and personalities, see *Tnuas Hamussar* by Rabbi Dov Katz. The primary source on the movement and on its founder, Rabbi Yisrael Lipkin of Salant, is the book *Ohr Yisrael* by Rabbi Yitzchak Blazer (Peterburger) published in Vilna in 1900.

cern regarding the Day of Judgment have to do with me? He is obligated to answer me courteously, *for that is the way of pleasantness and grace.*"[14]

Another example of this rule of pleasantness as developed by the great Lithuanian masters of *Mussar* is found in a letter written by Rabbi Simchah Zissel Ziev, the *"Alter"* of Kelm. He writes, "How great is the requirement that a person care about the feelings of others, that they should not be pained by him! We see that the prophet Jeremiah, while in great personal mental agony over the prophecy of the impending destruction of the Temple, nevertheless did not forget to greet and bless others whom he chanced to meet on the way."[15] In short, the Alter states, "Concern about the welfare of others is in reality the ultimate concern regarding one's own self and one's own soul."[16]

The *Alter* was differentiating between courtesy – manners that are learned and superficial (and often a manifestation of innate smugness and self-aggrandizement) – and sincere concern for others, which is rooted in true pleasantness of character. That trait, in essence, is a characteristic of one's soul, revealing itself in every venue and interplay with others. It rests upon a feeling about one's self, about others, about the world generally; and it stems from the recognition that everything God created in our universe is very good. Character traits of appreciation and thankfulness are developed, as well as a sense of satisfaction with one's lot in life. In that sense, concern for others is a product of one's own relationship with God, a pleasantness that is nourished by deep spiritual roots.

The renowned spiritual counselor Rabbi Yerucham Levovitz, *Mashgiach* of the Yeshiva of Mir in the 1920s and early 1930s, pointed out that pleasantness is the key to justice. The attitude of two people who enter a case in a rabbinic court should not be "What can I gain from the other person?" but rather "How can I rid myself of the doubt that I may have in my possession wealth or objects that are 'stolen' in that they are not really mine?"[17] The key to pleasantness, and hence to

---

14. *Ohr Yisrael*, p. 118.
15. *Chochmah U'Mussar*, Brooklyn, 1957, p. 13.
16. Ibid., p. 12.
17. *Da'as Chochmah U'Mussar*, vol. 1, Brooklyn, 1966, p. 254, et al.

justice and fairness in life, is judging one's own behavior in the light of how it affects others. Justice is found only in the ability to glimpse the other person's plight, needs, and opinions.

Inner serenity derives from consistent pleasantness in demeanor, behavior, and character. The prophet Yishayahu stated that "evildoers rage like [the waves of] the sea."[18] Beset by jealousy of others, unsatiated desires, and overwhelming frustrations, the evildoer is not a pleasant person and therefore will never achieve inner serenity.

Rabbi Levovitz stresses that that this serenity is a spiritual accomplishment, approaching Godliness itself, which is the ultimate goal. "Serenity of the spirit is the crown and sum of all positive traits and accomplishments. The opposite of this, the *lack* of inner serenity, contains all of the character defects of a person. From a lack of serenity, negative traits such as anger and irascibility emerge. It also causes failure in achieving proper intent during prayer and lack of devotion to Torah study."

The mindset that the Torah is not a burden on Jews – but rather a privilege and a badge of honor – permeated Lithuanian Jewry and is found in every vibrant Torah personality and community. Our leaders generally strived to make living a halachic life in the midst of an often hostile non-Jewish society a pleasant and attainable goal. For example, Lithuanian rabbis were in the forefront of finding ways to free women who were *agunos* (women who were trapped in a limbo of distress because their husbands had disappeared and they had no knowledge of their whereabouts, nor a divorce). The learned responsa of the Lithuanian rabbis on this matter always show their compassion and ways of pleasantness as a guiding lodestar in these efforts.[19]

These rabbis did not search out defects in others; and in their rational view of the world, they tolerated different views and approaches to Jewish life. As mentioned previously, traditional Jewry fought and

---

18. Isaiah 57:20.
19. See, for example, the responsa of Rabbi Chaim of Volozhin, *Chut Hameshulash*, section eight; the responsa of Rabbi Yitzchak Elchanan Spektor, *Be'er Yitzchak*; Rabbi Isaac Halevy Herzog in his responsa on *Even Haezer*; and the works of many other Lithuanian sages over the centuries.

opposed Jewish secularism and the Marxist ideas of the nineteenth and early twentieth centuries. Yet even in regard to these critical issues, the battle was fought with less personal acrimony and lasting bitterness in Lithuania.[20]

There were historical exceptions to the idea of conducting a "pleasant" struggle between vastly conflicting and opposing streams in Jewish Lithuanian society. Many of the bitter struggles regarding eighteenth-century Jewish life in Lithuania were marked by bans, excommunications, betrayal to the Czarist authorities, and even physical violence. Yet after the initial decades of strife, the "ways of pleasantness" in Lithuanian Jewry reasserted itself. By the middle of the nineteenth century, the dispute between Chasidim and Misnagdim – though always simmering beneath the surface – was removed from the public life of Lithuanian Jews. In the mid-nineteenth century, Rabbi Yitzchak of Volozhin, the titular head of non-Chasidic Lithuanian Jewry, cooperated openly and sincerely with the Lubavitcher Rebbe of his time on matters of mutual interest and public benefit.

There were strong, though small, pockets of Chasidim scattered throughout Lithuania in the nineteenth and twentieth centuries. Chasidic life there closely mirrored this way of pleasantness that was the overall direction of both the rabbinic and Chasidic leadership. In general, there was a great deal of cooperation and mutual respect between the different Jewish religious groupings in Lita (Lithuania).

The attitude of rabbinic Lithuanian leadership on the whole was moderate and thoughtful, not given to extremism and fanaticism. In the world of ideas and political action in general at that time, there were many competing groups – yeshivas, secularists, Marxists, "enlightened ones," Zionists and anti-Zionists, followers of *Mussar* and anti-*Mussar* scholars – but their ideological struggles were conducted in the public

---

20. It is important to note that the Lithuanian rabbinic leadership was almost totally wiped out in the Holocaust. Because of this, those who embodied this idea of pleasantness and its value system – and had been in the forefront of its dissemination in the wider Jewish world – virtually disappeared from the Jewish scene. Certainly, their presence and influence are still sorely missed.

arena in a much more muted, scholarly, and intellectual fashion than in other countries.

With the rise of Communism in the twentieth century, this began to change slowly. The ruthlessness and violence practiced by the extreme Left victimized the Jewish community in new and shocking ways. Despite their penchant for moderation, rabbinic Lithuanian leaders were forced to take a more militant attitude to counter dire threats.

An age of brutality was ushered in. By the atrocities of Hitler and Stalin, Lithuanian Jewry was destroyed. But its spirit, legacy, and values remain vital in Jewish life in Israel and the Diaspora until today.

The great Rav of Ponivezh, Rabbi Yosef Shlomo Kahaneman, told me in 1964, "The Jews of South Africa are in the main Litvaks. Many have forgotten observances and Torah learning. But still they have retained the good character traits and ways of pleasantness which were so characteristic of Lithuanian Jewry. Because of this, the Lord will help them find their way back to Torah observance and study as well." The rabbis taught us that "a wise man [in his foresight] is even greater than a pure prophet."[21] In large measure, the Rav's prediction has come to fruition in South African Jewry. One should never underestimate the spiritual and historical power of the ways of pleasantness in Jewish society.

---

21. Bava Basra 12a.

Chapter Two

Being a Mensch

Rabbi Warren Goldstein

Literally translated, *mensch* means "person," but "to be a *mensch*" conveys so much more. A *mensch* is infused with morality, goodness, and kindness; adheres to proper manners; demonstrates basic human decency; is scrupulous in keeping the *mitzvos* governing interpersonal relationships; and develops good character traits.

THREE BASIC PRINCIPLES

The concept of being a *mensch* is multi-faceted, but can be distilled to three basic principles: *derech eretz* (appropriate behavior), *middos tovos* (good character traits), and, of course, the *mitzvos bein adam lechaveiro* (the actual commandments that relate to human interactions). These principles will be explained, but their common goal is to produce a highly refined, emotionally balanced and developed person, one who interacts with others sensitively and kindly and in a manner that brings honor to himself and to Hashem.

Principle I: Derech Eretz Came Before Torah

According to the Midrash, *derech eretz* was given to humanity through Adam and Eve at the beginning of human history, and the Torah was given to the Jewish people 26 generations later. Thus, concludes the Midrash, "*derech eretz* came before Torah." The chronological order reflects a logical order.

The Maharal explains *derech eretz* in the context of two wisdoms: that of the lower world and that of the upper world.[1] The former concerns living as part of human civilization in the physical world, and the latter to living in accordance with the eternal values of God's will as expressed in the Torah. *Derech eretz* is the science of appropriate human behavior in the lower world and is very wide-ranging in its field of application: from personal hygiene to earning a living; from social etiquette to decency and integrity in all circumstances. It includes anything that a person needs to do in order to function well as a member of human society, from the most basic level to the morality of interpersonal relationships and good character, such as being careful not to cause any unnecessary anguish or irritation to anybody.

As *derech eretz* represents the basics of decent human behavior (lower world), while Torah is the wisdom of the upper world, logically *derech eretz* must come before Torah. Torah is addressed to people who are already assumed to be properly developed, civilized human beings who have mastered *derech eretz*. The Torah can elevate a person to the highest levels of spiritual development, but first he must achieve the full glory of all that entails being a good person.

The Maharal contrasts the term *eretz* (land) with that of *olam* (world). *Eretz* refers to the areas of human society and habitation, and *olam* includes areas of the wild where human beings do not live. The human dimension is crucial because *derech eretz* is not about living as part of nature. On the contrary, it is about taming our animal instincts, elevating us to refined behavior.

So it is not surprising that the Gemara lists learning Torah, good

---

1. *Nesiv Derech Eretz*. It consists of only one chapter. All references to the Maharal can be found in that chapter unless otherwise indicated.

deeds, prayer, and *derech eretz* as requiring extra effort and support.[2] The Maharal explains that in order to achieve any of these, a person must overcome the natural physical urges of the body and strive for greatness of the spirit. A person who always follows his natural physical instincts is like an animal and cannot behave with *derech eretz*. He is lacking in the fundamentals of civilized living in accordance with the wisdom of the lower world.

While the obligation of living with *derech eretz* predates the obligation of living according to the Torah, the Torah incorporates the moral principles of *derech eretz* and *middos tovos*, thereby elevating them to the level of Torah sanctity and *mitzvos*. Violating them is considered a breach of the very basics of civilized behavior.

The Definition of Civilized Behavior

The Mishnah says that a person who does not behave with *derech eretz* is not part of the *yishuv* (the civilized world).[3] A person who lacks learning may be referred to as an *am ha'aretz*, but is still part of civilized society. It is the lack of *derech eretz* that changes the very identity of a person and excludes him from being considered part of civilization.

The Gemara adds that such a person is also disqualified from giving testimony in a Jewish court of law. The Rambam and *Shulchan Aruch* rule accordingly, explaining that a person without *derech eretz* is presumed to be a *rasha* (an evil person) whose serious sins disqualify him from testimony.[4] A person who lacks basic *derech eretz* is presumed to live a life without any moral restraint. *Derech eretz* marks the minimum entrance level to be considered human and part of the civilized world. The Maharal provides yet another reason for disqualification as a witness: such a person is detached from reality due to his uncivilized behavior. Consequently, his testimony – which must be connected to a framework of reality to be valid – cannot be accepted.

---

2. Berachos 32b.
3. Kiddushin 40b.
4. Rambam, *Edus* 11:1. *Shulchan Aruch* c.m. 34:17. The *Aruch Hashulchan* c.m. 34:18 defines the lack of *derech eretz* as not working for a living.

As an example of a lack of *derech eretz*,[5] the Gemara cites a *braisa*: "One who eats in the marketplace is like a dog; and some say such a person is disqualified from giving testimony."[6] Rabbeinu Tam stipulates that this refers specifically to eating a proper meal with bread, while the Maharal contends that it deals with a person who regularly eats in public. He cites the Yerushalmi statement that a *talmid chacham* (Torah scholar) should not do so even occasionally.[7] Rashi explains that a lack of *derech eretz* disqualifies a potential witness from testifying because such a person has no self-respect or dignity, which are important safeguards against lying to a court. The Maharal says that the comparison is to a dog, an animal regarded by the Tanach (Bible) as the most undignified.[8] The Rambam and *Shulchan Aruch* rule that this disqualification extends to other types of grossly undignified behavior.[9] The indignity and disgrace of being caught lying to the court is not a deterrent to such a person.

The Gemara elsewhere says that to eat in a gluttonous way exhibits a lack of *derech eretz*.[10] And so it is forbidden, according to the Gemara, to eat the flesh of a slaughtered animal before its skin is properly removed, because the indecent haste indicates a wild and greedy attitude. Like-

---

5. Rashi (s.v. *vepasul*) explains the case of eating in the marketplace as an example of a lack of *derech eretz*. It seems that the Rambam and *Shulchan Aruch* regard it as a separate rabbinic disqualification of people who embarrass themselves publicly, for example, by going naked in public. Hence they set it out as a separate *halachah* in Rambam *Edus* 11:5 and *Shulchan Aruch* c.m. 34:18.
6. Kiddushin 40b.
7. The Maharal makes the distinction as an answer to Tosafos (s.v. *veyeish*) on Rashi from the Yerushalmi. There is much discussion in the commentaries about how to reconcile the Yerushalmi. Tosafos, for example, cites different opinions on the matter.
8. The Gemara itself does not say that to eat in the marketplace is prohibited. It implies that it is forbidden because such conduct is regarded as so wrong as to disqualify a person from giving testimony. Rav Moshe Feinstein applies this principle of dignified living to the issue of hypnosis. Rav Moshe says that it is prohibited to be hypnotized because to do so is to place oneself in an inherently and grossly undignified state but, deferring to the terminology of the exact nature of the prohibition, calls it "the spirit of prohibition" (*Igros Moshe* y.d. 3:44). The fact that it is not a direct negative prohibition *mede'oraisa* allows for some flexibility in assessing a situation in which there are medical reasons for hypnosis.
9. Rambam *Edus* 11:5, *Shulchan Aruch* c.m. 34:18.
10. Beitzah 25b.

wise, the Gemara refers to draining a cup of liquid in one gulp as another example of such behavior. There is strong emphasis on eating because *derech eretz* is about civilizing and transforming a person from the level of an animal to that of a human being. Eating as a human being means eating with acceptable manners, dignity, and refinement. For example, when the Telzer *Roshei Yeshiva* arrived in America, they were appalled to see yeshiva students drinking soda directly out of a bottle. They used to say that only a drunkard drinks out of a bottle.[11]

Some other practical examples, provided by Rabbi Aharon Kotler, give a sense of what *derech eretz* can mean in a yeshiva setting: throwing a paper on the floor of the yeshiva displays a lack of *derech eretz* and *middos tovos*. Not only is it a violation of the laws of the proper sanctity and awe due to a place of holy learning, it also bespeaks a lack of concern and sensitivity to the dignity of one's fellow students. Another example would be taking a book from the library of the *beis midrash* (house of study) and not returning it to its place, which, in addition to being a lack of *derech eretz*, can cause time to be wasted from Torah learning. (He adds that it may even be a problem of theft of time.)

Other examples of *derech eretz* relate to physical appearance such as dress, personal hygiene and neatness, and the importance of being well-groomed and well-presented in all respects.

There are some *halachos* that overlap the requirements of *derech eretz*. For example, washing hands before eating bread is a *mitzvah de'rabanan*. The Gemara compares eating bread without washing to being with a prostitute because, in both cases, physical acts are debased to an animal level and not elevated or refined to that of a human being.

Principle II: The Mandate to Develop Middos Tovos

In addition to *derech eretz*, there is a second concept crucial to being a *mensch*: the development of good character traits, or *middos tovos*, which is one of the most important Torah objectives. Based on a Midrash that the Torah was given to purify its adherents, the Ramban holds that there are many *mitzvos* designed to inculcate compassion in people.[12]

---

11. Told to me by Rabbi Azriel Chaim Goldfein, *zt"l*, my *rebbi* and *Rosh Yeshiva*.
12. Ramban Deuteronomy 22:6.

The Vilna Gaon says that *middos tovos* are not explicitly mentioned in the Torah "because they encompass the entire Torah, as it states [in the Talmud], 'Whoever becomes angry – it is as if he worships idols,' and 'Whoever speaks *lashon hara* – it is as though he denies God.'"[13] In another passage, he writes that the main purpose of the Torah is refinement and the inculcation of good character traits.

The Rambam states that to cultivate *middos tovos* can be counted as one of the 613 *mitzvos*. The Torah commands: "You shall walk in His ways,"[14] and the Gemara explains: "In the same way that He is compassionate, so should you be; in the same way that He is gracious, so too should you be." Every Jew is commanded to develop *middos tovos* in emulation of God.

The Gemara's examples relate to helping people in need. It says that God clothes the naked, visits the sick, comforts the mourners, and buries the dead; therefore, we too should do all these deeds of lovingkindness. The Rambam extends this principle of emulating God to all areas of character development. He notes that the prophets described God's qualities, such as strength, uprightness, and kindness, in order to "make known that these are good and straight ways and that a person is obligated to conduct himself in accordance with them and to become as similar to Him as his abilities will allow."[15] He teaches that to accomplish this, one should follow the middle path of balance between two extremes. For example, when it comes to possessions and money, a person should be neither parsimonious nor attached to physical things, but on the other hand, should treat property with respect and not waste or squander it. The only exception to taking the middle path, says the Rambam, is in the area of arrogance and anger, where one should strive to be extremely humble and slow to anger.

As the only *mitzvah* based on the fact that God Himself performs it, possessing *middos tovos*[16] has a level of importance not shared by any other *mitzvah*. The Rambam says that to follow the path of *middos tovos*

---

13. *Perush HaGra, Megillas Esther* 10:3.
14. Deuteronomy 28:9.
15. Rambam *De'os* 1:6.
16. I heard this idea from my *Rosh Yeshiva, zt"l.*

is called "the way of God"[17] and is part of the legacy of Avraham, sourcing his contention in the verse where God says of Avraham: "I have loved him because he will instruct his children and his household after him that they keep the way of God, to do righteousness and justice."[18] Thus, developing *middos tovos* is incorporated not only as one of the *mitzvos*, but as one of the most important *mitzvos* in the Torah.

The Rambam demonstrates this significance in the structuring of his *Yad Hachazakah*.[19] *Hilchos De'os* (which deals with all aspects of *derech eretz, middos tovos*, and many *mitzvos bein adam lechaveiro*) comes second in the entire monumental work only to *Hilchos Yesodei Hatorah – Laws of the Foundations of the Torah* – which includes *mitzvos* of belief, and fear and love of God. The Rambam cites a number of different verses as sources for all the different topics dealt with in *Hilchos De'os*, and at the center of so many of them is the *mitzvah* to emulate God's kindness. If one is obligated to reach out to others with kindness, how much more so is one prohibited from causing pain or damage to another person?[20]

Principle III: Mitzvos Bein Adam Lechaveiro

The third foundational principle involved in being a *mensch* is expressed through many of the 613 *mitzvos*. Traditionally, the *mitzvos* are divided into two categories: *bein adam leMakom* (between a person and God) and *bein adam lechaveiro* (between one person and another). This division goes back to the Ten Commandments, which are often divided into two groups of five, with the first one referring to duties toward God, and the second toward other people. Interpersonal *mitzvos* govern every aspect of social interactions in all areas, from marriage and business to honoring parents and the elderly, to ethics of speech and charity.

Some of the most important *mitzvos*, such as *tzedakah* and *chesed*, fit into this category. The Gemara accords unique importance to *tzedakah*, placing it in a category of its own in relation to the other commandments, as is clear from the following statements: "Rabbi Asi said, '*Tzedakah* is

---

17. Rambam *De'os* 1:7.
18. Genesis 18:19, translation based on Rashi.
19. Heard from my *Rosh Yeshiva, zt"l*.
20. Heard from my *Rosh Yeshiva, zt"l*.

equal [in value] to all of the other commandments [combined];"[21] and "Rabbi Yehoshua ben Korchah says, 'Whoever ignores [the responsibility] of *tzedakah* – it is as if he worships idols.'"[22] Idolatry is one of the most severe transgressions in Jewish law. Consequently, the comparison of idolatry to not giving *tzedakah* is significant. The Rambam, based on the Talmud, writes:[23]

> We are obligated to be careful with the commandment of *tzedakah* more than any of the other positive commandments…. Whoever ignores [the responsibility] of *tzedakah* is called 'lawless' in the same way that an idol worshipper is called 'lawless.'… And he [such a person] is called wicked…and he is called a sinner.

The importance of *tzedakah* is also manifest in the reward promised for its fulfillment. It is interesting to note how the *Shulchan Aruch* (based on the Talmud) goes beyond its normal confines of stating legal principles, and offers:[24]

> No one ever becomes poor from [giving] *tzedakah*, and no bad thing or damage comes as a result of it, as it states, 'The product of *tzedakah* shall be peace' [Isaiah 32:17].
> Whoever has compassion on the poor – the Holy One, Blessed Is He, has compassion on him. A person should recognize that he requests sustenance from the Holy One, Blessed Is He, and in the same way that he requests [Him] to take heed of his plea, so should he take heed of the pleas of the poor….
> *Tzedakah* sets aside all harsh decrees, and in a famine it saves from death…and it brings wealth. And it is forbidden to test God, except in this matter [that is, that giving charity brings wealth].

---

21. Talmud Bava Basra 9a.
22. Talmud Bava Basra 10a and Kesubos 68a.
23. Rambam *Hilchos Matnos Aniyim* 10:1.3.
24. *Shulchan Aruch* Y.D. 247:2–4.

The Talmud points out that the Torah begins and concludes with God's acts of kindness to people.[25] Elsewhere, the Midrash says that *chesed* (loving-kindness) is the central value of the Torah.[26] The Talmud claims that *chesed* is even greater than *tzedakah* because the former has broader application than the latter in three ways: *tzedakah* is performed with one's material possessions, while *chesed* can be performed even with one's person; *tzedakah* is given to the poor, but *chesed* can be done for rich and poor alike; *tzedakah* is giving to the living, but *chesed* can be done for the living and dead alike.[27] The Mishnah also says that *chesed* is one of three values for which the world was created and, therefore, upon which the continued existence of the world is predicated.[28] It also states that *chesed* is rewarded more than most other commandments.[29]

INTERTWINING THE THREE BASIC PRINCIPLES

Although *derech eretz*, *middos tovos*, and interpersonal *mitzvos* are three distinct principles, they often are intertwined. The Mishnah states: "If there is no Torah, there is no *derech eretz*; if there is no *derech eretz*, there is no Torah."[30] Rabbeinu Yonah comments that this Mishnah highlights the connection between Torah and *derech eretz*. He defines the term *derech eretz* as *middos tovos*, explaining that without Torah, a person cannot be truly complete in goodness and *middos*, because there are so many *mitzvos* connected to being kind, compassionate, and ethical. Without these *mitzvos*, a person cannot reach completeness in *derech eretz*.

On the other hand, explains Rabbeinu Yonah, without *derech eretz*, a person cannot receive Torah into his life. Good character and human decency are prerequisites to receiving the Torah; therefore a person "must correct himself with *middos tovos* – and through this, the Torah will dwell with him because it [the Torah] does not dwell with anybody who does not possess *middos tovos*."

Derech eretz operates on two levels: it has a pre-Torah dimension

---

25. Sotah 14a.
26. *Lekach Tov*, Proverbs 31:26.
27. Sukkah 49b.
28. Mishnah Avos 1:2. See also the commentaries of Rashi and Rabbeinu Yonah ad loc.
29. Mishnah Pe'ah 1:1.
30. Pirkei Avos 3:17.

that is accessible to (and required by) all human beings, yet there are many *mitzvos* that enhance aspects of *derech eretz* for those who live by the Torah.

Rabbeinu Yonah cites specific *mitzvos*, such as those relating to pledged objects and accurate weights and measurements, as examples of how the Torah incorporates and elevates the basic ethics of *derech eretz* and good character. There are other examples of how principles of *derech eretz* were crystallized as *mitzvos* when the Torah was given.

One of them is the obligation to honor parents, which came to the world as part of *derech eretz* before the Torah was given.[31] When the Torah was given, it became a *mitzvah*: "Honor your father and mother as you have been commanded by the Lord, your God."[32] The phrase "as you have been commanded" means the basis for honoring parents is no longer only *derech eretz*; as part of God's Torah, it is now a *mitzvah* and is accorded a loftier and holier status than before.

Here is an example of integrated values: The Telzer *Roshei Yeshiva* in America[33] would often tell their students (before the students went home for *bein hazmanim*) to be mindful of the *braisa* in *Maseches Derech Eretz*: "Do not be one who sits among those who stand, and be not one who stands among those who sit," i.e., it is basic *derech eretz* that one should respect the norms of a place. Of course, such respect is also consistent with *middos tovos* in general. To differ publicly from the established customs reflects brazenness – one of the worst of the bad *middos*. Such public behavior also is often rooted in haughtiness – another of the worst *middos*. It is possible that the *Roshei Yeshiva* wanted to address the expected arrogance of yeshiva students returning to their home towns, prideful in their newly acquired Torah knowledge, as they

---

31. See *Igros Moshe*, Y.D. 2:130, who says this, and therefore holds that non-Jews are also obligated to honor their parents even though this rule is not part of the seven Noahide laws.
32. Deuteronomy 5:15. This example and the next (about the bathing), I heard from my *Rosh Yeshiva, zt"l*, among many others he used in order to illustrate this concept of incorporation. The *Aruch Hashulchan* 240:3 also draws this conclusion from the phrase "as you have been commanded."
33. I heard this from my *Rosh Yeshiva, zt"l*, and he would instruct us, his students, accordingly.

interact with members of their families and communities who had not learned in a yeshiva.

Behaving in a way that differs from local customs can also lead to terrible outcomes of conflict, disunity, and *lashon hara*. This practice is part and parcel of the *halachah, lo tisgodedu* (do not form separate groups). The Gemara warns that such divisive behavior leads to *Chillul Hashem*, for it gives the impression that there are two Torahs in the world.

Another example is bathing and personal hygiene, which are duties of *derech eretz*. The Midrash[34] relates that when Hillel the Elder once took leave of his students, they asked where he was going and he answered that he was going to fulfill the *mitzvah* of going to the bathhouse. They questioned him, what kind of a *mitzvah* is bathing? He explained that a human being is created in the Image of God. Therefore, to respect the totality of the person – which includes the body and not only the soul – is to respect God Himself. Among other things, respect and honor for the human body means keeping it clean, living healthfully, and dressing appropriately. Bathing and personal hygiene are rules of *derech eretz* that result in living with dignity. Yet Hillel the Elder saw them as more: he pointed out that these activities go beyond the basic level of *derech eretz* to that of *mitzvos*. The concept of dignified living is thereby elevated into the broader Torah value of *kavod habriyos* (human dignity).

The Rambam also treats the pursuit of bodily health as a *mitzvah*: "For the body to be healthy and complete is from the ways of God, because it is impossible to understand or know of the knowledge of God when a person is sick."[35] Famously, the Rambam then proceeds to give detailed instructions concerning diet and exercise.

There are numerous instances of the Torah itself teaching *derech eretz*. Perhaps the most famous example occurs when God says, "Let us make man in our image."[36] The plural form is used, says Rashi (based on the Midrash), to indicate that God consulted with the angels before creating man in order to teach us *derech eretz*: we should consult with others when making important decisions that affect them, even though

---

34. *Leviticus Rabah* 34:3.
35. Rambam *De'os* 4:1.
36. Genesis 1:26.

we have the power to make the decision alone. Consulting them is respectful and sensitive to their dignity, and, on a utilitarian level, also ensures that they will be supportive. The utilitarian benefits are recognized components of *derech eretz*, which includes the recognition of the value of a well-functioning, peaceful society. Surprisingly, the use of the plural form gives rise to the heretical impression of plurality of the Divine, in direct conflict with the central tenet of Torah that there is only one God! Our sages comment that teaching *derech eretz* to mankind is so important to the Creator that He is prepared to risk heretical implications to demonstrate the lesson.

The Book of Proverbs is devoted to teaching *derech eretz*. The Talmud also deals extensively with *derech eretz* in entire dedicated tractates (Tractate Derech Eretz, Raba and Zuta). *Derech eretz* is one of the main themes of Pirkei Avos, which is so revered and famous throughout the Jewish world.

Becoming a Holistic and Integrated Torah Personality

Not only are the three principles of *menschlichkeit* intertwined, all aspects of being a Torah person are intertwined. Torah should create a holistic person whose entire life is permeated by the will of Hashem. The Gemara says: "One who wants to be a truly righteous person" should focus on three areas: matters of damages, matters of blessings, and matters of *avos*.[37] The Maharal, the Maharsha, and the Vilna Gaon explain that these three areas refer respectively to relationships *bein adam lechaveiro* (between man and man); *bein adam leMakom* (between man and God); and *bein adam le'atzmo* (internal completeness achieved through *middos tovos*).[38]

---

37. Bava Kama 30a. The Gemara cites these three items as separate opinions; however the Maharal and others say that they should be interpreted as three complementary opinions, all referring to the three different aspects of Torah, as explained in the main body of the text.

38. The Maharal in his Introduction to Pirkei Avos, *Chidushei Agados Bava Kama*; the Maharsha *Chidushei Agados Bava Kama*; *Bi'ur HaGra Yeshayahu* 1:2. The Maharal notes that the Gemara does not give outstanding *chesed* as an example of this area of Torah because acts of kindness are mandatory and cannot be considered exceptionally righteous. However, to be very sensitive and proactive in avoiding causing pain to others, even in the most indirect form, is exceptional righteousness.

To be a true servant of Hashem, it is insufficient to embrace one's duties in respect of only one relationship or another.

"Matters of damages" involves going to great lengths to avoid causing any harm to another person, no matter how indirect that harm may be. A righteous person is someone who goes beyond the letter of the law in this respect. The Gemara gives an example of the "early saintly people" (the great people of earlier generations) who buried broken glass or pottery deep in the ground so that no one could be injured by the sharp edges of the broken pieces. This conduct exemplifies excellence in *bein adam lechaveiro*.

"Matters of blessings" refers to the blessings that are recited in praise and thanksgiving to God, as instituted by our sages, for various activities and experiences, for example, eating or seeing the wonders of nature, such as lightning or the ocean. These blessings should be recited with great devotion and sincerity, and with punctilious attention to the appropriate time, place, and circumstance. This obviously symbolizes the broader principle of striving for excellence in the Torah area of *bein adam leMakom*.

"Matters of *avos*" refers to the Tractate Pirkei Avos, which focuses on *derech eretz* and *middos tovos*. This refers to the relationship with oneself and it is about achieving *shleimus bein adam le'atzmo* (internal completeness through the refinement of one's character).

The key message is that the Torah requires complete holistic commitment and goodness in all aspects of life.

APPLYING PRINCIPLES OF MENSCHLICHKEIT WITH SPECIAL CARE

Holistic Torah living means embracing all areas of *halachah* and *mitzvos*. Nevertheless, the great Lithuanian rabbis placed special emphasis on being a *mensch*, with all that it involves. The famous student of the Vilna Gaon, Reb Chaim of Volozhin, continues this train of thought in a remarkable interpretation of the Mishnah in Pirkei Avos cited above:[39] "If there is no Torah, there is no *derech eretz*; if there is no *derech eretz*, there is no Torah." Reb Chaim explains the first component: without

---

39. *Ruach Chaim* on Pirkei Avos 3:17.

Torah, true *derech eretz* is not possible, since Torah has so much hala-chic and aggadic (conceptual, philosophical) content devoted to how to be a good person that to understand and practice the principles of *derech eretz* without Torah is impossible. His explanation of the second component, "If there is no *derech eretz*, there is no Torah," is "If there is no *derech eretz*, the Torah [knowledge] one acquires will be without benefit, and it will be useless."

In this connection, he cites another statement in the same Mish-nah: "If there is no flour, there is no Torah; if there is no Torah, there is no flour." Reb Chaim explains that without flour, i.e., financial and physical support, there is no Torah. On the other hand, "if there is no Torah, there is no flour" conveys that without Torah, sustenance has no purpose or meaning. The parallels are startling! According to Reb Chaim, just as Torah gives significance and purpose to physical sustenance, so too do *derech eretz* and *middos tovos* give significance and purpose to Torah. He seems to follow the opinion of his great mentor, the Vilna Gaon, that the very purpose of Torah is to create a refined, noble person who attains the highest standards of ethical conduct and *middos tovos*.

Failures in Menschlichkeit Are Judged Severely

The Book of Ecclesiastes states: "For God will judge every deed – even everything hidden – whether good or bad."[40] The Gemara interprets "even everything hidden" as any *inadvertent* discomfort caused to another person, such as killing an insect or spitting in front of someone who finds these actions repugnant. Rashi explains that since the discomfort is "hidden" from the perpetrator, the deed falls into the halachic category of *shogeg* (an accidental transgression) for which one is not normally held liable. Nevertheless, if another person suffers, the perpetrator is liable and will be judged accordingly. The Gemara adds that the phrase "whether good or bad" includes hurting another person, even when try-ing to benefit that person. It gives the example of dispensing charity to a poor person in a way that embarrasses the recipient in public.

Rav Chaim Shmulevitz, Mirrer *Rosh Yeshiva* and *Mashgiach*, cites numerous sources to prove that misconduct *bein adam lechaveiro* is

---

40. Ecclesiastes 12:14.

judged much more harshly than any other infraction of Torah, and that difficult circumstances or good intentions do not mitigate responsibility for causing pain (or even discomfort) to another person.[41] It is well known that Yom Kippur does not atone for sins *bein adam lechaveiro* unless one is forgiven by one's victim and has made amends, if possible, for the harm caused.[42] Reb Chaim writes: "And so, our situation on this holy day [Yom Kippur] with respect to sins *bein adam lechaveiro* is a frightening and terrible situation."[43]

In Chapter Four, you will be introduced to the *Mussar* Movement (a program for self-improvement) and its impact on the Jews of Lithuania and the world. There are many anecdotes concerning that movement that reflect its sincere dedication to the values described in this chapter. The stories told about its founder, Rabbi Yisrael Salanter, exemplify these values. It is told that Rabbi Salanter was in a Paris *shul* for Shabbos when the *parshah* that lists curses for transgression of Torah law (*Tochachah*) was being read. Traditionally, the *shul* had given the dreaded *aliyah* of the curses to a poor person, because everyone else was afraid to be associated with its negativity. At the moment of the *aliyah*, the congregation was looking for a poor person, and there was a resultant delay. Reb Yisrael himself immediately walked up to the *bimah* for the *aliyah* and read it himself. After the service, he rebuked the congregation severely, saying that they should have been more afraid of hurting the feelings of a poor person, who is vulnerable and oppressed, than of the curses.[44]

On another occasion, Reb Yisrael was invited to the Friday night Shabbos meal at a prominent student's house. Before accepting the invitation, he asked his student how he conducts the meal. The student told him that everything in his house is done according to the highest levels of the *halachah*: the meat is bought from a well-known, devout *shochet* (kosher butcher), that it is *glatt* kosher and that the entire meal is prepared at the highest standards of *kashrus* by the widow of a *talmid chacham*. The student said also that they sing many songs, share words

---

41. *Sichos Mussar* 31:74, 32:105.
42. Gemara Yoma 85b, Rambam *Teshuvah* 2:9.
43. *Sichos Mussar* 32:105.
44. *Tnuas Hamussar* vol. 1, p. 326.

of Torah between courses, and even learn passages of *Shulchan Aruch* at the table. Of course, the meal finishes quite late. Reb Yisrael accepted the invitation on condition that the meal will be completed within two hours. That Friday night, they rushed through the meal, serving each course immediately after the last. Just before *benching*, the host asked Reb Yisrael why he had made them rush, and whether the Rav found something wrong with the way he normally did things. Rabbi Salanter explained that the length of the dinner meant that the widow who was responsible for cooking the food and running the kitchen had to stay up for the duration of the meal. For that reason, it must not be prolonged! He told his student that his conduct was very nice, provided it did not harm others.[45]

MAINTAINING THE HIGHEST MONETARY ETHICS

The Epstein family was one of the renowned Lithuanian rabbinic dynasties. Rabbi Baruch Halevi Epstein, the famous Torah Temimah, writes about the scrupulous ethical halachic standards of his grandfather, Rabbi Aharon Yitzchak Halevi Epstein (father of Rabbi Yechiel Michel Halevi Epstein, the esteemed Aruch Hashulchan):[46]

> All those who had business dealings with my grandfather, Jew or non-Jew, recall their relationship with him with the utmost admiration. Not only was he more than fair in paying his workers a proper wage, but whenever the slightest question arose as to whether he owed money, he would immediately agree to pay, no questions asked. He used to say, 'If a spoon with even the slightest trace of suspicion of being *treif* became mixed up with many kosher spoons, I would certainly *kasher* all of them as the *din* (law) requires. Why should I treat a monetary question with any less gravity than a question in *kashrus*? On the contrary, in a question of *kashrus* the sin is only between myself and Heaven, whereas in a monetary matter it includes both Heaven and my fellow man.'

45. *Tnuas Hamussar* vol. 1, pp. 332–333.
46. *Recollections* (English translation of *Mekor Baruch*), p. 18.

Other notables shared this exacting approach since they were
more fearful of sins involving monetary matters than traditionally religious issues, such as *kashrus*. For example,[47] a *shochet* once told Rabbi
Salanter that he was leaving his profession because he was afraid of making mistakes that would cause others to sin by eating non-kosher meat.
He had decided to run a shop to make his living, instead. Reb Yisrael
remarked that it is a mistake to think that running a business would lead
to fewer serious sins. He explained that when it comes to *shechitah* (ritual slaughter), there is only the one negative commandment of *neveilah*
(non-kosher meat) at stake, but running a shop involves the potential
transgression of the many *mitzvos* governing monetary matters, which
involve some of the most complex areas of *halachah*. And so as a shop
owner, he would be much more likely to sin in many serious respects
than he would as a *shochet*. Reb Yisrael pointed out that one of the first
questions a person is asked in the Heavenly court is: "Did you deal faithfully, honestly in business?"[48]

Rabbi Salanter was even concerned about indirectly causing a loss
of money. He once visited the Admor, Reb Yitzchak Meir, the Rebbe of
Gur, who accorded him great honor. The word soon spread that a great
Lithuanian *rav* was in town.[49] The two rabbis went to *daven Minchah*, and
a very large crowd gathered to see Rav Yisrael Salanter. He *davened* the
Amidah so quickly that the Chasidim were disappointed: they expected
more from a *Gadol*. Reb Yisrael noticed their reaction and explained
that when he saw so many tailors, shoemakers, and other workmen who
had taken off time from their work, he felt it would be wrong to *daven*
for too long. The longer the interruption of their working day, the more
money they would lose.

One *erev* Yom Kippur, people were shocked to see Rabbi Salanter
chasing after a cat, in order to get it into his house. His explanation was
simple: he had borrowed some books and was concerned that during
Yom Kippur, when the house would be completely empty, rodents would
come in and damage them (for they were likely to chew the leather

47. *Tnuas Hamussar* vol. 1., pp. 321–322.
48. Gemara Shabbos 31a. (Translation of *emunah* is both "faithfully" and "honestly".)
49. *Tnuas Hamussar* vol. 1., p. 332.

bindings). As he had to protect the property of others, he needed a cat in the house![50]

Financial Dealings with Non-Jews

This sensitivity and dedication to *bein adam lechaveiro* and monetary matters applies as well to a Jew's treatment of non-Jews. Even on a *de'oraisa* level, the *mitzvah* of emulating God includes[51] behaving with kindness and compassion to all human beings; as the verse states: "His compassion is on all His works."[52] Again, we can look for guidance to Rabbi Baruch Epstein:

> My grandfather was particularly careful [from an ethical point of view] when doing business with a non-Jew. A general order went out to all his clerks and business managers that if there was even one chance in a hundred that a non-Jewish worker might be owed wages, to pay him anyway, lest [the oversight] would cause a *Chillul Hashem*. Even though one isn't expected to spend more than twenty percent of one's assets on [positive] *mitzvos*, he explained, one is required to give up *all* of one's possessions to prevent a *Chillul Hashem* or dishonoring the Jewish people. Indeed, as the Smag explains, stealing from a non-Jew is worse than stealing from a Jew because of the *Chillul Hashem* involved. Grandfather would often quote the moving words of the *Be'er Hagolah* commentary on *Choshen Mishpat* 348 in this respect: 'I am recording this for all generations, for I have seen those who have become wealthy from deceiving non-Jews in business. They eventually lose all their wealth and leave nothing after them. Many others sanctified God's Name and returned mistaken gains – even large amounts – and they eventually became wealthy and left an inheritance for their children.'

---

50. Ibid., p. 324.
51. Rambam *Hilchos Melochim* 10:12. There is so much material about a Jew's moral obligation to non-Jews, but this one source will suffice for the purpose of highlighting Litvishe philosophy on these issues.
52. Psalms 145:9.

My grandfather pointed out that these words were especially significant coming as they did from the Be'er Hagolah,
who suffered so terribly at the hands of gentiles. He wrote them
soon after he and his entire community in Lithuania had fled for
their lives from the terrible pogroms of 5415 (1655). They were
miraculously saved and escaped to Amsterdam, as he himself
writes: 'The entire congregation fled with nothing in their hands
except a calendar showing the dates of the holidays. Those who
had wagons and horses took them, while those who did not
set out on foot with their children on their shoulders. They ran
wherever they could, and the earth shook with the pounding of
their feet. Those who did not get out in time fell into the hands
of the Cossacks, who laid siege to the city of Vilna and burned
it to the ground.' (These words are not printed in most editions
of the *Shulchan Aruch* with the Be'er Hagolah's commentary. My
grandfather told me that he had seen them in his youth when he
was studying with the Gaon Rav Shlomo Eiger in Warsaw. I have
quoted the words as they appear in the book *Kiryah Ne'emanah*.)

If such a person, who had suffered so much from the cruelty of gentiles, could be so dedicated to treating all people with
honesty and integrity, how much greater is our obligation to do
so when we live under the protection of a government which
has blessed us with peace, security, and equality, in a country
in which we are allowed to prosper, my grandfather concluded.

Let us analyze the Torah values reflected in this approach to
non-Jews. As we have seen, the emphasis on *derech eretz* and *middos
tovos* is based in part on the concept that it is important to attain the
level of a good human being – a *mensch*. *Derech eretz* and *middos tovos*
cannot be compartmentalized. A person either has integrity, decency,
and uprightness, which he applies in all situations in dealing with all
people, or he does not.

That, too, is part of the Talmudic principle of *dina demalchusa
dina* (the law of the state is also the law for Jews living in that state[53]),

---

53. See, for instance, Nedarim 28a and Gittin 10b.

which, for example, elevates the obligation to pay taxes from a legal to a religious one. Provided the state laws are based on equality and fairness, the *halachah* demands that one should behave as a loyal citizen. To break the laws of the land makes one a criminal, which cannot be reconciled with any notion of *derech eretz* and *middos tovos*.

The *mitzvah* of *Kiddush Hashem*, and, more importantly, the severity of the sin of *Chillul Hashem*, are major driving forces in the Torah worldview regarding ethical conduct involving non-Jews and governments. In fact, *Kiddush Hashem* affects all of the concepts mentioned above. This precept will be dealt with more extensively toward the end of this chapter.

LETTERS FROM THE PAST: THE VILNA GAON

Powerful messages can be learned from the ethical wills written by great rabbis to their own families. The centrality of *middos tovos* in the Torah worldview comes through very strongly in the letter of the Vilna Gaon to his family. As noted in the Introduction to this book, it was written when he was planning to leave them for an extended period of time during his travels to the Land of Israel and while making arrangements for them to join him. He leaves detailed instructions on how the household should be run. The Gaon's plan to live in Israel did not materialize, but his letter remains an important document, and has since become well known. On what did he choose to focus, given that he was leaving for a long time?

Much of the letter discusses *middos tovos*, emphasizing the severity of speech-related sins, such as *lashon hara*. Consistent with his view that *middos* "encompass the entire Torah," the Vilna Gaon connects the rules against *lashon hara* with the building of good character. Although these laws are part of the actual *mitzvos* of the Torah, they are also rooted in a person's character.

The Gaon broadens the concept of sinful speech beyond *lashon hara* to include scoffing, breaking vows and oaths, and conflict-laden speech, all of which constitute bad *middos*. He urges his wife to guide everyone in their household to speak in ways that avoid conflict, "rather, everything [said] must only be in peace, in love, and in affection and in gentleness."

The supreme importance of the matter is demonstrated in the following passage from the letter:

> Every word is brought in judgment [before God]; not even a small utterance will be lost [and not judged by God]…because the sins of the tongue are above all else, as expressed in the statement of our sages, z"l, '…and *lashon hara* is equal to them all.'[54] And why should I elaborate on this sin which is the most severe of all the sins? 'All man's toil is for his mouth, [yet his wants are never satisfied.]'[55] [In reference to this verse] our sages, z"l, have said that all a man's *mitzvos* and Torah will not suffice [to save him from] that which comes out of his mouth…. In forbidden matters [of speech], such as *lashon hara* and scoffing and oaths and vows and conflict and curses, and especially in *shul* and on Shabbos and Yom Tov…not even one word will be lost and not written down [by God].

The passage continues at some length about punishment and accountability for sins of speech. The Vilna Gaon repeats the importance of ethical and good speech a number of times. For example, at one point in the letter, he cites a Midrash: "Every moment that a person closes his mouth [so as not to speak *lashon hara*] he merits a hidden light that no angel or creature can imagine."

The disproportionate attention given to the issues of *middos tovos* and proper speech shows how these Torah values were of enormous importance to this great leader.

The Chayei Adam's Letter

Rabbi Avraham Danzig, known as the Chayei Adam, was a distinguished Lithuanian sage whose life overlapped that of the Vilna Gaon. The Dayan of Vilna in his later years, the Chayei Adam left an ethical will[56] dealing with many subjects, but he focuses disproportionately,

---

54. *Tosefta Pe'ah*, chap. 1.
55. Ecclesiastes 6:7.
56. *Sefer Asher Yetzaveh*, p. 55 et seq.

both quantitatively and in intensity of language, on issues of *derech eretz,* *middos tovos,* and special care with *mitzvos bein adam lechaveiro.* Like the Vilna Gaon's letter, the Chayei Adam's will indicates what he regarded as the most important values he wished to convey to his family. In fact, he instructs them to read a part of it each day, going over it at least once every two months. The will follows the order of the *mitzvos* of the day, and much of the first portion deals with the correct approach to *davening* and learning. Moreover, he urges his family to eat in order to be healthy to serve God – and to eat with *derech eretz.*[57]

The Chayei Adam exhorts his children to do business in accordance with *halachah,* whether dealing with Jew or gentile, recounting to them the general principle: "All property acquired without integrity will not remain in one's hands."[58] He also speaks at length about the prohibition against lying and deceiving, which he describes as "the father of fathers of impurity."[59] He explains that the foundation of ethical business practices is faith in God as the source of all sustenance. This belief precludes jealousy, for it is understood that a person earns precisely what God's judgment decrees – which makes unethical practices ultimately unnecessary and ineffective. A person who truly believes in Divine providence will not cheat in business.

Furthermore, the Chayei Adam strongly emphasizes the severity of the prohibition of *onaas devarim* (emotional pain inflicted through words by insulting).[60] He warns his children not to take these matters lightly and says, based on the Mishnah, "And how would a person not take notice [of such a serious prohibition] that would destroy all efforts – fasts and *mitzvos* – that he does?" He cites the Rokeach: to hurt someone with words, even in private, is like murdering the victim. The only remedy is to beg for forgiveness.

The Chayei Adam deals severely with a number of negative character traits such as arrogance, brazenness, hatred, and anger.[61] Declar-

---

57. Ibid., pp. 68–69.
58. Ibid., p. 69.
59. Ibid., p. 70.
60. Ibid., pp. 71–72.
61. Ibid., pp. 75–77.

ing that a brazen person tends to become involved in conflict, he cites sources to show that such a person is regarded as wicked and is sentenced to *Gehinom*. Central to Torah values are the qualities of gentleness and humility, which include "not speaking harshly to any person." The Chayei Adam describes these as "very praiseworthy" attributes, among the essential defining characteristics of being a Jew, according to the Gemara.

Anger, he says, is a "repugnant" character trait; and he also notes that "hatred itself destroyed our house [the Temple] and exiled us from our land, and [involves] transgressing many negative commandments." Consequently, compassion – as the opposite of hatred – is praiseworthy. He warns that one must be very careful to do the *mitzvah* of *tzedakah* properly. Moreover, he warns that one should treat servants with dignity, "and just because they serve you, does that render them of lower status than you?"[62]

Toward the end of the letter, the Chayei Adam pleads, "My dear children – my friends whom I love! – beware of the four groups of people who do not receive the Face of the *Shechinah*: liars, scoffers, speakers of *lashon hara*, and flatterers. Be very careful with these matters; for even if such a person has Torah and good deeds, he will be lost from *olam haba*."[63]

Though intended as his last ethical will and testament to his family, the Chayei Adam's letter extends beyond them, speaking to us as well, movingly informing us of eternal Torah values and principles of *menschlichkeit*.

62. Ibid., p. 82.
63. Ibid., p. 83.

Chapter Three

A Matter of Direction

Rabbi Warren Goldstein

Chapter two presents the three main practical behavioral principles of *menschlichkeit*: *Derech Eretz, Middos Tovos,* and *Mitzvos Bein Adam Lechaveiro*. This chapter looks at how these principles actually could and should shape the entire Torah *derech* and direction of individuals, society, and history.

ASSESSING OUR DERECH

Rabbi Chaim Shmulevitz candidly states that a person can keep all the *mitzvos* and still be on the wrong *derech* (path) in life, and be held accountable by God for his mistakes.[1] He writes that even good intentions and devotion cannot save a person from the responsibility of not properly examining his *derech*, and for not seriously considering the possibility that he may be on the wrong path.

Apart from praying for guidance – which is important – Reb Chaim gives guidelines for how one can assess the authenticity of one's

---

1. *Sichos Mussar* 31:99.

derech. He cites the verse from Psalms as the standard by which all of one's Torah should be measured: "The commandments of Hashem are *yesharim*,"[2] meaning that the commandments of God reflect the value of *yashrus*, which literally means "straight," but reflects much broader values of integrity and uprightness. This, says Reb Chaim, is the ultimate test of one's *derech*: if the Torah and *mitzvos* one performs reflect the value of *yashrus*, one is on the right path. If not, even though on the surface one appears to be doing everything in accordance with God's will by obeying His *mitzvos*, in fact he is fundamentally at odds with Hashem.

Reb Chaim says that *derech eretz* is one important part of what *yashrus* means. Therefore, everything that a person does, including in the realm of *mitzvos*, must be guided by values of *derech eretz* and *middos tovos*. He notes that according to a Midrash cited by Rashi, Moshe questioned God's command to count the tribe of Levi, including the babies of at least one month, saying that he was unable to fulfill the instruction because it would mean infringing on the families' privacy. Granting his objection, God told him to go to each tent, and while Moshe stood outside, a Heavenly voice called out to him the number of people in each household. Reb Chaim explains that though Hashem had given an explicit command to count the people, Moshe fulfilled the task in a way that would not violate the principles of *derech eretz*. Yet, the Torah states that Moshe followed God's instruction "as commanded."[3] He contends that the phrase "as commanded" is to be understood literally, for it was as if God actually commanded him not to enter the houses, but to wait outside for the Divine voice to supply the needed information. Reb Chaim concludes that any instruction from Hashem must be interpreted as consistently as possible with the principles of *derech eretz* and *middos tovos*.

Hakoras hatov (gratitude) is another critical aspect of *yashrus*. Reb Chaim again cites the example of Moshe. Commanded by God to go to war against Midian, Moshe sent Pinchas to lead the people into battle. Viewed superficially, Moshe did not do as he was told by God. The Midrash cited by Rashi recounts that Moshe felt it would be wrong for him to fight against Midian, for he owed that country a debt

2. Psalms 19:9.
3. Numbers 3:16.

of gratitude. It had provided him with refuge when he fled from Egypt. As gratitude is an important Torah value, it follows that Moshe had to interpret God's command to go to war against Midian in a way that was compatible with it.

Reb Chaim cites a Midrash that is very harsh in its criticism of a *talmid chacham* who does not conduct himself with *derech eretz* and *middos tovos*, saying that "a carcass is better than him."[4] The Midrash makes this comment in the context of praising the exemplary *derech eretz* of Moshe Rabbeinu. The Book of Leviticus begins with God's invitation to Moshe to enter the *Mishkan* (the tent of meeting) in order to hear the contents of the Torah as part of the ongoing revelation that had begun on Mount Sinai. Despite his familiarity and closeness to God, Moshe was not so presumptuous as to enter uninvited. The Midrash points out the extent of Moshe's humility and sensitivity: "Go and learn from Moshe, father of wisdom, father of the prophets, who took Israel out of Egypt, and through him many miracles and wonders were done on the Red Sea; and he went up to the heights of Heaven and brought down the Torah from Heaven and was involved in the work [of building] the *Mishkan*, and yet would not go into the inner chamber until [God] called to him."

Good character and *derech eretz* prevented Moshe from entering without being called to do so. In contrast, one of the worst character traits from the perspective of our Sages is brazenness. "The brazen-faced [go] to *Gehinom*," says the Mishnah. The opposite quality is gentle sensitivity, a quality connected to humility – epitomized by Moshe Rabbeinu.

Reb Chaim[5] notes that from this Midrash we learn that even with all of Moshe's greatness and awesome achievements for Hashem, Torah, and *Klal Yisrael*, even a carcass would have been better than him if he had acted with a lack of *derech eretz*. This example reinforces the principle that a lack of *menschlichkeit* puts a person on the wrong *derech*, no matter what other good qualities he may have.

---

4. *Leviticus Rabah* 1:15. The literal meaning of the words of the Midrash is a *talmid chacham* who lacks "*da'as*" – which literally translated means knowledge or intellect. The Radal says this means *derech eretz* and *middos tovos* as the context of the passage so clearly indicates.
5. *Sichos Mussar* 32:5.

In reference to this, Rabbi Aharon Kotler comments, "Not only are we obligated to the priority of *derech eretz* before Torah, but also if there is a lack of *derech eretz*, all of a person's Torah is to be considered nothing; and not only is his Torah…considered unimportant, even his very essence is nullified." Reb Aharon explains that the reason *derech eretz* comes before Torah is that Torah was given to a person to elevate him and bring him into a state of closeness to Hashem and to eternal life – but these levels of Torah were given only to a person who has *already reached* the level of completeness of what it means to be a human being. And it is only through attainment and practice of the values of *derech eretz* that a person becomes a human being in the complete sense of the word. The image of a carcass conveys the seriousness with which our sages regard the precept of *derech eretz*, implying that without *derech eretz* and character refinement a person is sub-human.[6]

Reb Aharon explains that the reason the Midrash refers to a *talmid chacham* – even though everybody has similar duties of *derech eretz* – is that a breach of *derech eretz* by a *talmid chacham* is considered even more severe because of the *Chillul Hashem* that is caused. Disgrace to the Torah is brought about by a person who is recognized as having such a strong bond to the Torah and yet "is dirty and despicable with bad deeds and bad thoughts." He cites sources to explain that the Torah is like the daughter of Hashem who is taken in marriage by a person who learns. If the princess marries a coarse and crude person, she is brought into a state of disgrace by her husband. So too, the Torah is brought into a state of disgrace by a learned person who does not conduct himself with *derech eretz*.

Reb Aharon further comments on the comparison to a carcass based on the writings of Rabbi Chaim Vital, who explains, on a mystical level, that whereas the Torah and its *mitzvos* relate to the higher soul within a person, *derech eretz* relates to the animal life force within a person.

---

6. My *Rosh Yeshiva, zt"l,* would speak of a person who lacks *derech eretz* as a "barbarian." In support, he would often cite the sources in Gemara and Maharal that appear in Chapter Two.

TWO CRUCIAL MOMENTS IN HISTORY

Derech eretz and *middos tovos* should direct the very path and destiny, the *derech* of *Klal Yisrael* as a whole, and should shape the direction of Jewish history. Rabbi Kotler explains that the foundational nature of the principles of *menschlichkeit* has manifested at two crucial moments in Jewish history: the giving of the Torah on Mount Sinai and the tragic deaths of Rabbi Akiva's students.

At Sinai, Moshe Rabbeinu did not eat or drink for 40 days and nights while receiving the Torah. This required tremendous dedication on his part and miracles from God to ensure his survival. The Midrash explains that Moshe fasted because of *derech eretz!* He was adhering to the dictate: "When you go to a city, follow in its customs."[7] As Moshe was among God and the angels, who do not eat or drink, Moshe did not eat or drink out of sensitivity to the prevailing custom.

According to the Midrash, the Torah is known as "the Torah of Moshe" in the merit of this self-sacrifice on the mountain.[8] Certainly, according to the all-important principle of *pikuach nefesh* (the saving of a life), Moshe should not have fasted for so long. Then why should he endanger himself and transgress the principle of preserving life, relying on miracles to survive without food and drink? Reb Aharon says that at the moment the Torah came into the world for the first time, Moshe's *derech eretz* had to be perfect because without *derech eretz*, the Torah itself is defiled and corrupted. Without *derech eretz*, the Torah is not Torah. Consequently, life-saving miracles were necessary to ensure that his *derech eretz* and the transmission of the Torah would be without flaw.

The other episode in Jewish history cited by Rav Kotler is the tragic deaths of the students of Rabbi Akiva. The Gemara states that they died because they did not treat each other with proper respect and honor.[9] Reb Aharon brings sources to support his opinion that the loss of such *talmidei chachamim* was an even greater loss than the destruction of the Holy Temple, going so far as to question whether the terrible consequences were proportionate to their wrongdoing. His answer is

---

7. *Exodus Rabah* 47:5.
8. *Mechilta Beshalach.*
9. Yevamos 62b.

illuminating. He explains that, historically, this was a crucial time of consolidation and transmission of the Oral Torah for all future generations. Rabbi Akiva was to the Oral Torah what Moshe was to the Written Torah. Hearkening back to the example of Moshe on Mount Sinai, any lack of *derech eretz* would have corrupted the Oral Torah that Rabbi Akiva and his students were bringing into the world. As the custodians of the Oral Torah, the students of Rabbi Akiva were held up to exceptionally high standards of *derech eretz*, and were found wanting. Their fate prevented their lack of *derech eretz* from damaging the Oral Torah for all future generations. Reb Aharon thereby reiterates the point that a person who has Torah without *derech eretz* does not in fact have Torah at all, despite all appearances to the contrary.

"A PERVERSE AND TWISTED GENERATION"

One of the greatest calamities of Jewish history is attributed directly to the negation of the values of *menschlichkeit*. The destruction of the Second Holy Temple in Jerusalem and the ensuing exile of the Jewish people at the hands of the Roman Empire had a catastrophic effect, which is felt to this day; we still await the Redemption and rebuilding of the Temple. The Gemara asserts that the devastation came as punishment for the sin of *sinas chinam* (causeless hatred).[10] It points out that the people of that generation "were involved with Torah, *mitzvos*, and doing acts of kindness," and yet, because of their baseless hatred for each other, the Temple was destroyed. The famous Netziv of Volozhin pinpoints their sin as failure to act in accordance with *yashrus*. He writes that the generation of the destruction of the Second Temple was "righteous and saintly and dedicated learners of Torah, and yet they were not *yesharim* – upright and good – in the paths of their world."[11]

The Netziv defines *yashrus* as the central value from which everything flows; literally translated as straightness, but much broader in its implications that include integrity, uprightness, sensitivity, kindness, compassion, and highly developed character traits (such as being slow to anger and quick to forgive). According to the Netziv, the Book of

10. Yoma 9b.
11. Introduction to his commentary, *Haamek Davar* on Genesis.

Genesis teaches the highest principles of *derech eretz, middos tovos,* and *bein adam lechaveiro* through the lives and deeds of our Patriarchs and Matriarchs.

Citing the Gemara that the Book of Genesis is called *Sefer Hayashar* (the book of the forefathers who lived with *yashrus*),[12] the Netziv furnishes numerous biblical proofs that all the forefathers demonstrated their outstanding capacity to avoid conflict and pursue peace through generous and forgiving spirits. Avraham was accommodating to Lot when conflict erupted between their shepherds; Yitzchak forgave Avimelech very easily in spite of the harm the latter tried to inflict on him; and Yaakov spoke to Lavan at all times with quiet dignity, despite the latter's duplicity and attempts to kill him. Moreover, Yaakov was easily appeased when the two parted ways.

Part of their *yashrus*, says the Netziv, was the forefathers' love and concern for all people. Avraham, in particular, demonstrated his identity as "father of a multitude of nations" by begging God to spare the cities of Sodom and Gomorrah from destruction. And he did this despite the fact that the people of those cities opposed his core values of kindness and compassion, and were about to be destroyed for their evil, particularly for their cruelty to the poor and the wayfarer. The Netziv contrasts Avraham's generosity – even with those who opposed him – with Jews who have *sinas chinam,* causeless hatred in their hearts even for fellow Jews.

The Netziv addresses the question of what transgression triggered the destruction of the Second Temple. He refers to a biblical verse that describes the society of the Second-Temple period as a "perverse and twisted generation."[13] Perverse and twisted is the very opposite of straight and upright. The Netziv explains the verse is from the prophetic song of *Haazinu,* which in part justifies God's punishment of that generation: "The Rock – perfect is His work, for all His paths are just; a God of faith without iniquity; righteous and upright is He."[14] The

---

12. The Gemara Avodah Zarah 25a explains this in the reference to what the Books of Joshua (10:13) and Samuel II (1:18) call the *"Sefer Hayashar."*
13. Deuteronomy 32:5, ArtScroll Chumash translation based on Rashi.
14. Deuteronomy 32:4, translation mainly based on ArtScroll Chumash.

word upright in Hebrew is *yashar*. The next verse reads, "Corruption is not His – the blemish is His children's, a perverse and twisted generation." As one Who is the epitome of *yashrus*, God could not tolerate a "perverse and twisted generation" whose fundamental sin was living in opposition to all values of *yashrus*.

The Netziv contends that "because of the hatred in their hearts for each other, they suspected anyone whom they saw behave not in accordance with their opinion in the service of God of being a *tzeduki* and an *apikores* [categories of heretics]." Adding to this shocking statement, he says that they did this *leshem Shamayim* (for the sake of Heaven), for they were very religious people. Their good intentions could not save them from annihilation because their approach and behavior to other people were the very converse of *yashrus*.

Comparing the destructions of the First and Second Temples, the Gemara notes that the first was destroyed for the three cardinal sins of murder, idolatry, and sexual immorality, teaching us that the sin of causeless hatred is equal in severity to the three cardinal sins. In fact, the Gemara observes that the exile after the destruction of the First Temple lasted only 70 years, as was pre-ordained, and the exile of the second has already lasted much longer – which indicates that the sins of the Second Temple were even worse than those of the first.[15] The Gemara also points out that the duration of the exile of the First Temple was revealed to our sages but the duration of the second one was not because the societal sins of the former were openly known, while the sins of the latter were hidden. Just as the sins were hidden, so is the fate of the Jewish People in this long exile.

Commenting on this comparison, the Maharsha explains that, on the surface, the generation of the Second Temple observed *mitzvos* and were even friendly to one another; but in their hearts and behind closed doors, they hated one another and behaved treacherously towards each other. This was worse than the open sins of the generation of the First Temple destruction, because hidden sins demonstrate a greater fear of people than of God, whereas revealed sins show a similar disrespect for

---

15. Yoma 9b.

both.[16] This is the problem of the "perverse and twisted generation": they appear righteous, but beneath the surface, they lack, as the Netziv put it, *yashrus* – basic integrity, goodness, and uprightness. It is noteworthy that the Gemara says that they actually did do acts of kindness, but it seems that they did kindness only for those whom they did not hate. Furthermore, according to the Netziv's explanation, even their kindness could not compensate for a fundamental lack of integrity and uprightness.

THE LITMUS TEST OF ONE'S DERECH

Rav Chaim Shmulevitz suggests that another defining test of the *derech* and direction of one's life is whether it reflects the verse referring to the ways of Torah as ways of pleasantness and the paths of Torah as paths of peace. The values of "ways of pleasantness and … peace" are a litmus test for the correct *derech*. If a person is fulfilling all commandments – but in a manner that is not pleasant or peaceful – such a person is not living according to authentic Torah values.

Reb Chaim demonstrates his approach by referring to the Gemara's discussion about the kinds of tree branches that satisfy the requirements of a *lulav* (palm branch) for the *mitzvah* on Sukkos.[17] The Gemara rejects a particular branch purely on the grounds that it has thorns and therefore conflicts with "ways of pleasantness," even though the branch complies in all other respects. He notes that the principle underlying "ways of pleasantness" is actually used to interpret the *mitzvos*: a branch with thorns – runs the legal argument – could not possibly be the branch that God had in mind, simply because it does not conform to the Torah's defining characteristic of "pleasantness." It follows that all aspects of one's Torah living must be an expression of peace and pleasantness.

Another aspect of "ways of pleasantness and … peace" is to not cause pain to another person. Reb Chaim shows how the entire

---

16. The Maharsha cites as support the law that a thief (who took something when no one was looking) pays a fine of double the value of the stolen object, whereas a robber (who took in view of his victim) merely replaces the value of the stolen object because the former is more afraid of man than God, whereas the latter demonstrates equal disrespect for both.
17. Sukkah 32b.

redemption from Egypt was subject to this value.[18] Moshe objected to accepting the task of leading the people for fear of hurting the feelings of Aharon, his older brother.[19] God countered that, on the contrary, Aharon would be happy for him. Reb Chaim points out that God didn't dismiss Moshe's concerns about his brother's pain, nor would it have been less important than God's explicit instruction to lead the historic and eternal exodus from Egypt. Reb Chaim concludes that from this example, we learn that even the crucial and lofty project of the redemption from Egypt could not override basic principles of decency, *derech eretz*, and *middos tovos*. Everything, no matter how important, must be examined through the prism of these values.

"THE NAME OF HEAVEN IS BELOVED THROUGH YOU"

There is another vital test of whether one is on the right *derech*, says Reb Chaim. The Gemara[20] says that the injunction "you shall love the Lord your God"[21] is fulfilled "by making the name of Heaven beloved through you." This is achieved when a person has studied Torah "and his dealings with people are with integrity and his speaking to people is with gentleness." Then, continues the Gemara, "What do people say about him? 'Fortunate is so-and-so who has learned Torah, fortunate is his father…fortunate is his teacher who taught him Torah.'" We are to behave in ways that will inspire others to exclaim, as the Gemara puts it, "'Have you seen how so-and-so, who has learned Torah – how beautiful are his ways and how refined are his deeds.' Of him the Scripture says, 'And He said to me, you are my servant Israel, through you I will be glorified.'"

The Gemara then describes the situation of a person who has learned Torah and does not behave with integrity and does not speak to people gently. The reaction of others is to perceive Torah very negatively, saying, "Woe to so-and-so who has learned Torah…. Fortunate are those people who have not learned Torah."

---

18. *Sichos Mussar* 32:5.
19. *Exodus Rabah* 3:16.
20. Yoma 86a.
21. Deuteronomy 6:5.

Therefore, Reb Chaim concludes, according to this Gemara, one reliable test of whether a Torah person is on the right *derech* is when objective outsiders look at his conduct and see moral beauty and refinement. But if people are repulsed by what they see, it is a sign that such a person is on the wrong path even if he technically fulfills all the *mitzvos*.

The sensitivity required to respect ordinary people also relates to another significant Torah value: *meurav bein habriyos* (the ability to mix easily with people). It is about engaging easily with people, and having the humility and sensitivity to relate to their issues, concerns, and interests from their perspectives. It also means that Torah should not transform one into a strange and aloof person who is detached from society and this worldly life to the extent that others experience him as alien and difficult to relate to.

THE MEANING OF KIDDUSH HASHEM

The Gemara discussed above also highlights one of the most crucial Torah values: *Kiddush Hashem*. Our Creator becomes universally beloved and sanctified when Torah Jews are exemplary in their behavior.

The actions of any person associated with Torah, especially *talmidei chachamim*, reflect on the reputation of God and His Torah. A lack of *derech eretz* or basic morality can cause *Chillul Hashem* – bringing God and His Torah into disrepute.

The Gemara recounts that the Amora Rav said that if he were to take meat from a butcher and not pay immediately, it would be a *Chillul Hashem* because people may think that he was stealing.[22] The rule against *Chillul Hashem* even applies to physical appearance. Accordingly, the Gemara[23] says that a *talmid chacham* who goes out with a stain on his clothing is liable for his life because of the bad impression he creates, which people then attribute to the Torah itself. This may explain the ruling of the Rambam[24] (based on the Gemara) that it is permitted to teach Torah only to students whose actions are good and decent in

---

22. Yoma 86a, Rashi (s.v. *velo*), Rambam *Hilchos Yesodei Hatorah* 5:11.
23. Shabbos 114a.
24. *Hilchos Talmud Torah* 4:1. The *Kesef Mishneh* cites one of the opinions in a dispute on this matter in Gemara Berachos 28a as the source. The case there is of a person

accordance with *derech eretz* and *middos tovos*. To teach a person who may bring disgrace to the Torah is forbidden.

The Gemara states that *Chillul Hashem* is the only sin for which full atonement cannot be achieved before death.[25] Even after repentance and suffering, one has to wait for the moment of death to receive full atonement. Hence, the seriousness of a stain on the clothing of a *talmid chacham*! Significantly, the Rambam deals with the laws of *Kiddush/Chillul Hashem* under his section of the Mishneh Torah, "Laws of the Foundations of the Torah."

The Torah mandate is to be very careful with one's appearance, conduct, and manner of engaging with people so that one never brings God or His Torah into disrepute. This applies even to the way one performs *mitzvos*. The *Mesilas Yesharim*, by Rabbi Moshe Chaim Luzzatto, (Ramchal) says that even when doing a *mitzvah*, a person must be careful not to cause people to mock Torah, thereby causing a *Chillul Hashem*. Obviously, when a person fulfills the basic requirements of *halachah*, he must proceed regardless of ridicule. But if a person observes a *chumrah* (stringency) that causes ridicule of the Torah, the Ramchal says that he is held responsible for the *Chillul Hashem* he caused.

In fact, all of the values mentioned above are connected to potential *Chillul* or *Kiddush Hashem*. A failure in *derech eretz*, *middos*, monetary ethics, and *mitzvos bein adam lechaveiro* cause *Chillul Hashem*. The Gemara is also concerned about *Chillul* and *Kiddush Hashem* when it comes to non-Jews and their impression of Jews and Torah.

FOLLOWING THE DERECH OF TIFERES: REFLECTING A TORAH OF BEAUTY

The value of *tiferes* brings together many of the values discussed in this chapter. It literally means "beauty" but actually has a more profound meaning that includes harmony, balance, and glory. The multi-faceted meaning of this word reflects the multi-faceted values that are bound

---

who is insincere – "his inside is not like his outside." This ruling is also found in the Tur Y.D. 246 but not in the *Shulchan Aruch*. I heard this explanation of the Rambam – that the concern is for *Chillul Hashem* – from my *Rosh Yeshiva, zt"l*.

25. Yoma 86a.

together by this concept. We noted above that when a Jew behaves in a way that makes God more beloved by others, it fulfills the Divine goal: "Through you, I will be glorified." The Hebrew word for "glorified," *pe'er*, is from the root of the word *tiferes*.

The main quality of the Telzer approach to everything (according to Rav Avraham Yitzchak Bloch, the Telzer *Rosh Yeshiva*) was *tiferes*,[26] and the Telzer students were taught that this should be a person's dominant character trait. His devoted *talmid*, Rav Mordechai Gifter, confirmed that this was the "Telzer way"[27] in his writings as well. Rav Mottel Katz, the Telzer *Rosh Yeshiva* in America, used to teach that his *talmidim* must be *Torah b'kli mefoar* (Torah in a beautiful vessel).

What, exactly, does such a mission entail? It is multi-faceted. The Mishnah states: "What is the correct path that a person should choose? A path which brings *tiferes* to him, and *tiferes* to people."[28] In one explanation of this passage, Rabbeinu Yonah says this refers to doing *mitzvos* in a physically beautiful way. The Rambam maintains that the Mishnah is referring to the *tiferes* of *middos tovos*, which are generally dependent on following the middle path of moderation in all things. In his commentary on this Mishnah, Rav Yisrael Lipshitz explains that the quality of *tiferes* includes fulfilling one's basic duties arising from the *mitzvos*, nurturing *middos tovos* such as humility, and living with *derech eretz*. It follows that *tiferes* is about holistic goodness in all areas of life.

Rabbi Avraham Yitzchak Bloch taught that *tiferes* should permeate every aspect of how one exercises control over his time, conduct, and appearance. *Tiferes* manifests in a neat, dignified, and elegant physical appearance, which also reflects a moral beauty and refinement that brings glory to God and His Torah. *Tiferes* is even revealed in the way one thinks about the world. The main difference between animals and mankind is that animals function in the world through instinct and automatic natural reflexes; but human beings can exercise control over their actions and thoughts. Human beings have this ability, and the more developed it is, the more elevated the person.

---

26. *Shiurei Da'as Reb Avraham Yitzchak*, p. 67 et seq.
27. *Pirkei Emunah*, p. 159.
28. Avos 2:1.

Tiferes, therefore, involves living with the highest levels of control over one's thoughts and actions. When such control is always in operation, a person will naturally be slow to anger and of even temperament. His *middos* will shine. In particular, he will display the *middah* of *mesinus* – literally translated as patience, but on a deeper level, it means inner tranquility and control, as opposed to frenzied, instinctual reactions, which can have negative consequences. Anger is one of the worst *middos*, according to the Gemara. The Rambam who advocates the middle path on all areas of character, makes an exception of anger and arrogance. One must go to the opposite extreme to avoid anger and arrogance at all costs.

Continuing these thoughts, Reb Avraham Yitzchak taught that people must invest effort in performing *mitzvos* with beauty, dignity, and whole-heartedness. This concept is in line with the translation in *Targum Onkelos* of "I will glorify Him" in the biblical statement "This is my God and I will glorify Him."[29] Onkelos renders the meaning as "I will build for Him a sanctuary," i.e., I will make my home a beautiful sanctuary for God.[30] The *Shechinah* (the Divine Presence) rests in a home where *mitzvos* are performed with *tiferes*; and a life of service of Hashem with *tiferes* makes this world a home for the *Shechinah*.

The Gemara notes that contained in the statement "I will glorify Him" are the two words "I" and "Him" referring to the commandment to emulate God, particularly in His kindness and compassion. It would follow, therefore, that part of the beauty one must bring into the world is God's kindness and compassion.

The *mechilta* cited by Rashi explains that "I will glorify Him" means "I will tell the world of God's praises and glories." That is ultimately how the quality of *tiferes* is fulfilled – by bringing awareness of the beauty and greatness of God and His Torah to all mankind, which is the ultimate *Kiddush Hashem*.

Reb Avraham Yitzchak[31] says in the name of his father, Rabbi

---

29. Exodus 15:2.
30. This passage is also understood by the Gemara in Shabbos 133b to mean that one must do the *mitzvos* beautifully.
31. *Shiurei Da'as*, pp. 92–93.

Yosef Yehudah Lev Bloch, that the three following verses are the pillars of a Torah worldview:

1. *"Shma Yisrael*…Hashem is one."[32]
2. "The nations will acknowledge You, Hashem, the nations will acknowledge – all of them."[33]
3. "'Peace, peace for the far and near,' says Hashem, 'and I will heal him.'"[34]

These verses provide a comprehensive framework for the concepts of *tiferes* and *Kiddush Hashem*, and indeed many of the concepts of the right *derech*. They create the framework for service of Hashem in this world.

Shma Yisrael – the unity and authority of Hashem – is the foundation and overarching concept of the entire Torah. Everything we are and do comes from Hashem.

From the second verse we learn the importance of proclaiming the truth of the Torah to the entire world. Reb Avraham Yitzchak writes, "We must try to spread the knowledge of truth in the world, not concentrate the truth in a small narrow circle. Rather, our goal and purpose is to sanctify the Name of Heaven in the world and to spread it throughout earth."

In elaborating on "Peace, peace for the far and near…and I will heal him," the Telzer *Rav* invokes the Gemara, which explains it like this: through the power of peace, those who are far are brought closer to the healing presence of Hashem.

According to this verse, everything we do to promote truth must be done in a peaceful manner. It must be peace rooted in truth, as modeled by Aharon the High Priest: "Love peace, pursue peace, love people and bring them closer to Torah."[35]

---

32. Deuteronomy 6:4.
33. Psalms 67:4.
34. Isaiah 57:19.
35. Pirkei Avos 1:12.

Chapter Four

The Mussar Movement

Rabbi Berel Wein

To this day, *Mussar* is a major Torah philosophy, influencing Jewish life across the ideological spectrum. Initially, the *Mussar* Movement profoundly shaped Lithuanian Jewry; it later extended throughout the Jewish world, fostering deeper understanding, sharper focus, and greater emphasis on key Torah values and principles. To better understand how and why *Mussar* evolved, we must look at both its historical context and the life of the one man most responsible for this sociological sea change: Rabbi Yisrael Lipkin of Salant.

Due to the pressures of persecution by the Czarist regime and the secularization of large sections of European Jewry by the *Haskalah* ("Enlightenment") movement, weaknesses began to appear in the ethical foundations of Lithuanian Jewry. Fortunately, in 1810 a phenomenal prodigy was born who would counter this negative development with outstanding creativity, perseverance, and spiritual strength. As a child, Yisrael Lipkin was especially gifted in the art of *pilpul*, displaying an ability to connect very disparate Talmudic subjects with one another through complicated mental gymnastics. However, at the age of fifteen he began to study under the rabbi of Salant, Rabbi Tzvi Hirsh Broida, who was famous for his deeply analytical approach to Talmud. Reb Yisrael forsook his pilpulistic brilliance in favor of his mentor's method, and thereafter, pursued simplicity, intellectual honesty, and accuracy in his study of Torah. His fame as a genius accompanied him even in this intellectual transformation.

In Salant, Reb Yisrael came under the influence of a disciple of the Gaon of Vilna, Rabbi Yosef Zundel of Salant, who encouraged him to study *Mussar* – the four basic books of Jewish ethics and morality. They are *Chovos Halevavos* (Rabbi Bachya ibn Pekuda, eleventh-century Spain); *Orchos Tzaddikim* (anonymous, fourteenth-century Spain); *Sha'arei Teshuvah* (Rabbi Yonah Ibn Gerundi, thirteenth-century Spain); and *Mesilas Yesharim* (Rabbi Moshe Chaim Luzzatto, eighteenth-century Italy and the Netherlands). The term *Mussar* literally means chastisement, and these works urge scrupulously honest appraisal of oneself and self-improvement through a stronger attachment to God and man. Accordingly, Rabbi Yosef Zundel advocated devoting time daily to personal introspection and spiritual contemplation.

In 1840, Rabbi Yisrael left Salant and settled in Vilna taking a position there as the head of the yeshiva "Remailles." Because of internal faculty friction, Rabbi Yisrael left to found his own yeshiva in Zorace, a suburb of Vilna. His was a rare combination – a charismatic holy personality, a talent for oratory, a logical and coherent approach to unraveling complicated Talmudic issues, and exemplary personal behavior. He attracted many great people to study with him. He not only conducted classes in Zorace, but visited many of the synagogues and study houses of Vilna on a regular basis, teaching Torah to many different groups. His fame spread and his reputation as one of the leading Talmudists of the era was solidified. From this position of recognition, acceptance, and admiration, he turned to his life's work – the establishment of the *Mussar* Movement.[1]

---

1. There have been many exhaustive works written about the *Mussar* Movement and its founder Rabbi Yisrael Lipkin of Salant. Works in English include Hillel Goldberg's *The Fire Within*, Brooklyn, 1987, and Jacob Glenn's *Rabbi Israel Salanter*, Philadelphia, 1948. In Hebrew, see Rabbi Dov Katz, *Tnuas Hamussar*, Tel Aviv, 1952,

Rabbi Yisrael crafted his program in response to inroads made by the Reform and *Haskalah* movements, envisioning the defeat of these forces not so much by attack and dispute as by the elevation and restructuring of traditional Jewish life and behavior on superior ethical, moral, and behavioral grounds. Rabbi Yisrael sought to elevate Jewish religious life by restoring the primacy of ethical behavior as the key to meaningful Torah observance and study. He sought to deepen the sincerity of religious commitment and rejuvenate the value system of Jews, individually, and of Jewish society in general. All aspects of life – even community relations with the government and with the non-Jewish world – were to be measured by the standards of *Mussar*.

By 1845, Reb Yisrael was ready to launch his idea in Vilna. His plan consisted of four parts:

1. the printing and dissemination of the classical works of *Mussar* (listed above);
2. lectures delivered regularly in all synagogues, study houses, and public forums on *Mussar* topics;
3. the establishment of special "*Mussar* houses" where *Mussar* would be constantly studied and taught in all communities and neighborhoods; and
4. the development of an elite cadre of disciples who would commit their lives and futures to spreading and strengthening the *Mussar* Movement.

Rabbi Yisrael demanded ethical improvement in society and personal commitment to moral values. He required punctilious observance of Torah law and commandments, but with a soul; with the understanding that good deeds are necessary to create a good person and becoming that good person was the end goal of Jewish life. Lithuanian *Mussar* therefore lent a new dimension to all of the time-honored aspects of

---

Emmanuel Itkes, *Rabbi Yisrael Salanter*, 1982, and Rabbi Yechiel Weinberg's *Sidrei Aish*, vol. 4, p. 276, Jerusalem, 1969. The classic Hebrew biography of Rabbi Yisrael Lipkin is that of his disciple, Rabbi Yitzchak Blazer, *Ohr Yisrael*, reprinted many times. The thrust of this chapter is derived from these works of scholarship and research.

Judaism. It was to be prayer with *Mussar*, Torah study with *Mussar*, communal activity with *Mussar*, commerce with *Mussar*, charity with *Mussar*, domestic relations and family life with *Mussar*, life itself with *Mussar*.

Mussar was meant to successfully challenge and combat the blandishments of the secular humanism of the nineteenth century. It was also meant to infuse Jews with internal pride and self-worth in an age of Czarist oppression.

This ambitious program began to take root in Vilna and it initially achieved wide popularity. It was well received in the scholarly community, and to a limited extent, in the wider Jewish community as well. *Mussar* is intellectually rigorous, spiritual, and introspective. It also has a spirit of serenity about it. It preaches care for others, sensitivity in word and deed, and an optimistic view of a better world.

Nevertheless, the *Mussar* Movement never became a truly popular movement among the masses of Lithuanian Jewry; its direct success was in the yeshivas, where it achieved prominence and presence in almost all of those institutions. Naturally, since the yeshivas provided the spiritual leadership for Lithuanian Jewry, the influence of *Mussar* eventually filtered down to the masses, restoring ethical behavior and perspective. The movement was destined to influence not only Lithuanian yeshivas in Rabbi Yisrael's sphere, but would have an impact on worldwide Jewish life for generations until today.

A tragic misreading of Rabbi Yisrael and his movement would eventually force him to flee Vilna. In the 1840s, the *Haskalah* movement was on the ascent. Nowhere was this more evident than in Vilna, where a number of the movement's leaders lived and were very active in propagating its cause. The leaders of *Haskalah* initially were fascinated by Rabbi Yisrael's personality and philosophy. They felt that as a societal "reformer," he was an ally to their cause. In 1848, the Russian government established two new official rabbinical seminaries in Vilna and Zhitomir[2] under the auspices of the *Haskalah*. The goal was to produce modern

---

2. These institutions were failures from every point of view. Their graduates were not accepted by the Jewish communities as legitimate rabbis. Some of these "rabbis" even converted to Christianity! The Russian government recognized their failure and closed these institutions approximately a decade after their founding.

rabbis. Rabbi Yisrael was asked to teach Talmud in the Vilna *Haskalah* seminary. Because of the Russian government's support of *Haskalah* positions and institutions, the offer made to Rabbi Yisrael was laden with ominous personal consequences if he refused. He fled Vilna and took up residence in Kovno, where he continued teaching and strengthening the growing *Mussar* Movement.

Rabbi Yisrael's adherents spread the movement throughout Lithuania. His main disciples were Rabbi Yitzchak Blazer, Rabbi Naftali Amsterdam, Rabbi Simchah Zissel Ziev, Rabbi Eliezer Gordon, and Rabbi Jacob Joseph. Also counted in the *Mussar* Movement in the nineteenth and twentieth centuries were Rabbi Yisrael Meir Kagan (Chofetz Chaim), Rabbi Yosef Bloch, Rabbi Nosson Tzvi Finkel, Rabbi Yoseph Y. Horowitz, Rabbi Yerucham Levovitz, Rabbi Yechezkel Levenstein, Rabbi Eliyahu Dessler, and Rabbi Yechezkel Sarna, among many others.

Of course, no innovation is without its opponents. As it gained momentum, the *Mussar* Movement caused an upheaval in the yeshivas. A number of institutions became embroiled in internal controversy for many years over whether or not to include *Mussar* in their daily schedule, ostensibly taking time away from pure Talmud study. Moreover, the inclusion of *Mussar* could be divisive, as not everyone in the yeshiva was willing to study *Mussar* formally. The climate of controversy gave rise to a provocative question advanced to Rabbi Yisrael Salanter: If one has only ten minutes a day to study, should he study *Mussar* or Talmud? His riposte: "*Mussar* – for if he studies *Mussar*, he will soon realize that he has more than ten minutes a day to study Torah and Talmud."

Like all young believers in a new ideal, many of the *Mussar* advocates proselytized openly, tenaciously, and successfully. Some of them undermined the authority of the established rabbi of the community or of the head of the yeshiva, and they cast themselves as an elitist, exclusive group. By the end of the nineteenth century, this activity and attitude evoked the opposition of some important rabbinic figures and heads of yeshivas to the *Mussar* Movement. Eventually this opposition had a salutary, calming effect upon the proponents of *Mussar* who reined in their extremists and answered logically and convincingly all questions raised against them. *Mussar* became a mainstream movement in Lithuanian Jewish society and in its institutions of Torah learning.

While the original opposition of some of the rabbinic leaders of Lithuania to *Mussar* had a positive effect on the movement and Lithuanian Jewish society, the opposition of the *Haskalah* supporters was negative, fierce, and unrelenting. They ridiculed the piety and exactitude of *Mussar* and used every means at their disposal, including Czarist governmental pressure and broad media propaganda, in their attempts to crush the movement. Since the *Haskalah* was basically a small, *avant garde* elitist movement, it reacted violently to the success of the *Mussar* Movement in attracting young men of leadership, intellect, and promise away from *Haskalah* and into the ranks of yeshivas and Torah study houses. This *Haskalah* war against *Mussar* soon descended into violent and shameful polemics and behavior, with little philosophy, thought, or ideas being seriously debated.

As evidence of the nature of this conflict, the following incident is revelatory: Rabbi Yisrael's youngest son, Yom Tov Lipman Lipkin was a child prodigy in mathematics. Though he had no formal secular education, he was accepted at the age of seventeen to the University of Königsberg in Prussia. His father opposed his choice, knowing it would lead to his assimilation and abandonment of observant Judaism, but was powerless to stop his son from going. The young Lipkin eventually received a PhD in mathematics at the University of Vienna and discovered a technological mathematical breakthrough in applied mathematics, still known today as the "Lipkin parallelogram." Lipkin moved to St. Petersburg where he was showered with honors by the Czarist government. By this time, he had given up Jewish observance and had become a hero and role model for the followers of *Haskalah* as to how the "new Jew" should look and behave. They bearded the old lion in his den by publishing a congratulatory article in their newspaper in honor of "the great rabbi and teacher Rabbi Yisrael Salanter of Kovno...whose son Lipman is a crown to his sainted and learned father, who did not prevent his son from studying in the university so that thereby Torah and wisdom will be united in the person of his son for the glory of our people."[3]

In the following issue of the newspaper, Rabbi Yisrael inserted this letter:

---

3. *HaMaggid* (1865) vol. 7, p. 49.

Since truth has been the guiding light in my life, I am compelled to publicly announce that my son is not the 'crown' to me as the editor indicated but rather the opposite is true. He is a source of disappointment and sadness to me and my heart weeps over his way of life. Anyone who loves him and can influence him to change his ways and not go counter to my soul and wishes will do a great favor to me this very day.

     Yours in faith,
     Yisrael of Salant[4]

This vignette sums up the struggle between *Mussar* and *Haskalah*, and illustrates the deep inroads that the ideas of *Haskalah* and secular humanism made in the traditional Jewish community, especially among the youth of the time. It was a known fact that many of the sons of prominent rabbis defected to the ranks of the *Haskalah*, thereby granting it legitimacy and acceptance, even in the ranks of the largely traditional Lithuanian world.

Unable to defeat the *Mussar* Movement directly, *Haskalah* leadership would often claim that their movement was somehow allied with the goals of the *Mussar* Movement. But nothing could be farther from the truth. *Mussar* stemmed from authentic Torah sources developed and refined over the ages and was intensely loyal to Torah values and traditional behavior. Even ideas and methods that were adopted from outside Judaism were thoroughly Judaized in their presentation and adaptation to Jewish life and thought. Everything was viewed through the prism of Torah and the Oral Law. The *Haskalah*, on the other hand, derived its ideas and goals almost exclusively from non-Jewish outside sources and concepts. Even the Jewish ideas and content of its program were thoroughly secularized and cleansed of Jewish tradition and perspective in its presentation and goals.[5] This basic divergence was readily apparent by the beginning of the twentieth century, but in the 1850s and 1860s – the

---

4. *HaMaggid* vol. 11, p. 83.
5. An example of this would be the adoption of Biblical Criticism as a method of studying the holy Torah.

formative decades of the *Mussar* Movement – this fundamental difference was not yet clearly understood by the Jewish masses of Lithuania.

Looking back from our twenty-first century view, it is clear that *Mussar* survived while *Haskalah* has largely disappeared from the Jewish world. The greatness of *Mussar* and its influence on the Jewish world has become more readily recognizable in later generations, when the movement was past its peak, than in its earlier stages when the movement's dynamism and popularity was surging.

Though *Mussar* is no longer defined as a movement in our current Jewish life, it has become part of the fabric of our lives in its various expressions. Its scope and influence is felt throughout the Jewish world, shaping traditional Jewish society, just as Rabbi Yisrael Salanter intended. It is certainly one of the greatest contributions of Lithuanian leadership to general Jewish society in all places and times.

THE ROLE OF DVEIKUS:
RELIGIOUS FERVOR IN MUSSAR

While *Mussar* enveloped its followers with quiet devotion to God, it would be a mistake to view them as purely intellectual or emotionally unfeeling. Anyone who has had the privilege of participating in a "*yeshivishe*" prayer service is well aware of the devotion and emotion underscoring such *davening*. Though fervent and sincere, this kind of prayer service is conducted in a non-obtrusive, private fashion without shouting, dancing, or commotion.

Followers of the *Mussar* Movement sought and achieved *dveikus* (a feeling of connection and adherence with the Almighty) in a disciplined fashion. They were not prone to exhibit acts of piety and devotion publicly, for excess in this area could appear hypocritical in the service of God.

Those of us who still saw the remnants of the *Mussar* world after the Holocaust were always struck by the serenity and devotion, the care and love that were apparent in every word of their prayers. When they were engaged in prayer, it was obvious that all of the distractions of this world – that ever-present cacophony of sound and noise – somehow melted away and that their souls spoke directly to the Creator. This was also true in the study of Torah. There was a well-known aphorism among Lithuanian Jews: prayer is when Jews speak to God, and Torah study is when God speaks to Jews. Both are forms of *dveikus* that form a continual, eternal conversation between Jews and God. It is interesting to note that Torah study was always carried out with a vocal volume of sound, and even melody; while prayers were conducted more softly and quietly. *Dveikus* comes in many forms and expressions, and even in different decibels.

Dveikus was not confined or defined by prayer or Torah study alone. It was a goal in everyday activities as well. Every action in life was seen as forging a link of eternity with Heaven. Rabbi Yisrael Lipkin of Salant once said, "Helping another human being in this world's mundane matters is the foundation of my eternity in the next world." Serene demeanor can mask the turmoil of a soul reaching for eternal connection to its Creator.

The great *Mussar* teachers preached that only through order and discipline could one reach Godliness and truly emulate the Creator. Simply looking around at the almost incomprehensibly perfect world of natural order in which we live commands us to cleave to our Creator in that same fashion – with perfect order. Order and discipline are not the enemies of emotion and *dveikus*.

I remember that when I was ten years old, my father and grandfather enrolled me in Beis Midrash L'Torah in Chicago. My teacher was the kind, sagacious, warm and caring Rabbi David Silver, a quintessential product of the Lithuanian yeshivas. I was terribly nervous the first few weeks of the school year, and for good reason. The bigger boys picked on me, and I became physically ill. Rabbi Silver consoled me, telling me the following anecdote about his own life: "When I was eleven years old, my father sent me away to study in one of the famed Lithuanian *Mussar* yeshivas. When I arrived, one of the rabbis told me to hang up my coat in the clothes closet and then to come see him. I did so, but I hung up my coat as a child does – one sleeve in, one sleeve out – in a completely crooked fashion. The rabbi – who had been watching me all that time – said to me gently, with a wry smile on his face, 'If this is how disordered you are on the outside, one can only imagine how chaotic you must be within your soul!'" When my revered *rebbi* revealed to me that he, too, had suffered turmoil as a child, I felt instantly encouraged and I took his advice to persevere. Looking back on it, I see that his story was a perfect illustration of the *Mussar* worldview – that our outside behavior reflects the inner state of our soul.

Spiritual leaders of Lithuanian Jewry took seriously the Talmud's emphasis on imitating God's ways, so to speak, as the key to a truly religious way of life. One of "God's ways" is to be self-effacing (again, "so to speak," for we are viewing Him in human terms). Charity given anonymously, prayer uttered silently from the heart rather than loudly from the throat – these were the attributes that the prophet Amos praised so greatly when he demanded that Israel must understand what it means to "walk humbly with your God." "Walking humbly" achieves a firm connection – sincere *dveikus* – with the Creator of all.

This inner emotion of connection is the secret of Jewish life even in the worst moments and terrible circumstances. The love of Torah study and the intellectual appreciation of Judaism remained constant and primary, as did the profound sense of closeness to God for Lithuanian Jewry.

Moreover, one who does not indulge in overly fanciful expectations is not easily disappointed or depressed by life's realities and society's unavoidable shortcomings. Wry humor and an appreciation of human folly and foibles became an integral part of Litvishe Jewish life. Lithuania was a country with few natural resources, a relatively small population, and a chronically weak economy. It featured brutally cold and snowy winters and dry, steamy summers. The Jewish population also suffered from a bitter, deeply implanted anti-Semitism. Yet the great Lithuanian rabbinic leaders taught their followers not to be depressed; rather to remain creative, cheerful, firmly idealistic, and optimistic. These traits are also products of *dveikus* since they are, as mentioned earlier, a higher form of imitating God's ways.

Rabbinic leaders also maintained a dignified, yet humble, presence in their communities. Their understanding of leadership was rooted in the fact that Moshe Rabbeinu was given the title "servant of God." In being a true servant, he was constantly attached to Heaven and became the greatest of all prophets. Like Moshe, they identified themselves as servants of their people and of God. And in that very servitude, they attained religious fervor and attachment to the Eternal One.

Reserve, humility, and discipline do not necessarily signal coldness. In Lita, self-containment of emotion was transformed into the highest form of *dveikus,* investing all aspects of life with a warmth and intensity that carried them aloft in the bleakest of circumstances.

To the outsider, however, that intensity was not always apparent, and indeed, could be easily missed. Avraham Kariv, a noted Hebrew writer and author wrote a small memoir about his birthplace of Lithuania and the Jewish society that lived there for centuries before being destroyed in the 1940s. Written with blood and tears, not merely ink, the 48-page essay is hauntingly beautiful. His concluding lines underscore the subtlety of Lithuanian Jewish character: "A visitor to Lithuanian Jewry will require a deeply analytical and discerning eye in order not to come back empty. Just as Torah and *Mussar* were studied in Lithuania on a deeply analytical and critical basis to plumb their depths, so too is it necessary to listen carefully and see deeply in order to recognize and truly appreciate the character of the Lithuanian Jew."[6]

---

6.   Kariv, *Lita Makurasi,* Tel Aviv, 1958, p. 48.

Chapter Five

Eirlichkeit: Honesty, Integrity, and Humility

Rabbi Warren Goldstein

There's an old Lithuanian Yiddish saying that expresses a unique worldview: "A Jew is not *frum* – a Jew is *eirlich*." *Frum* means religious and *eirlich* means honest and upright. The ultimate accolade, the very essence of a Jew is not his level of religiosity, but his level of *eirlichkeit*, connoting his honesty, integrity, and uprightness.

On the other hand, this saying is also puzzling. Isn't being a good Jew about religious duties as well? In this chapter, we will explore the true meanings of *eirlichkeit* and *frumkeit*.

SPEAKING THE TRUTH

Truth is a central Torah value. The Gemara says: "The seal of the Holy One, Blessed Be He, is truth."[1] This value manifests itself in many different ways, from the most simple to the most profound. On a basic

---

1. Shabbos 55a, Yoma 69b.

level, it is about honesty in speech – telling the truth. The Torah says: "Distance yourself from falsehood."[2] The Gemara cites this verse in the context of the requirement to tell the truth.[3]

The *Sefer Hachinuch* teaches that the unusual language of the verse "distance yourself" indicates how serious this prohibition is and "there is nothing more repulsive than falsehood" which is "abominable and corrupt in all eyes."[4] We must distance ourselves from falsehood because truth is part of God's essence and we are required to imitate Him. The strong wording of the *Sefer Hachinuch* gives some indication of the significance of this value in Torah philosophy.

Lying is part of the general immorality of deception, what the Gemara calls "speaking one way with the mouth and another with the heart."[5] The Rambam expands this Talmudic principle to include all aspects of verbal deception: "It is forbidden for a person to conduct himself with words of false smoothness and enticement."[6] And he includes in this prohibition the Talmudic principle of *geneivas da'as*,[7] which means to knowingly deceive a person in order to attain his good will. The Rambam cites an example of selling non-kosher meat to a non-Jew while giving the impression that the meat is kosher, leading the non-Jew to believe that the meat is more valuable to the Jewish seller than it really is. The Rambam concludes with his description of verbal integrity: "truthful speech, and a correct spirit, and a heart free from corruption and deceit."[8]

2. Exodus 23:7.
3. Kesubos 17a. There is much discussion concerning the exact legal status of the prohibition. Some say that it is a negative commandment. Others say that telling a lie is a transgression of a positive commandment, or that outside of the courts, it is rabbinic prohibition. See *Tzitz Eliezer* 15:12 for an analysis of the exact nature of the prohibition.
4. *Sefer Hachinuch Mitzvah* 74.
5. Bava Metzia 49a, Rashi Bava Metzia 49a (s.v. *shelo*) gives a specific example of verbal deception: at the moment of promising to do something having no intention of fulfilling it.
6. Rambam *Hilchos De'os* 2:6.
7. Chulin 94a, b.
8. Rambam *Hilchos De'os* 2:6.

Keeping One's Word

Fulfilling verbal commitments made to others is another important Torah principle connected to the value of truth.[9] The context of the Gemara's discussion is commercial negotiations, where breaking one's word is considered so serious that, in certain circumstances, those who do so are described as *mechusrei emunah* (people who lack basic trustworthiness),[10] with whom the "the spirit of the sages is displeased." In the more serious circumstance of breaking a verbal commitment, a guilty person is subjected to the official halachic sanction of a court declaration: "The One who exacted punishment from the generation of the flood and the generation of the dispersion will exact punishment from the one who has not stood by his word."

The Rambam says that dealing with people in an honest and trustworthy manner – especially fulfilling verbal commitments – is an absolute, unconditional moral requirement, from a Torah perspective.[11] The first question a person's soul must answer to the Heavenly Court

---

9   Talmud Bava Metzia 49a. Rashi's interpretation, Bava Metzia 49a (s.v. *elah*). Rashi Talmud Kesuvos 81a (s.v. *pri'as*) invokes this Torah law as the basis for the duty of repaying a debt. See the *Torah Temimah* Leviticus 19:36, no. 265 for a discussion of the Ritva who disagrees with Rashi. The *Gilyon Hashas* on Bava Metzia refers to Rashi, seemingly agreeing with Rashi's expansion of the law. The *Minchas Chinuch* (259) proves that, according to Rashi, fulfilling verbal commitments is *de'oraisa*. He says that it would be *de'rabanan* according to the Rambam's general principle that anything learned from a verse that the Talmud does not explicitly state to be *de'oraisa* is presumed to be *de'rabanan*.

10. This paragraph is based on the Talmud's discussion in Bava Metzia 49a. There are many details of the different situations where these principles are applied.

11. *Kesef Mishneh* on Rambam *De'os* 5:13. Rav Yosef Karo explains that this point in the Rambam is based on the Talmud's (Yoma 86a) description of how people are inspired to love God and His Torah when they see those who learn Torah displaying outstanding moral qualities. Dealing faithfully and honestly is one such quality, defined by Rav Yosef Karo as including integrity of verbal commitments. The *Torah Temimah* questions the *Kesef Mishneh* on the basis that the simpler source for the Rambam is the passage in the Talmud Bava Metzia 49a with which we have been dealing. See the *Ain Mishpat* on Bava Metzia that links the Rambam to Bava Metzia as the *Torah Temimah* does.

is: "Did you deal faithfully and honestly with others?"[12] This includes the integrity of verbal commitments.[13]

"Say Little and Do Much"

Shammai states in the Mishnah: "Say little and do much."[14] This means promise less than you deliver and deliver more than you promise. The Gemara[15] says this quality defines a *tzaddik* (a righteous person). Converse conduct defines a *rasha* (a wicked person), who promises much, then does not deliver. Our role model of integrity in this regard is Avraham, who offered only a little bread and water to the famous three wayfarers (who, unbeknown to him at the time, were angels). They accepted his humble offer and he then presented them with a lavish feast, which, we are told, could have graced the table of King Shlomo.[16] The example of the converse is Ephron the Hittite, with whom Avraham negotiated to purchase the Cave of Machpelah as a burial site for his beloved wife, Sarah. In public, Ephron promised much by offering Avraham the burial site for no payment. But in the end, Ephron asked for, and Avraham paid, an exorbitant amount for the land.[17] Ephron's lack of integrity in promising much and not delivering on his promise is regarded by the Talmud as the classic behavior of a wicked person.

When Rav Moshe Feinstein addressed the 56th National Convention of Agudath Israel of America, he chose to speak on integrity.[18] He cited the biblical example of Rivkah when she passed the tests Eliezer had devised and proved herself a worthy wife for Yitzchak. Reb Moshe noted that she offered to water the camels only after she had given water to Eliezer. This impressed Eliezer because she didn't promise to water the

---

12. Shabbos 31a. See also the second answer of Tosafos Sanhedrin 7a (s.v. *elah*).
13. Rav Yosef Karo does not say so explicitly. However, the words are exactly the same as those in Talmud Yoma 86a, where he does interpret them to include the integrity of verbal commitments.
14. Avos 1:15.
15 Bava Metzia 87a.
16 Ibid.
17. See commentary of Rabbi Aryeh Kaplan in *The Living Torah*, where he explains how exorbitant the price was by comparing the price to what things cost in those days.
18. *The Jewish Observer*, January 1979, p. 3.

camels initially. Integrity demands being careful not to make promises that you may not be able to keep. Moreover, Rivkah's demonstration of "say little and do much," a value so central to the house of Avraham and to the Jewish people forever, was part of what qualified her to marry into such a family.

Vows and the Sanctity of Speech

The critical significance of keeping verbal commitments is linked to one of the most stringent areas of *halachah*: the laws of vows. That breaking a vow is one of the most serious sins is evidenced by the particular attention this issue receives before and during the High Holy Days of judgment and atonement. The custom for every individual to annul his vows commences before Rosh Hashanah. Furthermore, Yom Kippur is ushered in with the famous *Kol Nidrei* prayer, which is also about confronting the sin of broken vows. Great care is taken so that people do not enter the holy day bearing such sins.

A vow is binding in very specific circumstances, and therefore, very often, an ordinary verbal commitment is not necessarily covered by the law of vows. Nevertheless, the law of vows reflects the Torah's concern with the sanctity of speech and commitments that are made verbally, albeit in accordance with a very specific formula.

The Torah states: "He shall not desecrate his word,"[19] indicating that speech is holy. *Targum Onkelos* translates the verse, "and Adam became a living soul" as "and Adam became a speaking being." The Maharal explains that while other creations are either purely spiritual or purely physical, man is a combination of physical, emotional, spiritual, and intellectual components. The power of speech is a product of all elements of the human being, and is therefore the quintessential expression of human uniqueness. In fact, the Talmud defines a human being as the *medaber* (the speaker). Speech is sacred, and through it we fulfill some of the most important commandments, including prayer and Torah study. Conversely, some of the worst sins – gossip, slander, insult, breaking vows, and ignoring verbal commitments – are committed through speech.

---

19. Numbers 30:3.

Personal Integrity

There is another dimension of breaking commitments that goes beyond the issue of the sacredness of speech, and that is being true to oneself – what we might call "personal integrity." This includes promises made to oneself, even if not communicated to others, because personal integrity is an essential element of integrity itself; and it is a prerequisite to developing integrity toward others.

The Gemara[20] says that Rav Safra was the epitome of "one who speaks truth in his heart."[21] The Rashbam recounts an illuminating incident in this regard: one day, when Rav Safra was reciting the *Shma* (and therefore was not permitted to interrupt his prayer with talk), someone came to him to buy merchandise. The buyer offered to pay a certain price that satisfied Rav Safra, but he was unable to interrupt his prayer to accept the offer. The purchaser misinterpreted Rav Safra's silence as non-acceptance of the offer, and then began increasing the offered purchase price while Rav Safra continued to recite *Shma*. Upon concluding his prayer, Rav Safra informed the purchaser that he would accept the first offer because Rav Safra had already agreed to the bargain in his heart. With this outstanding demonstration of integrity, Rav Safra certainly earned the accolade of "one who speaks truth in his heart."

Rav Avraham Yitzchak Bloch,[22] comments that Rav Safra teaches us that integrity of verbal commitments is part of a commitment to inner truth, and to faithfully fulfilling the undertakings of one's heart. Such an undertaking is accorded the same status as if it were verbally articulated. This is part of being honest because it means that the external is made to conform to the internal state of mind, establishing congruency between the two. Consistent with this, the Talmud teaches us that "a *talmid chacham* whose inside is not like his outside, is not a *talmid chacham*."[23]

---

20. Bava Basra 88a.
21. Psalms 15:2.
22. *Shiurei Da'as*, p. 9.
23. Yoma 72b.

Modesty and Inner Truth

Truth resides in the hidden world and not the world of externalities, a value the prophet Michah called "walking modestly with your God."[24] This verse is a "great principle in the service of God,"[25] according to Rabbi Pinchas, the son of Rabbi Yehudah (known as the Maggid of Polotzack), student of the Vilna Gaon. He says that a person should conceal his good deeds as far as possible because such modesty leads to purifying one's intentions when serving God.

The Gemara expounds on the verse "walking modestly with your God" to include the manner of fulfilling the commandment of burying the dead, and assisting a bride to get married.[26] As funerals and weddings are public events, it says that one should be involved in these modestly; how much more so, the Gemara goes on to say, should one be modest in the performance of other good deeds, which are private by nature. Rav Chaim Shmulevitz writes that good deeds performed publicly provide ulterior benefits such as receiving honor and recognition from others. Therefore, great effort is required to purify one's motives by doing these deeds in as modest a manner as possible.[27] Consistent with this concept is one of the foundational pillars of the *Mussar* Movement: one must purify one's inner thoughts and emotions even when performing good deeds.[28]

Focusing on consistent inner truth and sincere devotion – as opposed to superficial religiosity, which is focused on externalities – is a central Torah pillar. The connection between "inside" and "outside" is clearly articulated by Rabbeinu Bachya in his book, aptly titled "Duties of the Heart":[29]

> Regarding one whose inside is not like his outside, Scripture says, 'His heart was not whole with Hashem his God' (Kings I, 11:4). As is well known, if someone contradicts himself or proves

---

24. Micah 6:8.
25. *Asher Yetzaveh*, p. 111.
26. Sukkah 49b.
27. *Sichos Mussar* 31:46.
28. *Tnuas Hamussar* vol. 1, pp. 63–64.
29. Feldheim 1996 ed., pp. 37–38.

himself a liar, whether in speech or in deed, people no longer believe in his integrity and have no confidence in his sincerity. Similarly, if our outer and inner selves are in contradiction, if our talk is not matched by our intentions, if the actions of our limbs are at odds with the convictions of our hearts, then our worship of God is imperfect; for God does not accept insincere service, as it is written: 'For I, God, love justice; I despise robbery in a burnt offering' (Isaiah 61:8).

According to Rabbi Avraham Grodzensky, the famous *Mashgiach* of Slabodka, the *Alter* of Slabodka taught that one principle in particular is of vital importance in the service of God: focusing on real internal change, not external superficialities.[30] This concept is encapsulated in a famous passage from Isaiah:[31] "The Lord said: 'Inasmuch as this people has drawn close, with its mouth and with its lips it has honored Me, yet it has distanced its heart from Me – their fear of Me is *like rote learning of human commands.*'" The key phrase is "like rote learning" which implies empty, external service and not deep change. According to Rav Grodzensky, the *Alter* emphasized the importance of real transformation resulting in the emergence of a "new person" through real change, in contradistinction to a "rote learning" approach to service of God. This is connected to the foundational Torah values of truth, sincerity, and modesty.

"OUTSIDE LIKE INSIDE"

Central to these values is the statement of the Gemara:[32] "Whoever takes pride in wearing the cloak of a *talmid chacham* and is not a *talmid chacham*, will not be allowed into the inner partition of the Holy One, Blessed Is He." Rabbeinu Gershom explains that this passage refers to a special hat or turban, which, in Talmudic times, only a *talmid chacham* was entitled to wear.

Appropriate clothing – clean, presentable, and dignified – is

---

30. *Toras Avraham* p. 236 et. seq.
31. Isaiah 29:13.
32. Bava Basra 98a.

required in terms of *derech eretz* and *Kiddush Hashem*; as Rav Mordechai Katz, the Telzer *Rosh Yeshiva*, used to say, the Torah must be in a *kli mefoar* (a beautiful vessel).[33] On the other hand, the general approach of many Lithuanian rabbis was to stress humility of dress and to discourage the egotism involved in externalities. Those who did not hold official rabbinic office dressed in ordinary apparel. There are many stories of how the Chofetz Chaim was not recognized in public because he wore a simple worker's cap, and not a rabbinic hat. Despite his towering stature as a *talmid chacham* and writer, he held no official position and therefore deemed it inappropriate to wear rabbinic garb. The father of Rabbi Eliezer Gordon, *Rosh Yeshiva* of Telz, was a brandy maker who dressed in sheep skins, though he was an accomplished *talmid chacham* and a student of the legendary Reb Chaim Volozhiner. It is told that when Rabbi Gordon's father walked into the *beis midrash*, Reb Chaim stood up for him. Amazed onlookers were privileged to see the renowned Reb Chaim rising respectfully for a man who looked like a peasant in sheep skins.

"The cloak of a Talmid Chacham"

An alternative interpretation of the Gemara passage cited above, "Whoever takes pride in wearing the cloak of a *talmid chacham* and is not a *talmid chacham*, reflects another dimension of personal integrity. While Rabbeinu Gershom presumes the allusion is to a distinctive turban, the Rashbam explains the passage differently, saying that it refers to extra piety in dress that a *talmid chacham* would appropriately observe: "The cloak of a *talmid chacham*" refers to a long frock that would cover the body and legs, ensuring extra levels of modesty.[34] The manner in which one dresses presents a particular image to oneself and to the outside world. Integrity and honesty demand that the outward appearance of extra piety reflect an inner reality, that a person not dress up in the "clothing" of piety when it does not reflect his true self.

The Gemara relates that Mar Ukva said about himself, "I am like

---

33. All of the examples in this paragraph I heard from my *Rosh Yeshiva*, HaRav Azriel Chaim Goldfein.
34. Rashbam, Bava Basra 98a (s.v. *kol hamisga'eh*).

vinegar, the son of wine, relative to my father; because if my father would eat meat now, he would not eat cheese until tomorrow at the same time. Whereas I do not eat [cheese] at this meal [where I ate meat], but I would eat it at the next meal."[35] Rabbi Avraham Yitzchak Bloch[36] points out that Mar Ukva clearly regarded his father's actions as praiseworthy because he describes himself as vinegar in comparison to wine for not doing as his father did. Reb Avraham Yitzchak then asks: if that is so, why did Mar Ukva not do as his father did, considering how highly he regarded his father's conduct? Reb Avraham Yitzchak answers that a person should not do anything that is disproportionate to his other deeds. Mar Ukva was bemoaning the fact that he was not on the high level of his father. His own level would make keeping the stringency of a 24-hour wait between meat and milk incongruent with his character and conduct in other areas of life.[37] Righteous conduct that is incongruent with one's life and conduct as a whole is dishonest and lacks integrity. A person acting in this way is not being honest with himself, and his visible deeds of piety do not reflect the truth of his real inner character.

THE "YUHARAH" PRINCIPLE

Since Torah philosophy is molded by *halachah,* it is not surprising that its rejection of disproportionate external piety is based on a Talmudic legal principle called *yuharah,*[38] translated literally as arrogance. *Yuharah* embodies a general legal principle that has a wide-ranging impact on the implementation of *halachah.*

Yuharah is discussed in a Mishnah relating to the question of whether it is permissible to work on Tisha B'Av. Different places have different customs, with some permitting work and others forbidding it.[39] The Mishnah rules that *talmidei chachamim* must follow the strict custom of not working, even if they live in a place where the custom

---

35. Chulin 105a.
36. *Shiurei Da'as,* pp. 174–175.
37. In the *Shiurei Da'as,* Rabbi Bloch does not explicitly connect this analysis to the issue of honesty and integrity, but it seems that these values are implicit to the idea he presents.
38. Berachos 17b, Pesachim 55a.
39. Pesachim 54b.

permits work. Raban Shimon ben Gamliel says that even a layman can conduct himself on the stricter level of a *talmid chacham*. However, the opinion of the majority of sages differs with him, based on the idea that to act as a *talmid chacham* would constitute *yuharah*. The Gemara explains that while Raban Shimon ben Gamliel agrees to the principle of *yuharah*, as the cited Mishnah indicates, he holds that in this case, there is no violation of it because abstaining from work could imply that the person simply has no work to do and is not necessarily abstaining for religious reasons.[40]

Although the Talmud discusses the *yuharah* principle in specific cases, its application is much wider. Any action, in whatever area of *halachah*, which goes beyond the letter of the law and can be described as an act of extra piety must be assessed to determine whether it violates the *yuharah* principle.[41] Obviously, the principle applies only to acts of extra piety, or *chumros*, and not to mandatory halachic duties. The philosophical implications of it are far reaching.

Like Achashverosh in the Garments of the High Priest

The laws of *yuharah* demand the honesty of being the same inside and out, of not wearing the "cloak of a *talmid chacham*" and not pretending to be someone else. One of the harshest condemnations of *yuharah* comes from a strongly worded document authored by Rabbi Pinchas, Maggid of Polotzack, a disciple of the Vilna Gaon. In an ethical will addressed to his children, he devotes considerable space to *yuharah*.[42] The Maggid

---

40. Pesachim 55a. The passage of the Talmud follows the same pattern as Talmud Berachos 17b that all opinions hold for the *yuharah* principle, differing only about the interpretation of its application.
41. The Mishnah of Talmud Sukkah 25a states that notwithstanding one's obligation to eat in the Sukkah, one is not required to do so when eating a snack. It then gives examples of people who even insisted on eating snacks in the Sukkah. The Gemara (Sukkah 26b) explains that the purpose of citing such examples is to teach that this act of going beyond the strict requirements of the law is not a violation of the general *yuharah* principle. The fact that an entire passage in the Mishnah is devoted to giving a dispensation for this act of extra piety demonstrates that an act of extra piety is presumed to be a violation of the *yuharah* principle until indicated to the contrary.
42. *Asher Yetzaveh*, pp. 114–115.

compares arrogant people to King Achashverosh, who wore the garments of the High Priest to his infamous party described at the beginning of the Book of Esther. Even though he was wickedly celebrating the destruction of the Temple, he appeared as righteous as the High Priest. Similarly, says the Maggid, those who are guilty of *yuharah* wear the garments of a *talmid chacham* as if they were worthy of such garments.

This analogy is significant because it goes to the essence of the falsity of extra piety: wearing an outer garment that is not true to the inner reality undermines the difference between the great and the ordinary because both now appear the same.

After citing numerous examples, the Maggid rhetorically asks why the Talmud takes such a strong line on this issue: "What is this great noise? Why should I care if someone wants to take stringencies on himself or do an act of goodness? Whom does he harm or cause loss with this? After all, he is not doing a bad deed."

He answers that a person who transgresses the *yuharah* principle "destroys the entire world with his good deeds." The Maggid elaborates on the severity of *yuharah*. One aspect is that such arrogance undermines greatness and leadership because when those who are not great conduct themselves as if they were, they erode the distinction between leaders and followers, and between teachers and disciples. This leads to a situation where "the lowly are raised up and the elevated are brought down." In such an environment, there can be no greatness in Torah. He cites the Gemara, which relates that there was a time in Jewish history when the numbers of the arrogant increased; consequently the number of true students of Torah decreased.[43] In such an environment, the Maggid writes, moral direction is lost from the world: those qualified to rebuke and to correct the people are rendered incapable of doing so by the arrogance of those who need the rebuke. Due to their inappropriate actions of extra piety, they see themselves as morally equal or superior to those truly qualified to provide leadership.

According to the Maggid, this breakdown of recognizable Torah greatness "destroys the law of the Torah and the law of Israel in its

---

43. Sotah 47b.

entirety."[44] He condemns *yuharah* saying that it "allows for nothing good to exist in Israel, and darkens the faces of the *talmidei chachamim*; and through 'good deeds' the world is made lawless,[45] the path of truth is lost, the world is turned up-side down ... and deeds become ruined."[46] Realizing that his strong language may seem hyperbolic, the Maggid adds, "I have not written one meaningless word if you have eyes to see the truth."[47] (The Maggid also deals with *yuharah* in regard to the importance of being humble, which will be discussed below.)

It is quite possible that the Maggid's righteous passion about the nature of the foundations of Jewish society came from the Vilna Gaon, his mentor. The Mishnah states: "A community that is dedicated to Heaven (*l'shem Shamayim*) will endure forever; a community that is not dedicated to Heaven will not endure forever."[48] Many varied opinions are offered as to what qualities render a community "dedicated of Heaven," and of its converse. The Vilna Gaon taught that a community dedicated to Heaven is one in which the lines of Torah leadership and authority are properly drawn and recognized.

The Gaon cites support for this interpretation from the Midrash, which contrasts two occasions when the people approached Moshe Rabbeinu.[49] The first, which ended in disaster, was their request that spies be sent into the Land of Israel. The second occurred at the giving of the Torah when the people requested that Moshe teach them the Torah because hearing the direct voice of God would overwhelm them. In the latter case, the text reads: "and you approached me, all the heads of your tribes and your elders."[50] The Midrash points out that here the delegation consists of proper leadership enjoying the respect and recognition of the general population. In contrast, in the former case no mention is made of "heads of your tribes and of your elders." Moshe says, "and you

---

44. *Asher Yetzaveh*, p. 114.
45. Translation of *hefker*.
46. *Asher Yetzaveh*, pp. 114–115.
47. *Asher Yetzaveh*, p. 115.
48. Pirkei Avos 4:11.
49. Talmud Sifri Devarim 1:22, *Yalkut Shimoni* Devarim 804.
50. Deuteronomy 5:20.

approached me, all of you."[51] The term "all of you" denotes a group with no proper leadership structure – what is referred to as *irbuviah*, meaning a motley mixture, unruly rabble.

The influence of the Vilna Gaon and his students had a large impact on their *kehillah* (community) and Rabbi Yechiel Yaakov Weinberg writes that Lithuanian Jewry excelled in its *Kavod Harabbonim* – its respect for rabbis.[52]

Yuharah and the Individual

The *yuharah* principle addresses the damaging impact of extra piety on the individual, as well as on the society as a whole. A case discussed in the Gemara[53] indicates that a person can be guilty of *yuharah* even if the act of extra piety is performed privately. The great Tannaim, Rabbi Yehudah Hanasi and Rabbi Chiya, were walking together on private property adjacent to the public road. They were allowed to do so because of a special dispensation given by Yehoshua when he originally conquered and divided the Land of Israel. In the days of dirt roads, the winter rains made the roads of Israel difficult to walk on because the mud dries in such a way that there are hard spikes left behind. Yehoshua decreed that in such circumstances one could walk on private property adjacent to the public road. Since the land was given to the people with this decree in place, walking on private property in this instance is not regarded as a violation of private property rights.

While walking, Rabbi Yehudah Hanasi and Rabbi Chiya noticed that Rabbi Yehudah ben Kenusiah refused to rely on Joshua's dispensation and, instead, was walking in the middle of the public road, despite the spikes in the road. Not realizing the stature of Rabbi ben Kenusiah, Rabbi Yehudah Hanasi was outraged at the violation of *yuharah* and wanted to impose an excommunication ban on Rabbi Yehudah ben Kenusiah. Rabbi Chiya endorsed the outstanding character of Rabbi Yehudah ben Kenusiah, who was his student, assuring Rabbi Yehudah

---

51. Deuteronomy 1:22. Rashi on the verse cites this passage from the Sifri.
52. *Sidrei Aish* vol. 4, p. 278 et seq.
53. Bava Kama 81b.

Hanasi that his intentions were purely for the sake of Heaven. This endorsement saved him from the ban.

The Maharshal argues that Rabbi Yehudah ben Kenusiah was unaware that he had been seen.[54] If he had been aware of the presence of his mentor, Rabbi Chiya, he would have been guilty of not giving proper honor to his mentor (by acting more piously than his mentor). In such a case, even his pure intentions would not have saved him from sanction. Clearly, respect for Torah leadership is a matter of importance, and the absence of such respect in performing extra piety was regarded as very serious. The Maharshal derives the general principle from this case that the *yuharah* law is transgressed even if one is alone.

The fact that the *yuharah* principle applies even when a person is alone, and the act of extra piety is hidden from society, means that its damage goes beyond its societal impact. *Yuharah* is a negative character trait that is intrinsically problematic whether others observe it or not. We see that the *yuharah* principle advances another very important Torah value: humility.

Arrogance, argues the Maggid of Polotzack, invalidates a person's good deeds because the heart and mind have the power to ruin physical actions. A person who wears "the cloak of a *talmid chacham*" due to his arrogance would also (if given the opportunity) "wear the 'clothes' of the King of the world without concern for the honor of its Owner."[55] Thus, commitment to truth, integrity, and *Kavod Harabbonus* is also deeply connected to humility. *Yuharah* is the legal principle that brings all these values together.

The Maharshal derives another principle from the case of Rabbi Yehudah ben Kenusiah: in the absence of a clear indication of the greatness of the individual (and his exceptional dedication to God) anyone who performs an act of extra piety by acting stringently in the case of a well-established and well-accepted lenient halachic ruling dispensation, contravenes the *yuharah* principle and is liable to an excommunication ban. The Maharshal explains that the sanction for *yuharah* is actually

---

54. Rashi Bava Kama 81b (s.v. *gedulaso*) seems to indicate that Rabbi Yehudah ben Kenusiah was aware of them.
55. *Asher Yetzaveh*, p. 115.

part of a broader category of the sin of arrogance, which the Gemara elsewhere says is punished by excommunication.[56]

DEVELOPING HUMILITY

The Maharshal follows the approach already discussed, which seeks to extract broader principles of the rules of proper conduct from specific *halachos*. In so doing, he locates *yuharah* within a broader framework of values relating to arrogance and humility. The Gemara condemns arrogance in the strongest possible terms by citing different opinions comparing it to some of the worst sins, such as denying God's existence, committing severe sexual immorality (such as adultery or incest), and worshipping idols.[57] The Gemara cites further opinions that the *Shechinah* cries out in mourning for an arrogant person, for God says He cannot live together with an arrogant person.

The Rishonim follow the Gemara's severe approach to arrogance. The Rambam, a staunch advocate of balance and moderation in the area of character and ethics, holds that arrogance is one of two exceptions (the other is anger) in which extremism is encouraged: in the case of arrogance (and anger) a person should go to the opposite extreme and be excessively humble (and slow to anger).[58] As authority for this position, the Rambam cites no less a figure than Moshe Rabbeinu, himself, who is described in the Torah as *"very humble."*[59] The Rambam also mentions some of the Gemara's severe remarks about arrogance to support his approach that extreme behavior is valid in this case.

Similarly, the Ramban accords pride of place to the virtue of humility. In his famous letter to his son, he exhorts his son to be humble and explains how humility can be achieved. This is especially noteworthy, given the relative brevity of the letter. He says that humility "is the best of all the character traits" for it leads a person to awe of God, fear of sin, and a morally correct way of dealing with others. Similarly, the Rosh lists

---

56. Sotah 5a.
57. Sotah 4b.
58. *Hilchos De'os* 2:3.
59. Numbers 12:3. Emphasis added.

as the very first item of exhortations in his famous *Orchos Chaim*: "To distance oneself from arrogance in the absolute furthest manner possible."

The Ramchal's *Mesilas Yesharim* is one of the key classic texts that emphasizes humility. He first deals with it as part of general moral punctiliousness for living in accordance with Torah laws and values. Then he accords humility even greater significance by making it the subject of one of the major sections of his book, and in fact, one of the highest rungs on the ladder of spiritual and moral development in Torah.

On a basic level, humility ensures the capacity to learn and obey God's Torah. That is why the Gemara states, as we have seen, that when the number of arrogant people increases, the number of true *talmidei chachamim* decreases.

The opposite of humility – arrogance – as explained by the Ramchal,[60] is a sense of personal superiority and entitlement to praise for exceptional achievements or qualities. An arrogant person is disconnected from the truth, for there is a denial of his shortcomings. Awareness of personal flaws would temper feelings of superiority over others. Arrogance is predicated on a denial of the true reality that all of one's natural talents and achievements come from God, just as God gives a bird the ability to fly. It is not to the bird's credit. The Ramchal argues that natural talents impose duties upon the recipient to use them for the good. To be humble means understanding the truth that God is the source of all human talents and achievements. Arrogance, therefore, is a denial of God's role in the world; hence, the Gemara's comparison of arrogance to idolatry and atheism.

Consistent with this approach, the Ramban avers the intellectual folly of arrogance and its disconnection from truth:[61] "In what can a man's heart be proud? If it is wealth – it is God who makes one poor or wealthy. If it is honor – does honor not belong to God? As it is written, 'Wealth and honor come from You.' How can one take pride in the honor

---

60. This explanation of arrogance and humility is based on the Ramchal in *Mesilas Yesharim* chapters 11 and 22. The subject is vast. To merely give even a complete overview of the Ramchal's approach is beyond the needs of this chapter and, therefore, only a few aspects of humility and arrogance will be highlighted.

61. Aspects of this translation are based on *A Letter for the Ages*, Mesorah Publications, 1989.

of his Owner? And if he takes pride in wisdom, 'God may remove the speech of the most competent and take away the wisdom of the aged.'"[62]

Humility and Equality

"All people stand as equals before God," states the Ramban, "for in His fury He casts down the lofty and in His goodwill He elevates the downtrodden. Therefore, humble yourself, and God will raise you up."

Equality is about understanding that every person has been created by God with a unique purpose. The Ramchal offers the parable of a large mansion where there are many servants working for the owner. Each servant has a different task in the maintenance and service of the house and its occupants. Every task is necessary for the proper functioning of the house and therefore every servant is important to the master of the house. So too, every person in this world has a unique task to perform and is important to the One and Only Master.

Humility includes the appreciation of the unique value of every person. According to Rabbi Eliezer Yehudah Finkel, the early twentieth-century *Rosh Yeshiva* of Mir, such an appreciation inspired Moshe's legendary humility.[63] The verse describing Moshe's humility is conventionally translated: "And the man Moshe was very humble, *more than all other people.*" Reb Lazer Yehudah translates the Hebrew *mikol ha'adam* as literally "from all people," meaning that Moshe was so very humble because of the inspiration that he drew "from all people." He recognized the special hidden treasure of greatness within each person and was humbled by it. To be truly humble, one must value the unique contribution of every person. For example, it would be wrong to value only those who achieve distinction in Torah learning, and to not appreciate the special and different role that every person has to play in building human society. The Ramchal explains that humility and arrogance function at the inner level of thought and emotion and the physical level of action.

An inspiring example of humility can be found in a *teshuvah* (ruling) on the question of drinking blended whiskey, written by Rav

---

62. Job 12:20.
63. Cited by *Tallelei Oros* Numbers, vol. 1, p. 149.

Moshe Feinstein.[64] His opinion is that although there are good reasons to be stringent, there is sufficient authority to rely on for a lenient ruling. He then offers that he has taken upon himself not to drink blended whiskey due to the stringent opinions. He adds, however, that when he is in public, he drinks blended whiskey so that he will not appear to be guilty of *yuharah*.

An example of religious arrogance is explained by Rabbi Eliyahu Dessler,[65] a close disciple and nephew of Rabbi Chaim Ozer Grodzensky. Rav Dessler tells of a student who used to "bring in" Shabbos much earlier than everyone else. He would learn in the *beis midrash* on Friday afternoon in his Shabbos clothes, keeping the laws of Shabbos. The *Alter* of Slabodka discouraged this practice because while everyone else was hurrying to get ready for Shabbos on Friday afternoon, he would naturally feel superior – perhaps even harbor a momentary feeling that others were actually not keeping Shabbos properly.

Attaining Eternal Life

The importance of humility in the service of God is mentioned in the Gemara as a prerequisite for attaining eternity. The Gemara states:[66] "Who is a son of the world-to-come? A modest and humble person, who bows when entering, bows when leaving, and who learns Torah continuously but does not regard himself as worthy of credit because of it." In other words, one who earns a place in the world-to-come is someone who does the right thing, but does not view himself as deserving special recognition and praise because of it. He does not focus on his own goodness or elevation, but on his responsibilities. He goes about doing good in an unobtrusive manner (which relates to honesty, sincerity, and integrity, which we have discussed as important Torah values). At the core of religious humility is the Gemara's injunction: one should "not regard himself as worthy of credit" because of religious observance.

In his ethical will, the Maggid of Polotzack cites the above Gemara

64. *Igros Moshe* Y.D. 1:62.
65. *Michtav M'Eliyahu*, vol. 3 pp. 294–295.
66. Sanhedrin 88b.

and notes the sages' significant *omission* of certain actions that qualify one as a "son of the world-to-come":[67]

> They did not say: one who fasts continuously; one who does not eat from a living creature; one who says pleadings and requests continuously; one whose legs and arms shake during his prayers and who bows down to the ground; one whose spoken language is the Holy Language; one who makes his *tefillin* large and his *tzitzis* long; and so similarly all the imagined virtues that the masses view as important principles in the service [of God]. And possibly these things [that the masses think are important] are good to ensnare people and the ignorant masses [by creating the appearance of righteousness]. And it is these very things that desecrate the law of Israel.

The Maggid links the value of humility with the value of inner truth, as opposed to outer superficiality that is designed to impress others. He warns his children not be deceived by external manifestations of piety that may be insincere, but instead to focus on the Gemara's real test for humility, which includes the sincerity that makes a person "a son of the world-to-come." This exhortation brings together many of the major points of our discussion: Humility is connected to honesty, integrity, and sincerity. Arrogance is connected to superficiality, deception, and the cynical use of religion for self-advancement.

THE PERUSHIM

The Maggid cites the Talmud,[68] which strongly criticizes those who employ the appearance of piety to win respect, honor, and praise. A *braisa* lists several categories of people who use acts of extra piety to create a positive public image for themselves, calling them *perushim*

---

67. *Asher Yetzaveh*, pp. 116–117.
68. The Maggid cites the *braisa* from Talmud Sotah 22b. The *braisa* is brought by the Gemara in explanation for the Mishnah Sotah 20a. The *braisa* gives a list of seven kinds of *perushim*. The Mishnah mentions only one. The reference in the main text to a Mishnah is from Sotah 20a as mentioned.

(ascetics).[69] It refers to those who separate themselves from things that are permissible in order to create the false impression of outstanding piety.[70] They may be motivated by the love and admiration of others, or even fear of others' opinions of them.[71] One such category includes those who ask what acts of extra piety they can perform. They do so in order to impress others, implying that they are so righteous that they have already achieved all that is required of them.[72] Another example is those who try to demonstrate the extra piety of avoiding sin when a woman appears by "closing their eyes and colliding with a wall, drawing blood" as a result.[73]

There is the case of excessive humility – holding one's head very low – to create an impression of humility, but which actually masks arrogance. The Ramchal says that a person who acts in this way and "takes pride in his 'humility'" actually seeks superiority and praise in the eyes of society.[74] The arrogance of false humility is a complete lie, which eventually will be evident for all to see.[75]

The common denominator is that, in all of these cases, acts of extra piety are performed without sincerity. The intention is to create the appearance of saintliness in order to benefit from the resultant honor, praise, and esteem.[76] The Maggid writes further:[77]

---

69. Rambam *Perush Hamishnayos*. He explains that deception to create the false impression of great piety is the common denominator of the cases. See note below with similar approach to be found in the Maharsha.

70. Maharal *Chidushei Agados Sotah* 22b (s.v. *zayin perushim*).

71. Ibid. (Maharal's explanations for *parush meahavah* and *parush meyirah*.)

72. Rashi Sotah 22b (s.v. *mah chovasi*).

73. Rashi Sotah 22b (s.v. *mekiz dam*).

74. *Mesilas Yesharim*, chap. 11.

75. Ibid.

76. Maharsha Sotah 22b (s.v. *parush meduchia*). The first case of the *braisa* is called *parush shichmi*, which Rashi says refers to what the people of Shechem did when they circumcised themselves not to fulfill God's commandment but to gain acceptance by Yaakov and his family. Ben Yohadah explains that the people of Shechem were not obligated to circumcise themselves and therefore this is an example of doing an extra piety for the sake of honor and not for pure motives. When the deed is obligatory, one must do it even if one's motives are not pure – with the intent of purifying one's motives – as is clear from a later passage in the Gemara.

77. *Asher Yetzaveh*, pp. 116–117.

This is a general principle for you: any good deed which is not obligatory for a person, but rather an extra cautionary stringency, must be hidden from other people as much as possible. And if it is impossible to hide – then he should set aside that action completely for a time, and should not disturb [literally, make noise] the world with his actions.

The Mishnah says that the *perushim* "destroy the world." The *perushim* cause destruction by bringing falseness and deception to the world. A world in which image and appearance are more powerful than reality and substance is an unstable world. It lacks a key element vital for the sustainable survival of human society: truth.[78] The Rambam interprets "destroys the world" as "destroys the human being who is the world,"[79] for truth is the foundation of the human being as an individual, and not only of society as a whole. As already noted, truth is also the seal of God Himself.

The destruction of the world mentioned in the Mishnah also refers to the destruction of the moral world through a state of confusion; even the most basic values of goodness are called into question. The Maggid of Polotzack warns his children that falseness and deception in the service of God destroy sanctity because evil becomes mixed with good so that they become indistinguishable.[80] He compares falseness and deception to the skin of a fruit which smells like the fruit but has none of its life-giving nutrients; falseness in the service of God may smell like the real thing, and that creates mass moral and spiritual confusion. When truth and falsehood, good and evil, are confused, the moral world is destroyed.

Insincere External Piety

In concluding its discussion of the *perushim*, the Gemara says that those who deceive with their display of insincere piety will be judged by God,

---

78. Mishnah Avos 1:18.
79. *Rambam Perush Hamishnayos.* Tosfos Yom Tov explanation of the Rambam.
80. *Asher Yetzaveh*, p. 127.

Who sees through the charade:[81] "That which is hidden from people is hidden, and that which is revealed is revealed. However the Great Court [of God, before Whom everything is revealed] will exact punishment from those who wrap themselves in cloaks [of external piety]." Some explain the Gemara to mean that they wore cloaks with prominently displayed long *tzitzis* as a sign of piety.[82] The Aruch translates the Gemara as referring to black cloaks. From the Gemara, it appears that the saintly elite of that generation wore black. The Maharsha suggests that they wore black as a sign of mourning for the destruction of the Temple, so in this case, someone wearing black pretends to those around him that his exemplary piety leads him to mourn the destruction.

A society obsessed with external signs of piety – which nurtures a judgmental atmosphere around the competitive superficial criteria of religious saintliness – is a society that stands in stark opposition to the most fundamental Torah values of honesty, truth, integrity, and humility. The religious arrogance and emptiness of such a society will manifest itself in all areas of human interaction.

In fact, according to the Gemara, the nexus of arrogance and impressive superficial externalities affects *shidduchim* (matchmaking). The Gemara describes a time in Jewish history when "the daughters of Israel married the arrogant because our generation only sees the externalities."[83]

THE POWERFUL DRIVE OF FRUMKEIT

Rabbi Shlomo Wolbe,[84] the noted *talmid* of Reb Yerucham of Mir, offers a unique explanation of the *perushim*. Rav Wolbe says that the desire to be religious, to relate to one's Creator and Master, which he calls *frumkeit*, is a natural human drive similar to other natural desires, such as eating,

---

81. Sotah 22b.
82. Meiri Sotah 20a s.v. *klal*. Rashi Sotah 22b s.v. *demitamra* does not actually refer to *tzitzis* but does refer to a *tallis*, which could mean an ordinary cloak without four corners and *tzitzis*. It could mean that it does have four corners and *tzitzis*, or that it is a coat of special societal status.
83. Sotah 47b.
84. All the references to Rav Wolbe in the main text in this section are based on his chapter "Frumkeit" in *Alei Shur* vol. 2, pp. 152–155.

sexuality, and pursuit of wealth or honor. These basic drives share the common fact that they are self-centered: they focus on achieving self-gratification. If uncontrolled, natural human desires can cause damage because of their selfish egotistical nature. The Torah has many laws to uplift, sanctify, and purify physical drives in order to channel them in a positive way.

Rav Wolbe explains that like other natural drives, *frumkeit* – the desire to be close to God – is also found in animals, albeit in much more primitive form. He cites the following verse as support:[85] "The young lions roar after their prey, and seek their food from God." Rav Wolbe says that the verse can be understood literally because even animals have an instinctive sense, though primitive, that there is an ultimate provider of their food and they seek out that provider.

He contends that the natural desire of *frumkeit* can produce religious activity driven by self-interest and by raw instincts, which can cause destruction if unguided and uncontrolled by the higher moral code of the Torah. Like all natural drives, *frumkeit* has a positive side: the energy and desire to fulfill the requirements of the Torah, which would be burdensome without the drive of *frumkeit*. It also has the potential to cause harm, and therefore needs to be controlled and channeled, like all natural desires, by Torah knowledge and law so that it can be a force for the good.

In discussing the *perushim*, referred to above, most commentators place emphasis on the arrogance of displaying superior religious observance in order to impress others. But Rav Wolbe points out that all the categories of *perushim* are examples of people who demonstrate the excesses of *frumkeit*, whose religious instincts have driven them to override *da'as* (rational objective Torah standards that form the higher moral code and framework of Torah learning) and *halachah*, which should direct the way a person thinks and acts in all situations and provide the correct macro perspective of Torah values. This perspective is vital because, as Rav Eliyahu Dessler explains,[86] every extra effort invested in one area of Torah leads automatically to a weakening of efforts in

---

85. Psalms 104:21.
86. *Michtav M'Eliyahu,* vol. 3, pp. 294–295.

another area. He compares it to a man appearing before a king wearing a magnificent tie while his other garments are tattered and soiled. So too, a person may be exemplary in certain stringencies and, as a result, fail in other more fundamental areas of Torah. The best way to avoid such pitfalls is to focus on key important values, such as learning Torah and not speaking *lashon hara*, and to ensure that these are done with excellence.

"FRUMA NEGI'AH": RELIGIOUS BIAS

Primarily, the study of *Mussar* is about ensuring that *da'as* is the foundation of the service of God, according to Rabbi Wolbe. He warns that *frumkeit* poses the greatest danger in the area of interpersonal relationships, and to the *mitzvos* between man and his fellow. An egotistical religious drive can cause a person to hurt others, thereby violating explicit commandments of the Torah. In self-righteous indignation born of *frumkeit*, a person can feel totally justified in speaking *lashon hara* and creating *machlokes* (dissension), both of which are serious sins. Applying *da'as* would immediately reveal the flagrant violations of important Torah laws in this behavior.

Rav Wolbe credits Rav Yisrael Salanter as the originator of the expression *fruma negi'ah* (religious bias). It describes a mindset in which *frumkeit* causes a person to have such a skewed perception of a situation that it leads him to justify sinning against other people. Rav Wolbe's example of *fruma negi'ah*: people in opposing ideological Torah camps commit serious sins of speaking *lashon hara*, or insulting and humiliating each other under the misconception that they are doing good by fulfilling God's will in advancing their ideological cause.

There are many famous stories about Rabbi Yisrael Salanter's concern that religious fervor should not infringe on interpersonal *mitzvos*. For example,[87] he instructed his *shul* to *daven Maariv* early on Friday night even though that meant that *krias Shma* would not be said during the correct time with its blessings. The reason for his ruling was to enable Jewish maids to hear Kiddush earlier and eat the Shabbos meal: after the long and hard work of the day, it would be wrong to keep them

---

87. *Tnuas Hamussar*, p. 333. The importance of *bein adam lechaveiro* – interpersonal commandments – will be dealt with in great detail in a separate chapter.

waiting while the congregation fulfills the *hiddur*[88] (the extra enhancement) of saying *krias Shma* with its blessings at the right time.

CLOSENESS THROUGH HUMILITY

In the world of *frumkeit*, serving God can degenerate into climbing the ladder of status in religious society. In the competition of who is higher on the ladder, who is closer to God, an act of extra piety nurtures the self-gratification drive of *frumkeit*. The arrogance of *yuharah* is then another manifestation of the problem of *frumkeit*, for the religious drive spurs a person to perform acts of extra piety in a self-centered attempt to demonstrate religious superiority over others and to impress them in the process.

In contrast to this scenario, Rav Wolbe writes that one of the foundational principles of *da'as* is that a person becomes close to God through humility and submission. He builds his thesis on Rabbeinu Yonah's comments on the Mishnah: "Beloved is man created in the Image [of God].... Beloved is Israel who are called the children of God."[89] In Rav Wolbe's interpretation, Rabbeinu Yonah teaches that being close to God is not a product of our actions, but rather a gift from God. Therefore, people should focus not on bringing themselves closer to God but on simply doing the right thing in accordance with God's commandments. God grants His closeness as a gift, which we humbly accept; it is not some achievement for which we arrogantly strive.

This seems counter-intuitive because the concept of closeness to God is a familiar and ubiquitous one in our sources. For example, in his Psalms,[90] King David says, "My soul thirsts for You." Rav Wolbe understands that yearning in the context of the admonishment of his *rebbi*, Reb Yerucham, to his students, "Do not climb to the Heavens." This means that while closeness to God is a value, it is not attained through climbing up to the Heavens. It is not achieved by seeking to elevate oneself, but rather by humbling and submitting oneself before God in simple and loyal dedication to the fullfillment of His will.

---

88. The term *hiddur* comes from the cited passage from *Tnuas Hamussar*.
89. Mishnah Avos 3:18.
90. Psalms 63:2.

Frumkeit, on the other hand, drives a person to climb ambitiously in egotistical pursuit of becoming a highly spiritual, elevated person in order to convey his own personal achievements. The converse of *frumkeit* is humility, which drives a person to focus on doing the right thing without regard to the compensation of achieving some higher status. Rav Wolbe explains that this is because *frumkeit* is about the arrogance of self-centeredness, while humility is about transcending oneself. Furthermore, he says that the self-centeredness of *frumkeit* makes one particularly insensitive to other people and their needs, which explains the phenomenon of *fruma negi'ah.*

To sum up: egocentrism that excludes people excludes God too. As we have seen, the Gemara[91] compares arrogance to idolatry and atheism, both of which are forms of denial of One Almighty God. The denial of God inherent in arrogance results from the focus on self. The human religious drive – which arises naturally – is egotistical, and is the converse of humble submission before God. Paradoxically, *frumkeit* leaves no space for God because it is self-centered.

The meaning of that fine, pithy saying with which we began this chapter – "A Jew is not *frum;* a Jew is *eirlich*" – is now clear. We do not strive for *frumkeit;* we treasure and nurture *eirlichkeit,* which is about the integrity of inner growth rather than superficial religiosity or self-righteous ambitions. It is about profound humility, which leads to a genuine appreciation of other people, to a deeper connection to God, and to the sincere fulfillment of His will.

---

91. Sotah 4b.

Chapter Six

Torah Learning: The Basis for Everything

Rabbi Warren Goldstein

Though it is one of the 613 *mitzvos*, learning Torah is not merely another *mitzvah*; it is in a category all its own. It is qualitatively different because Torah learning is the foundation for everything.

TORAH LEARNING AS THE SOURCE
OF PERSONAL DEVELOPMENT

The Mishnah in Pirkei Avos says that a true *talmid chacham* is like a *ma'ayan hamisgaber* (an overflowing spring). Reb Chaim Volozhiner explains that even if there is mud on the ground covering it, the waters of a spring will pump right through. A *talmid chacham* is compared to this overflowing spring because he increases in spiritual strength through the life-giving waters of Torah learning. As long as the fresh waters of pure Torah are pumping, they will cleanse all impurities and give energy and perspective. This process occurs naturally through a shift in mindset: as a person learns Torah, he gradually absorbs more and more of

Hashem's thinking about the world, and becomes motivated and uplifted through understanding. The Torah emphasizes learning over coercion; persuasion over pressure. Torah learning changes a person's perspective on life, uplifts him through closeness to Hashem; and from that flows character development.

Bringing the Divine Presence into the World
On a spiritual level, Torah study uplifts a person and society because it brings the *Shechinah*, the Divine Presence, into the world. God is everywhere but there are certain places where His presence is felt more intensely, for example, in a *shul*; in the Land of Israel; and in the city of Jerusalem. These are places that have "extra" holiness because the *Shechinah* is more concentrated there. A similar principle holds true whenever and wherever we learn Torah: we draw the Divine Presence toward us. By studying the Torah, we bring the spiritual energy and holiness of God's presence into our day-to-day lives. As the Mishnah says:[1] "If there are two people sitting and there are words of Torah exchanged between them, the Divine Presence comes to dwell with them." The next Mishnah carries this idea further, saying that if there are three people sitting at a table conversing in Torah, "it is as if they have eaten from the table of Hashem."

The Midrash explains that God commanded the building of the *Mishkan* as a place for His presence to dwell because He desires to be near His Torah. Likening God to a king who has an only daughter, it relates that the king is reluctant to let her marry because he wants to remain near her. A prince comes to marry her and the king agrees to the marriage on condition that the prince builds a dwelling for the king so he can come and stay with them. So too, God said to the Jewish People, "I am giving you My Torah, but I cannot part with it. Build Me a *Mishkan* so that I can be with My Torah." The message of this analogy is that Hashem and His Torah are inextricably linked, and that Torah learning brings Hashem's presence into the world.[2]

---

1. Pirkei Avos 3:2.
2. I heard this explanation of the Midrash from Rabbi Azriel Chaim Goldfein, and then also saw it in the writings of Rabbi Aharon Kotler.

On the basis of this idea, Telzer *Rosh Yeshiva* Rabbi Mordechai Gifter explains why the Sanhedrin was located on the Temple Mount. Conventional wisdom would say that the members of the Sanhedrin wanted to be near the inspiration and devotion of the Temple service. Rav Gifter states that the reverse was true: The learning of the Sanhedrin's great sages would bring the *Shechinah* to the Holy Temple, ensuring that the service could be conducted in the immediate presence of Hashem.

Closeness to Hashem that comes from Torah learning defines our relationship with Him. "*Avinu Malkeinu* – Our Father Our King," the poignant prayer said on the Rosh Hashanah and Yom Kippur, refers to two kinds of relationships with Hashem. Reb Chaim Volozhiner[3] explains that describing Hashem as a king reflects our identity as His loyal servants who fulfill His commandments. A servant must obey even against his will. But describing Hashem as a father refers to our identity as His children, which is created by learning Torah. Through teaching us Torah, Hashem relates to us as a loving parent, as a father who sits down with his child to explain what must be done and why. As the child learns, he understands the reasons for his parent's instructions in a spirit of love and respect. The exact sequence of the wording is significant: we refer to Hashem first as our father, and then as our king. This demonstrates that learning Torah is the primary foundation of our relationship to Him and to our duties in His world.

The Power of the Light within Torah

The words of the Midrash: "The light within it will bring them back to the good," refer to the spiritual energy of the Torah to transform and uplift people. This concept was an important pillar of the worldview of many great Lithuanian rabbis.[4] The Chofetz Chaim said that spiritual and moral darkness cannot be banished with force and aggression – only with the light of Torah. We learn this from the first day of creation: confronted with "chaos and void and darkness over the abyss," God said "Let there be light." According to the Midrash, this was a spiritual light reserved for the righteous. In this way, the act of creation, of bringing

---

3. As explained in *Pirkei Mo'ed* (Rav Mordechai Gifter) vol. 2, p. 39.
4. I heard this from Rabbi Azriel C. Goldfein.

light to chaos and darkness, is similar to that of Torah learning: it is the gentle way to change the world and people. Perhaps that is why the Gemara says: "*talmidei chachamim* increase peace in the world."[5]

Rabbi Moshe Chaim Luzzatto (the Ramchal) refers to a supernatural transformation precipitated by the spiritual light and energy that God has placed into the words of the Torah. He writes: "God granted us one particular means which can bring man close to Him more than anything else. This is the study of His Torah."[6] He explains that the most intense "Influence" of Hashem is brought into this world through the words and ideas of Torah:[7] "God chose a particular combination of words and sayings to constitute [the Torah, which consists of] the Five Books, and on a lower level, the *Nevi'im* [Prophets] and *Kesuvim* [Writings]. God then bound the aforementioned Influence to the words of these books in such a way that when a person actually pronounces the words of Torah, the Influence is transmitted to him…. An individual who wants to serve his Creator with complete devotion must therefore involve himself in every aspect of the Torah to the best of his ability. Through this, he can take part in the rectification of all creation." The deeper the level of the learning, the greater is the Influence of Hashem felt.

Rav Avraham Yitzchak Bloch explains this supernatural power of learning Torah using a Midrash:[8] "Bar Kapara said, 'The soul and the Torah are compared to a flame.' Of the soul it is written, 'the flame of Hashem is the soul of man,' and of the Torah it is written 'for the *mitzvah* is a flame and the Torah is light.' The Holy One, Blessed Be He, says to man, 'My flame [the Torah] is in your hand and your flame [your soul] is in My Hand. If you take care of My flame, I will take care of your flame.'"

Reb Avraham Yitzchak explains this Midrash by describing the cyclical interaction between the Torah and the *neshamah* based on kabbalistic teachings. The spiritual light and energy that Hashem has placed within the *neshamah* enables a person to see the light of Hashem in the Torah; and the light of the Torah infuses the person's *neshamah* with yet

---

5. Berachos 64a.
6. *Derech Hashem*, Feldheim translation (1997) p. 71.
7. *Derech Hashem*, pp. 257–259.
8. *Deuteronomy Rabah* 4:4.

more spiritual radiance and light, enabling him to learn more. And so a cycle is created. As the cycle continues, more and more of the *neshamah* is strengthened because the *neshamah* of a person can be expanded and become much greater – the person is surrounded by a potential "extra *neshamah*." The more he learns, the more that external *neshamah* is drawn into his internal *neshamah*.

The Ramchal cautions that the uplifting power of Torah learning is conditional upon the person's appreciation of the Divine origin of the Torah, the reverence with which he approaches it, and his devotion to living in accordance with the *mitzvos*. The Midrash[9] says: "If someone will tell you that there is wisdom among the nations you can believe them; but if someone tells you that there is Torah among the nations, do not believe them." There is wisdom among the nations because Hashem created every human being *b'tzelem Elokim*, in His image, i.e., endowed all of them with the capacity for wisdom and insight, and capabilities that enable incredible achievements in engineering, medicine, literature, technology, and every human endeavor. But our sages explain that Torah wisdom cannot be found anywhere else because it is the revealed wisdom of Hashem.

Rabbi Yerucham Levovitz of Mir expands on this concept. General, worldly wisdom and intellectual study are certainly very powerful, but, says Reb Yerucham, "Torah is a different reality and category altogether" and there is a qualitative difference between the concept of *chochmah* of the Torah, and the *wisdom* of the world. Our sages define four levels of existence in this world: inanimate objects, which are called *domem*; the plant kingdom, *tzomeach*; the animal kingdom, *chai*; and *medaber*, literally "speaker," referring to the level of human beings. Reb Yerucham likens the difference between Torah wisdom and general wisdom to the difference between an inanimate object and a plant, between a plant and an animal, or between an animal and a human being, which is a different kind of existence altogether.

While Torah is certainly very intellectual, deep, and sophisticated, it is more than that, for it operates in a completely different way. The experience of Mount Sinai was not just the handing over of information.

---

9. *Lamentations Rabah* 217.

There was thunder and lightning and all kinds of "effects": the mountain shook, the people shook, and according to one Talmudic tradition, the people's souls actually left their bodies because they were so awe-struck by the experience. Another passage in the Talmud (quoted by Rashi) reports that Hashem opened up the Heavens and showed the Jewish People the seven firmaments – all the way into the heart of the Heavens – so they were able to almost "see" Hashem Himself. It is generally assumed that all of those special effects were actually an external dimension of the experience; that the thunder, lightning, and sound effects were there to create wonderment and awe in order to announce the arrival of the Torah in the world.

Reb Yerucham says that the surrounding effects were not external but, in fact, intrinsic to the Revelation because in receiving the Torah we gained access to Hashem Himself. The Torah is His writing, His way of thinking, and through it we connect to Him. The whole world shook when the Torah was given – there were actual physical miracles felt throughout the world – because it gave human beings direct access to Hashem in a way that nothing else can. The depth of knowledge of everything in the universe and beyond opened up, and this is why it was such an awesome experience.

Reb Yerucham discusses acquisition of knowledge on a practical level as well. We can experience information in two ways: personally and from a distance. For example, when we hear about somebody who got married or had a baby – if we don't know the people personally, it is just a piece of information. If we know them and are close to the couple, hearing the information has an emotional effect on us. Similarly with bad news: when we hear about someone who is suffering illness or about a tragedy in some far-flung part of the world, we can process the information intellectually, but not personally. Obviously, we try to empathize with every human being, but the information does not have that same emotional impact as if we know the people affected. If, God forbid, somebody we know is terribly ill or has passed away, it shakes us to the core; it is not just a piece of information.

When we learn Torah, teaches Reb Yerucham, we are not just learning intellectual concepts in a cold, distant fashion, processing the information like a stranger who does not relate to it personally. Every word of Torah that we learn should have an enormous emotional and spiritual impact that goes to the core of our being. Torah is intellectually powerful, but the process of learning Torah cannot be just cold intellectualism. It needs to touch our hearts and souls and permeate every aspect of our lives. Every time we sit down to learn, we have the opportunity to experience a direct connection to Hashem. We need to feel that connection and bring our feelings and emotions to it in order for it to achieve its purpose.

Torah as the Source of Joy

And what is one of the most powerful emotions associated with Torah learning? Joy. "Were it not for Your Torah, which is my delight, I would have been lost in my affliction."[10] This verse from the Psalms was often quoted by the great Lithuanian rabbis during times of difficulty to express that it was only through Torah learning that they were not overwhelmed by hardships.[11] A specific example of the use of this fortifying passage is recorded in an event that took place in Vilna in the 1930s. Rav Eliezer Menachem Mann Shach had just experienced the tragedy of the death of his daughter, and Rav Chaim Ozer Grodzenski, who himself had lost his only daughter to illness, came to visit him during the *shiva* (the seven-day mourning period after the death of a loved one). "Remember what *David Hamelech* said," offered Reb Chaim Ozer. "Were it not for Your Torah, which is my delight, I would have been lost in my affliction." And when he saw Rav Shach again on other occasions, he would reinforce the thought, saying, "Remember, 'Were it not ....'"[12] According to later reports, "The words of the *pasuk* [passage] would become a life-song, accompanying Rav Shach through privation and hunger, through exile and anonymity, and ultimately, to the Holy Land."[13]

Reb Chaim Ozer and Rav Shach embodied the ideal of Torah study, of course. Yet learning Torah is a source of joy for anyone who

---

10. Psalms 119:92.
11. I heard this from Rabbi Azriel Chaim Goldfein. He used this verse often, and told us that it was a constant refrain of his *rebbeim*.
12. "Mishpacha Magazine" issue # 383, p. 32.
13. Ibid.

learns, on whatever level, for it creates a personal connection with Hashem. One enters a perfect world of the joy of closeness to Hashem, surrounded by all the concepts, principles, and laws that were given to us by the King of all kings. It is a world that is spiritually and emotionally nurturing, intellectually stimulating, indestructible; and it transcends time.

There was a widespread practice in Lithuania to get up in the middle of Friday night to learn Torah till morning. One can feel the joy and delight of this learning in a famous description by Rabbi Eliyahu Dessler:[14]

> Childhood memories crowd in. I remember how, when I was a boy of nine, my revered father and my uncle Gedalia (may the memory of both those *tzaddikim* be blessed) used to get up around midnight on those long winter Friday nights and learn together for about nine hours at a stretch, until the morning service. And I used to get up early and learn with my *rebbi* for a few hours. Mother (that *tzaddekes* of blessed memory) used to get up too, and she would study Midrash, Ramban, and Malbim on the weekly *sidrah* (Torah portion). When she came down, it was like a Yom Tov for me, for she used to serve us cups of steaming hot coffee accompanied by some very special and delicious-tasting latkes.

Rabbi Avraham Yitzchak Bloch once remarked to Rabbi Mordechai Gifter that he enjoys learning Torah so much that he feels it may not be considered *Torah lishmah* (for the pure sake of the love of Torah itself). Rav Gifter suggested that perhaps it is considered *lishmah* because one is supposed to enjoy it.[15] Rabbi Yaakov Kaminetzky articulates this approach with reference to the Mishnah, "Drink the words of our sages with thirst."[16] Learning Torah is compared to water because survival is dependent on both: water for physical sustenance and Torah for spiritual and moral survival. One could study the wisdom of Torah

---

14. *Michtav M'Eliyahu*, translation in *Strive for Truth, Part One*, pp. 97–98.
15. I heard this story from Rav Goldfein, who heard it from Rav Gifter.
16. Pirkei Avos 1:4. See Rav Kaminetzky's commentary *Emes L'Yaakov* on Pirkei Avos.

out of a sense of duty and necessity. According to Reb Yaakov, however, the Mishnah is teaching that we must be passionate about learning Torah, "thirsty" for its life-giving waters.

We should be naturally drawn to learning Torah, says Reb Yaakov, and in that respect, learning differs from other *mitzvos*. To explain the contrast, he cites a Midrash,[17] which says that the correct approach is not to feel a natural revulsion for pork; rather, we should feel that we want to eat it, but refrain from doing so because of God's command. On the other hand, we should not feel that the only reason we are learning is the Divine command to do so; rather, there should be a natural thirst for Torah.

Reb Yaakov argues that the enjoyment of learning is actually a halachic requirement of the *mitzvah*. In support, he looks to the blessing recited before learning, i.e., "Make the words of Your Torah sweet in our mouths." He notes that according to the Gemara,[18] the language of a blessing for a *mitzvah* reflects its halachic foundation, so the sweetness and joy of Torah learning is crucial to the proper fulfillment of this *mitzvah*.

Reb Yaakov cites the famous Rabbi Avraham Bornsztain of Sochatchov,[19] known as the Eglei Tal, who taught that the ultimate level of *Torah lishmah* is attained through enjoying the learning.

The question is why experiencing joy in the *mitzvah* of learning Torah is more important than it is in the performance of any other *mitzvah*. The Eglei Tal maintains that only when a person learns with joy, pleasure, and happiness are "the words of Torah absorbed into his blood." Reb Yaakov explains that the wisdom of Torah is acquired by the soul *only* through a person's love for learning, and then its power will transform and elevate that person.

---

17. *Toras Cohanim* cited by Rashi, Leviticus 20:26.
18. Shabbos 23a.
19. Introduction to *Eglei Tal*. Rav Bornsztain was a nineteenth-century *posek* who became the first Rebbe of the Sochatchover Chasidic dynasty. A descendant of the Rama and the Shach, he is also known as the Avnei Nezer, after his posthumously-published *sefer*.

TORAH LEARNING AS THE SOURCE
OF MITZVOS AND HALACHAH

The holiness of *mitzvos* derives from Torah learning. A verse in Proverbs states: *"Mitzvah* is a lamp and Torah is light."[20] Reb Chaim Volozhiner[21] explains the verse to mean that "Torah" – that is, the words and ideas of God Himself – is the source of the light of the *mitzvos*; and without Torah, the *mitzvos* are empty lamps that produce no light. The sanctity of *mitzvos* flows from Torah learning, reflective of God's wisdom. According to this explanation, the prescribed actions are not intrinsically holy; the source of their holiness is the Torah wisdom expressed through the Written Torah and the recorded content of the Oral Torah found in the Talmud and its commentaries.

Rabbi Mordechai Gifter explains Reb Chaim's view with the following illuminating analogy: on a superficial level, one might assume that turning on a tap creates a flow of water. The truth, however, is very different: water flows from the tap because it is connected through a complex and vast system of pipes to a central reservoir of water. Without the reservoir and pipes, water would not flow from the tap. The *mitzvos* are taps which can be turned on, allowing the life-giving waters of God's presence to flow into our lives. The reservoir at the source is the Torah – with all of its words, ideas, and principles.

This means that a life of Torah action must be rooted in a life of Torah learning. Rav Gifter has a novel explanation of the well-known statement of the Gemara: "Learning Torah takes priority because learning leads to action." The conventional explanation understands this statement at face value. Rav Gifter says that it means that the action of the *mitzvah* performed at the culmination of the Torah learning is actually the extension and the completion of the act of learning, and not something separate from it. There should be a seamless flow from learning into action as part of one process. The *halachah* translates the *mitzvos* into practical actions and can mistakenly be viewed as a superficial rule-book of dos and don'ts. Rav Gifter says that, instead, we must view *halachah* as an extension of Torah learning.

---

20. Proverbs 6:23.
21. *Nefesh Hachaim* 4:30.

Here is an example discussed by Rav Gifter. The Gemara debates the formula of the blessing that is recited before fulfilling the obligation to search for *chametz* on the night of Erev Pesach.[22] Because the blessing is recited before doing the action, it must be composed to reflect an action that is about to take place and not one that has already occurred. The Gemara says that the formula *leva'er chametz* (to burn or destroy *chametz*) is uncontroversial, because all authorities agree that the language refers to a future action. On the other hand, the formula *al bi'ur chametz* (on the burning or destruction of *chametz*) is controversial, because some authorities hold that it refers to a past action and is, therefore, invalid, while others hold that it refers to a future action and is valid. After some discussion, the Gemara rules that the formula to be used is *al bi'ur chametz* in accordance with the opinion that it is a valid formula.

The Rishonim ask why the Gemara chose to resolve the controversy with a contested formula when it could have ruled in favor of the formula *leva'er chametz*, which would accord with all opinions. Why take a chance on a controversial formula when an uncontroversial formula was available? The Rosh[23] bases his answer on a principle from the Gemara:[24] "From a person's [formulation of the] blessings he can be identified as a *talmid chacham*." According to the Rosh, using the controversial formula of *al bi'ur chametz*, there is a *chance to teach* that this formula refers to the future as well, and is therefore also valid; the opportunity would be lost if the safe option of *leva'er chametz* were used.

Rav Gifter[25] explains that we learn from the Rosh's answer that *halachah* must be an extension of Torah learning and that the *mitzvos* must flow from *chochmas hatorah* – the wisdom and intellect of the Torah in the area of *halachah* in particular, demonstrating Torah learning as the force and energy behind action. *Halachah* is *chochmas hatorah* in action: there is no separation between Torah learning and *halachah*, as if they were two totally separate parts of the Torah.

This approach mandates that *halachah* must be based on

---

22. Pesachim 7a, 7b.
23. *Rosh Pesachim* 1:10.
24. Berachos 50a.
25. *Pirkei Torah* 105 et seq.

intellectually deep Torah learning. The Talmud says of those who make halachic rulings based on the Mishnah alone, without understanding the underlying principles: "It is as if they destroy the world."[26] Rashi explains that the world is destroyed through errors in halachic rulings caused by superficial understanding of the Mishnah without its logical underpinnings.[27] The *halachah* is based on foundations of intellectual depth and cannot be applied accurately without them.

The Maharal contends that there is a deeper message in this statement. He points out that the Talmud regards even correct rulings arrived at through the simplistic method of applying the Mishnah (without regard to the depth of its deeper principles) as foreign to Torah, and it is actually an altogether different phenomenon. The Maharal's view: such casual methods remove the true essence of Torah from the world. This will lead to the destruction of the world because the world was created to be a place for Torah and is sustained in its merit. He adds that *halachah* is the process through which Torah learning is translated into action in the world and is, therefore, the highest level of Torah.

The Maharal decries the state of affairs during his time when the codifications of the Rambam and the Tur were being used as simple rule books. He maintains that if the authors had known how their work would be used to destroy the process of determining *halachah*, they would not have written at all. Their intention, he believed, was that the foundational principles in the original sources of the Mishnah, Gemara, and commentaries would continue to be rigorously analyzed in order to arrive at rationally- and intellectually-based conclusions. Only after an extensive intellectual process should the codifications be considered a part of the entire process of deciding the *halachah*.

Torah study at the highest possible levels, then, is at the heart of the *halachah*: there should be a natural flow from Torah learning into any halachic debate. Consequently, the more the final law reflects the nuance of the learning behind it, the better, as was demonstrated so clearly from the above example of the blessing before the search for *chametz*.

In fact, the Talmud goes out of its way to underscore that a super-

---

26. Talmud Sotah 22a. *Maharal, Nesiv HaTorah* chap. 15.
27. Rashi Sotah 22a (s.v. *shemorim*).

ficial approach to learning distorts the essence of Torah. The Mishnah states that a "cunningly wicked person … destroys the world,"[28] and the Gemara debates how to define such a person. One opinion is that the passage concerns someone who has learned Chumash and Mishnah, but has not plumbed the intellectual depth of Mishnaic rulings from a *talmid chacham* – the kind of learning that is found in the Gemara. His knowledge is superficial and simplistic – wide in content, but shallow in understanding. Rashi[29] explains that such a person will make mistakes in halachic rulings because he does not properly understand the intellectual concepts involved. He is called "cunning," says Rashi, due to the false impression he creates that he is a genuine *talmid chacham* (who is then accorded the honor due to such a scholar). In fact, according to one opinion in the Gemara, the person is considered an *am ha'aretz* – an ignoramus.[30]

Another opinion defines such a person as a *Cusi*[31] – a member of a renegade sect of Judaism. The Maharal[32] explains that the *Cusim* practiced only what they observed from their parents and elders: for them, the intellectual dimension of Torah was completely absent. Therefore a person who has merely learned the simple content of the rules is associated with the *Cusim*. Both are guilty of denuding the Torah of a core component of its identity: its intellectual dimension. The *Cusim* represent the notion of conventional religion, which is focused on a system of service of God through simple rules and ceremonies. Torah is an intellectual system. When divorced from intellect, the Torah loses its identity.

This loss of identity is so complete, according to a further opinion in the Gemara,[33] that the resulting practice ceases even to be a form of worship of God and becomes "witchcraft." Thus, the person who has not studied the intellectual principles and foundations of Torah is called a *magosh* – a sorcerer, to whom Torah is about incantations, spells, and magic. The Talmud says that for such a person, the intricate laws and

---

28. Talmud Sotah 20a.
29. Rashi, Talmud Sotah 22a (s.v. *lilmod*).
30. Talmud Sotah 22a.
31. Ibid.
32. *Nesiv HaTorah* chap. 15.
33. Talmud Sotah 22a.

rules of the *halachah* are mindless, irrational mumblings of a sorcerer. In contrast, true Torah is about providing an intellectual framework and foundation for the service of God. Without that intellectual dimension, what may look like Torah is so fundamentally different that it cannot be called by that name. Rav Mottel Katz, Telzer *Rosh Yeshiva*, used to say that to achieve greatness in Torah, one must have a passion for *chochmah*.[34]

Commitment to proper Torah learning is not just about depth but also about breadth. In terms of breadth, Rav Shach was an outspoken critic of the style of learning only a few pages of the Gemara during a yeshiva term. In a number of published letters,[35] he urges students to learn at least a page a day with Rashi and Tosafos, and to resort to other commentaries only if something remains unclear. He exhorts the students to review often and to master whole sections of *Shas*.

Creating Halachic Reality through Torah Learning

As the source of *halachah*, Torah study is the dominant organizing force of Jewish life on a practical, as well as a spiritual level. Torah learning creates the halachic reality – not merely discovers it.

In his introduction to the first published volume of his responsa, *Igros Moshe*, Rabbi Moshe Feinstein elucidates his philosophy of *halachah* to explain how he had the courage to answer the halachic questions that were put to him, given the fact that he might have erred in his interpretation of God's will and gotten it "wrong." In certain respects, his task as a *posek* was more difficult than that of many of his predecessors, because he had come to a new country – the United States of America – at a time when it was going through enormous technological, scientific, and economic expansion. There were so many new cases put before him that had no obvious precedent. He ruled on them boldly, often deducing principles directly from the Talmud. He confronted medical issues – such as heart transplants; financial questions – such as the status of a limited liability company in regard to the law prohibiting the charging of interest. He also confronted social phenomena that had never arisen in Eastern Europe – such as public school prayers designed to be religiously

---

34. As heard from my *Rosh Yeshiva*.
35. *Sefer Michtavim U'maamarim*, nos. 39–44, 46, 47.

neutral to allow Jews and people of differing faiths to pray together. Reb Moshe's responsa constitute an eloquent demonstration of the fact that the Torah was given by God to be applied in all eras and places, and therefore has within it the eternal Divine guidelines for all situations.

Reb Moshe explains that what gave him the confidence to *pasken* was the principle that when a *talmid chacham* who is properly trained and learned applies himself to deciding a question of *halachah*, delving into the Talmud and its *poskim* using "his full strength with seriousness and with fear of God," his conclusion is accepted by God as the truth even if it does not conform with the "right" answer as God Himself would have ruled.

It is generally accepted that God gave jurisdiction over the Torah to its great scholars when He said, "It [the Torah] is not in Heaven."[36] One of the most dramatic examples of the application of this principle is a case recorded in the Gemara:[37] There was a dispute between God and the Heavenly court on whether a particular kind of mark on the body constituted a *tamei tzara'as* or not. God ruled it to be pure and the Heavenly court ruled it to be impure. A mortal sage, Rabah bar Nachmani, was summoned to Heaven to decide the dispute between God and the court. The Ran[38] explains that Rabah bar Nachmani was called because the ultimate authority for interpreting the Torah is its earthly sages, for "It is not in Heaven."

The Ran and Reb Moshe cite another passage from the Gemara with a similar message, depicting an event which demonstrated the far-reaching consequences of the handover of authority from God to authentic *talmidei chachamim*.[39] During a halachic dispute, Rabbi Eliezer tried, unsuccessfully, to convince his colleagues of the validity of his dissenting opinion. In exasperation, he called on Heavenly assistance, and a Heavenly voice announced that the *halachah* accorded with Rabbi Eliezer's

36. Deuteronomy 30:12.
37. Bava Metzia 86a.
38. *Derashos HaRan*, Drush 7.
39. Talmud Bava Metzia 59b. Rav Moshe does not cite the Gemara, only the verse, "It is not in Heaven." Clearly, however, he is referring to the Gemara, because the verse on its own is ambiguous and could not be interpreted in such a way without the authority of the Gemara.

view. Despite this, Rabbi Yehoshua, the head of the Sanhedrin, overruled the Heavenly voice, citing the verse: "It is not in Heaven." The governing principle laid down by the Torah itself mandated that the majority of the Sanhedrin determines the law.

Only What His Eyes See

One of the key texts cited by Reb Moshe as support for his views of the validity of the deliberations of the *posek* deals with *dayanim* (Jewish law judges) but applies equally to any area of *halachah*, even that which does not come before a court. *Dayanim* are exhorted by the Gemara[40] to realize the seriousness of their responsibilities, yet not to avoid their duty to rule on the cases before them for fear of error, because God promises them: "I am with you in judgment."[41] The Talmud recognizes that "the *dayan* has only what his eyes see."[42] But while the halachic decision of a qualified *talmid chacham* is the product of "what his eyes see," that product is endorsed by the promise of God Himself.

Hashem endorses the decision of a *posek* provided that it is made with due diligence and application. The Gemara, citing the Mishnah in Pirkei Avos, says that the unintentional errors of a *talmid chacham* that lead to mistakes of *halachah* are regarded as if they are intentional sins.[43] Rashi and Rabbeinu Yonah explain that this applies only when the error results from a lack of diligent application in Torah learning.[44] The implication is that if the *talmid chacham* fulfills his obligations of proper application, he is not held responsible for any "errors."

So the *giving* of the Torah at Mount Sinai to the Jewish people was, in fact, literal. From then on, the future of Torah law lay in the hands of the great *talmidei chachamim* whose decisions would be accepted by God, even if He disagrees with them.

The Gemara describes how Moshe saw God putting crowns on the

40. Talmud Sanhedrin 6b and Rashi (s.v. *mah li*).
41. Chronicles II 19:6.
42. Talmud Sanhedrin 6b.
43. Talmud Bava Metzia 33b from Mishnah Avos 4:12.
44. Rashi Bava Metzia (s.vv. *le'ami, havei zahir*), Rashi Mishnah Avos 4:12, Rabbeinu Yonah, Mishnah Avos 4:12.

letters of the Torah at the time of the giving of the Torah.[45] Rav Moshe
Feinstein explains that the crowns represent the sovereignty that God
surrendered to the letters, i.e., the words of the Torah. Henceforth, they
would be sovereign to such an extent that any legitimate interpretation
given by a great and legitimate *talmid chacham*, arrived at with proper
diligence and with fear of God, would become the meaning of the Torah,
even if God had intended otherwise. The Torah, so interpreted, attains
the validity of God's own words. It follows that each of two conflicting
interpretations is legitimate if arrived at by great *talmidei chachamim*
with proper diligence and methodology and fear of Heaven. Thus, the
Gemara says of the conflicting opinions of the houses of Hillel and
Shammai: "Both are the words of the living God."[46]

According to the Gemara, Moshe Rabbeinu asked God why He
gave up his sovereignty of the Torah and handed it to be interpreted by
the *talmidei chachamim*.[47] God answered that the concise Torah allows
for "heaps and heaps"[48] of laws to be extracted for all future generations
and for all future situations. To retain sovereignty would have required all
future eventualities to be explicitly provided for, which, even if possible,
would have resulted in a voluminous and unwieldy Torah. That destiny
and eternity of Torah law was demonstrated by Rav Moshe Feinstein
himself in dramatic fashion throughout his long and illustrious career
as a *posek* whenever he tackled new cases of the fast developing world
of the twentieth century. Through Reb Moshe's life and work, one can
almost feel the force of Torah learning formulating the halachic framework to enable *Klal Yisrael* to live in the modern world in accordance
with the will of Hashem.

Reb Moshe held that every properly qualified *talmid chacham*
with proper integrity and *yiras shamayim* – fear of Heaven – is duty-
bound to rule as he sees the *halachah*. A distinguished *talmid chacham*
once asked him whether it was appropriate to live in Bnei Brak and to
teach there, even if he differed in opinion from the widely acclaimed

---

45. Menachos 29b.
46. Eruvin 13b.
47. See Rav Moshe Feinstein's extended discussion of the meaning of the Gemara.
48. Menachos 29b.

and revered Chazon Ish. (The Chazon Ish was no longer alive at the time, but he was the founding father of Bnei Brak and his halachic opinions are accepted there as a matter of course.)[49] Reb Moshe found the concern "incomprehensible." He answered that the Chazon Ish would never have said – nor even contemplated – that his opinions would not be challenged by other qualified *talmidei chachamim*. On the contrary, it is a mark of respect to the Chazon Ish that his views are considered so weighty that they are mentioned and analyzed in the course of halachic debate. A great Torah sage lives on after death, said Reb Moshe, through people learning his teachings, even when he is quoted by scholars who disagree with him. Reb Moshe writes that when differing from the Chazon Ish, the scholar in question should, obviously, do so with the utmost respect and *derech eretz*.

Reb Moshe's view was that the scholar was actually obliged to *pasken* as he sees the *halachah* and not as the Chazon Ish had ruled, and that he was not permitted to defer to the *psak* of the Chazon Ish. Reb Moshe cites the Gemara,[50] which records the following instructions given by Ravah to his students, both of whom were great *talmidei chachamim* and *dayanim* in their own right:

> If one of my rulings comes before you and you see a problem in it, do not tear it up until you have brought it before me – because I may give you a reason for it. And if I cannot, I will retract my opinion. If this happens after my death, still do not tear it up, but also do not learn from it. Do not tear it up because if I had been there I may have had an answer. Do not learn from it because a *dayan* only has 'what his eyes see.'[51]

The Rashbam explains that the reason for the instruction not to destroy his rulings even after his death was that scholars may eventu-

---

49. *Igros Moshe* Y.D. 3:88. The identity of the person who asked the question of Reb Moshe is not revealed in the text. The date of the *teshuvah* is 11 Nisan 5737 (1977).

50. Talmud Bava Basra 130b–131a.

51. Although the Gemara refers to a *dayan*, which normally means a judge in a monetary or marital matter, Rav Moshe Feinstein's view was that the same would apply to all areas of Torah law, since the general approach and principles apply throughout.

ally find a reason for it which had eluded them. And so Ravah clearly instructs his students that they have to follow their own reasoning, even if they disagree with him; yet his opinion should remain on record in case they may later change their views to accord with his. Until such time – which may never occur – they were instructed to rule as they understood the law. Therefore, argued Reb Moshe, a great *talmid chacham* duly qualified to decide *halachah* and who has a clear view of the correct ruling in a particular case is not allowed to defer to the *psak* of another, even if the other is a greater scholar.

Reb Moshe applied this approach consistently. Thus, in his introduction to *Igros Moshe*, he wrote that his intention in publishing his responsa was not to bind other *talmidei chachamim* to follow his halachic rulings; he was merely setting out the primary sources and his understanding of the issues involved, and every properly qualified *talmid chacham* should reach his own conclusions assisted by this work.

He took the concept of the independence of *psak* even further: a duly qualified *talmid chacham* was not allowed to refer a halachic question to another scholar. His authority for this view was the Talmudic[52] statement that King David ruled on intricate matters of *halachah* relating to individuals. The question arises, why did King David not refer these kinds of halachic questions to recognized *poskim*? There were many scholars who could have carried out the difficult process of research involved in each halachic decision, freeing the king to deal with his primary national responsibilities. The answer, infers Reb Moshe, is that once King David was asked for a ruling, he was not allowed to refer the case to others because he was duly qualified to rule on the matter himself.

TORAH LEARNING AS THE SOURCE OF HASHKAFAH

Torah learning determines our general *hashkafah* (the way in which we view everything around us) by molding the way we think to accord with the conceptual universe of God Himself. The Mishnah[53] states: "With ten statements the world was created. What does this teach us? Indeed, could it not have been created with one statement? This was to exact

<hr>

52. Berachos 4a.
53. Pirkei Avos 51.

punishment from the wicked who destroy the world that was created with ten statements, and to bestow good reward upon the righteous who sustain the world that was created with ten statements."

The Maharal[54] explains the significance of "ten statements" in this Mishnah and how that concept underscores the importance of Torah learning. The number ten represents two opposing qualities: unity, and diverse, disparate elements. There are only nine unique numbers, 1–9 (putting aside the discussion of "zero"). The number one represents unity, but it is a simple unity without any diverse, disparate elements. The number ten unifies the first nine as one composite whole. Eleven is just one plus ten. Therefore, in order to show us the nature of His world, Hashem created it with ten statements: it seems to be made of disparate, separate elements, yet there is the unifying cohesive whole.

The cohesive structure that holds together the entire universe in all its disparate elements, based on a central unity of God, is the Torah. Casting Torah as the blueprint of creation, the Midrash states: "Hashem looked into the Torah and created the world." The Torah, explains the Maharal, is the underlying order and framework of the entire world.

And so it stands to reason that the righteous who observe the commandments of the Torah sustain the basic spiritual infrastructure of the world, and the wicked undermine it. He goes on to explain that when studying Torah, one is learning to understand the underlying spiritual infrastructure and order of the world.

That is why the Mishnah says: "Turn it [Torah] over and over, for everything is in it."[55] In his commentary on that Mishnah, the Maharal explains that because the Torah is the blueprint of the entire universe, everything that is contained in this world is contained in the Torah. The more Torah one learns, the more is understood of the framework of concepts and ideas that underpin the entire universe. The Torah then becomes the source of our philosophy and how we view everything in this world. And so one of the most important dimensions of learning Torah is that it is the source for how we look at the world and understand the philosophy of everything around us.

---

54. *Derech Chaim* 5:1.
55. Pirkei Avos 5:26.

As Torah reveals how Hashem "views" the world, it is a guide to differentiating good from evil, important from trivial. Comparing this world to walking through a dangerous forest at night, the Gemara[56] quotes a verse from Proverbs: "For the *mitzvah* is a lamp and Torah [learning] is light" (mentioned above with the elucidations of Reb Chaim Volozhiner and Rabbi Mordechai Gifter). It explains that as we walk in the darkness, our *mitzvos* shed a little bit of light, just enough to illuminate the immediate area around us. Torah learning is like the sun rising and finding signposts in the forest. Torah learning gives us the vision and perspective to understand our world through the eyes of Hashem.

The Dubno Maggid (whose mentor was the Vilna Gaon) uses the following parable to show us how Torah is a light for us: Imagine a person who buys precious stones from a seller who turns out to be a fraud. He buys stones that look precious and is very proud of his purchase, which he bought for a great price but, in fact, the stones are worthless. He takes the stones to show them to a wise man, but arrives at night. The sage tells him it is too dark to have a look at the stones and they must wait till the morning. In the clear light of day, they see that these "precious" stones are forgeries. They put them under hot water and the color runs off; the stones actually melt.

This parable is used by the Dubno Maggid to explain a passage in the Gemara, which says the evil inclination is like a stone: if it tempts you to sin, drag it into the *beis midrash*, and it will melt. There are many things in life that people think are valuable and important, but when we examine these things under the bright, clear light of Torah, we see that they are actually not so precious; they melt away.

To say that Torah learning is the source of one's worldview goes to the heart of one of the great *chidushim* of Torah: morality and spirituality cannot be intuited. The careful intellectual analysis of Torah, in general, and *halachah* in particular, results in exact instructions on how to live and think. The correct approach to the service of God and morality is not instinctive; it is a science as revealed by God through His Written and Oral Torah. The *halachah*, with its rigorous, analytical

---

56. Sotah 21a.

approach has almost no place for any sentimentalism. Something may feel wrong, or feel like heresy, but after careful analysis is shown not to be. Sentimentalism must make way for real *halachah*. The preeminence of Torah learning means that action and attitude is always subservient to the intellectual guidance of God's wisdom, in contrast to *"frumkeit"* (feelings of religiosity) driven by emotion, instinct, and feelings of self-righteousness (as explained in Chapter Five).

Perspective and Clarity through Learning
Torah learning as the source for *hashkafah* provides a broad perspective of all Torah values so that the correct importance is attached when it comes to weighing a stringency that may have an impact on other *mitzvos*, very often on those that are *bein adam lechaveiro* – between man and his fellow. For example,[57] a number of decades ago, a group of yeshiva students came to complain to their *Rosh Yeshiva* about the "low" standards of kashrus maintained by the yeshiva cook, who was a widow. There were no allegations of actual breach of the laws of *kashrus*, rather of not maintaining certain halachic stringencies. The *Rosh Yeshiva* berated them, saying that for some stringency in *kashrus*, they were prepared to commit the most terrible sin of hurting a widow emotionally, and possibly, financially. His perspective, based on *chochmas haTorah* (wisdom of the Torah), clearly put the *mitzvos* into proper alignment. He was able to quickly point out to his students how severely the Torah regards any harm caused to a widow, and that implementing more stringencies in *kashrus* fell well below that priority.

Accuracy and careful commitment to the truth is part of the mind-set of Torah learning, which becomes crucial in evaluating how to respond to any situation in accordance with God's will. A question about a *mikveh* in Rochester, New York, was brought to Rabbi Yosef Eliyahu Henkin.[58] A rabbi had said that the old *mikveh* was invalid *mede'oraisa*, according to basic Torah law. In his response, Rav Henkin demonstrates

---

57 This account was told to me by an eye-witness. The exact identity of the Yeshiva and the *Rosh Yeshiva*, who was one the *gedolei hador* have been omitted for fear of embarrassing any of those involved (e.g., the cook) in this case.
58. *Kisvei HaGri Henkin* vol. 2, pp. 66–69.

that the problem raised by the rabbi concerned a *chumrah*, and not a basic Torah law. He cites the Rambam,[59] who says that to describe an *issur de'rabanan* as an *issur de'oraisa* constitutes a violation of the commandment: "You shall not add to the word which I command you."[60] Rav Henkin criticizes the rabbi for transgressing this commandment by describing a *chumrah* as basic *halachah* (and even as an *issur de'oraisa*). In this particular case, the rabbi had sought to forbid what was completely permissible in terms of basic *halachah*.

This *mikveh* case is a good example of the care that is required when using halachic terminology, and it relates to the broader issue of misrepresenting Torah, which the Maharshal says is akin to heresy.[61] He cites as support the Gemara,[62] which relates how two Roman officers were taught by Talmudic sages of their day. When they came to aspects of the law of damages that may have seemed so offensive to the Romans that a vengeful action may have resulted from the officers informing their superiors of the *halachah*, the sages were tempted to alter these laws when teaching the officers. But they did not do so, even though the truth could have offended the ruling Roman government and caused fatal reprisals, because to misrepresent the Torah is to be guilty of heresy. This is such a serious sin that the normal *pikuach nefesh* principle is set aside, and life must be sacrificed to avoid it. Rabbi Moshe Feinstein cites the Maharshal approvingly, in the context of defining the prohibition of *chanifah* (false flattery).[63] Related to the Maharshal's principle could be the imprecise and broad use of the term "heresy" (*apikorsus*), which could itself be a form of heresy when it amounts to misrepresenting *halachah*. To do so is, in effect, to add to Torah and actually to invent an altogether new doctrine.

59. *Rambam Maamarim* 2:9.
60. Deuteronomy 4:2.
61. *Yam Shel Shlomo* Bava Kama.
62. Bava Kama 38a.
63. *Igros Moshe* O.C. 2:51.

Halachah and Policy

Another area that could be affected by the Maharshal's principle is that a very clear distinction must be drawn between halachic and policy considerations. Very often the distinction between considerations of policy and *halachah* are blurred. To say that certain actions are *assur* – forbidden (intentionally using halachic terminology), when, in fact, the prohibition is based on policy considerations and not the *halachah* could, according to the Maharshal, be considered like heresy.

This does not mean that policy considerations cannot be taken into account. Sometimes it is very important to impose certain extra-halachic policies. There may be circumstances that require stringent policies that, in terms of the letter of the law, would otherwise be permitted. If that is the case, then such rulings must be clearly identified as policy and not *halachah* so as not to misrepresent the *halachah*. Policy issues are dealt with very differently from halachic ones. This worldview avoids sweeping, emotional and ideological pronouncements and instead favors the halachic methodology of case-by-case analysis. This approach to major issues begins with a careful halachic analysis, which may result in technical halachic permission, after which policy considerations can be weighed in a manner that is sensitive to local conditions.

A classic example of this approach is Rav Chaim Ozer Grodzenski's response to a question from Germany in 1913.[64] He was asked to rule on whether the Orthodox community should set itself up as a legal and social entity separate from the dominant Reform community. This question had been famously and hotly contested many years before, during the nineteenth century, by the great German rabbis, Rabbi Samson Raphael Hirsch and Rabbi Seligman Baer Bamburger. Rav Hirsch argued for separation and Rav Bamburger advocated cooperation. At the time, some followed the former and others followed the latter.

The questioner told Reb Chaim Ozer that since the passing of the original rabbis, certain new developments – including renewed assimilationist and secularist tendencies of the Reform movement – made it necessary to reconsider the matter. He requested that Reb Chaim Ozer

---

64. *Igros Reb Chaim Ozer* 2:51.

instruct all Orthodox German Jews to now follow Rav Hirsch's ruling and to separate from the Reform community altogether.

Reb Chaim Ozer refused to rule on the matter. He pointed out that the issue was not one of *halachah* but rather one of policy; and that the original debate between Rabbi Hirsch and Rabbi Bamburger was not one that could be determined with reference to the Talmud and *poskim* alone. Rather, it was dependent on the differing views of how best to further the cause of Torah Judaism politically, taking into account the consequences of separation and cooperation given the circumstances of the time and place. Reb Chaim Ozer's view was that the new developments did not change the basic fact that the issue was not one of *halachah* but rather of policy, which itself could not be separated from the original policy debate between Rav Hirsch and Rav Bamburger.

Reb Chaim Ozer's clear distinction between *halachah* and policy is a classic example of the approach of absolute accuracy and precision when it comes to *halachah*. If a behavior is halachically permissible, but regarded by distinguished rabbis as destructive either personally or communally, it must be presented as such, but not as halachically prohibited. To do so would be akin to heresy in terms of the Maharshal view cited above.

Furthermore, Reb Chaim Ozer felt that policy issues could not be addressed from a distance and, therefore, must be left to local rabbis who were best qualified to understand the unique local factors to determine what policy would be most beneficial for Torah Judaism in the long term. This approach is flexible enough to embrace different policies for different places. Thus, in a letter,[65] Reb Chaim Ozer clearly distinguished between the Berlin Rabbinical Seminary founded by Rabbi Azriel Hildesheimer and a proposal for a similar institution to be established in Israel. Reb Chaim Ozer pointed out that Rav Hildesheimer recognized that the German Jewish community needed such an institution, with its secular training for rabbis, because of the massive inroads made by the Reform and the *Haskalah* movements, while a totally different situation existed in Israel.

If the matter had been one of *halachah*, the same answer would

---

65. *Igros Reb Chaim Ozer* 2:525.

apply in Israel as it had in Germany. Policy issues, however, are not absolute and, therefore, can (and often should) differ, depending on local conditions, which vary greatly according to time, place, and historical forces, among many other factors.

The Hildesheimer Seminary issue related to a very controversial matter in the Jewish world today: the place of secular studies in Torah education. There are those who have made an ideology of the importance of secular studies, and there are those who have made an ideology of the evil of secular studies. In classic style, Rabbi Avraham Yitzchak Bloch clearly distinguished between the halachic and policy issues involved in regard to both the community and the individual. He articulated a number of non-negotiable halachic principles, but also stated that not all the issues involved are halachic; they are also philosophical and even practical. The specific circumstances of the individual concerned must be considered "because the answer to the problem is very dependent on the nature of the person and his particular path and is also dependent on the conditions of time and place and situation and surroundings."[66]

Another good example is a *teshuvah* written by Rabbi Elyah Meir Bloch about a symposium in honor of Yom Ha'atzmaut to be held in Cleveland under joint auspices of Agudath Israel and Mizrachi, where speakers would address the topic of Israel from their respective movement's perspective. Reb Elyah Meir analyzed the issues very carefully, and said that as long as there were no halachic issues (such as a violation of the laws of modesty) he fully supported the joint function. This approach was consistent with distinguishing clearly between halachic and other issues.

On ideological issues, Reb Elyah Meir stressed the importance of acknowledging the elements of truth in a matter, rather than taking a completely one-sided approach, which alienates people because of its lack of honesty. Therefore, he said, one ought to acknowledge that the "independence of Israel and the establishment of the state is an important event in the life of our people." He thought further that despite all the problems and deficiencies of the Israeli government, the actual establish-

---

66. This article is published in *Sefer Mitzvos HaShalom* edited by Rav Yosef Dovid Epstein and published by Torath HaAdam Institute.

ment of the State of Israel "through open miracles has an importance that we need to relate to with gratitude and satisfaction." He explained that this attitude is important because, without it, Agudath Israel will have no credibility; and also because "the truth needs to be said and to be revealed." He concluded that his approach had not been influenced by his being in America, and that in Lithuania the same approach prevailed.

"The truth needs to be said and to be revealed" goes to the heart of the approach of many Litvishe rabbinic leaders. For example,[67] Rav Yosef Dov Soloveitchik recounted this story about his grandfather, Reb Chaim:

It was during an era when a certain group of secular Jews decided not to circumcise their children. A rabbinic conference took place in St. Petersburg to consider whether Jewish communities should include in their registries of vital statistics (the *pinkas ha'ir*) the name of a Jewish baby boy whose parents refused to have him circumcised. Should such a child be recorded as being of the Jewish faith or not?

The overwhelming opinion of the rabbis present at the conference was that "an uncircumcised Jew is not a Jew," and such a child should not be registered as Jewish. Of course, if the name is not entered in the *pinkas*, it would be difficult, if not impossible, to later verify his Jewish identity.

In classic fashion, Rav Chaim Soloveitchik disagreed with the majority opinion and argued that the baby should be recorded in the Jewish registry. He argued that the law is that an uncircumcised Jew (*arel*) cannot eat the *Korban Pesach* (Passover offering/sacrifice) and cannot eat sacrificial meat (*kodshim*) and cannot eat *terumah* (tithe given to the priests of the family of Aharon in Temple times). Nowhere does it say, however, that an *arel* is not a Jew, argued Reb Chaim. Furthermore, in terms of the *halachah*, a baby is not responsible for the omission of his parents, and that only when the child becomes an adult and remains uncircumcised is he liable for the Divine punishment of *kareis*. He also pointed out that an uncircumcised Jew was not different halachically from one who desecrates Shabbos. If the former is to be excluded from the register, the latter should be excluded as well.

In telling the story, Rabbi Yosef Dov Soloveitchik explained that

---

67. *Halakhic Man*, Sefer VeSefel Publishing, Jerusalem 2005/5765, p. 90.

the other rabbis' intent was to make a "fence," which would be a strategic attempt to stop this anti-circumcision movement cold in its tracks. However, Reb Chaim insisted, "a *din* [law] is a *din*." One is not allowed to invent a new law for strategic motivations.

No matter how noble one's reason, it would be a misrepresentation of the Torah to invent a *halachah* that does not exist. Of course, it is often important to establish communal policies, which are enacted for practical or philosophical reasons, but these must be clearly identifiable as policy and not masquerade as *halachah*.

TORAH LEARNING AS THE SOURCE OF JEWISH IDENTITY

Torah learning is the driving force of the destiny of *Klal Yisrael*, for it is the source of energy ensuring the continuity of the Jewish People. At the heart of the question of Jewish destiny is the question that Raban Yochanan ben Zakkai had to answer when he was given a choice of asking for "anything" from Vespasian, who was a Roman military commander in Judea at the time, and had just been appointed as the new emperor. Raban Yochanan could have asked for Jerusalem and the Temple to be spared, yet he said, "Give me Yavneh and its sages."

This philosophy is based on the words of the Midrash: "If only they would leave Me but learn My Torah, the light within it will return them to the good."[68] Where there is Torah study, there will be growth and advancement for the individual, as well as for his community and the entire *Klal Yisrael*.

And so there is an imperative and a responsibility to teach and spread Torah. The Chofetz Chaim writes with horror of what he saw developing in his generation: "the worst affliction of all," that the Torah will be forgotten due to a lack of learning.[69] He explains that when Torah learning ceases *en masse* across *Klal Yisrael*, spiritual and national devastation occurs on every level. This is the root cause of all other spiritual afflictions. A classic example of this process is the destruction of the First Temple, which the Gemara attributes to the three cardinal sins of

---

68. *Midrash Rabah Lamentations.*
69. *Chomas Hadas* chap. 4.

murder, idolatry, and sexual immorality. Yet there is another statement of the Gemara that says the cause of the destruction was the lack of proper Torah learning, specifically learning without reciting the blessings beforehand. The Chofetz Chaim[70] resolves the contradiction by explaining that the lack of learning was the root cause of the other sins which ultimately condemned Jerusalem and the Temple to destruction. Even when it comes to the three most serious sins, the root cause of everything was the lack of Torah learning.

The Chofetz Chaim offers the following explanatory parable: "Someone falls into a deep pit and is injured severely. Bystanders call a doctor to treat the individual's wounds. The doctor says that before binding the wounds, the urgent priority is to ensure that the patient does not die. First revive the patient back to life, and then the wounds will heal themselves, is the doctor's advice. So too, when it comes to *Klal Yisrael*: the urgent priority is to revive the 'patient' by learning Torah; the 'wounds' of individual sins will heal naturally." He concludes that the greatest national calamity that can befall *Klal Yisrael* is Torah being forgotten.

At a time of terrible turbulence in 1939, Rav Elchanan Wasserman,[71] wrote that although there are many problems afflicting the Jewish People, the root cause of all spiritual demise of his generation was the neglect of Torah learning. He cites the Gemara[72] that the prophet Chavakuk said that all the commandments rest on one foundational *mitzvah*: faith in Hashem, which, says Reb Elchanan, can be achieved only through learning Torah. Therefore, if the neglect of Torah learning can be reversed and the light of Torah learning can be spread, from there will emerge the vitality and vibrancy of *Klal Yisrael.* Reb Elchanan declared that the only way to do that is to start with the Torah education of children. He specifically advised that they should be taught Chumash with Rashi, and only by teachers who live a Torah lifestyle with faith.

The loss of Torah learning on a mass scale – such as the deaths of

70. The Chofetz Chaim does not explicitly set it up as a contradiction. He explains it in such a way that implies that he is dealing with it as a way to solve the contradiction.
71. *Kovetz Maamarim, Michtav Shenishlach L'Yisrael HaTza'ir* pp. 68–73.
72. Makkos 24a.

the 24,000 students of Rabbi Akiva – is worse than the destructions of the Temple, according to Rabbi Aharon Kotler.[73] He cites the Sifri that the purpose of the *mitzvah* of *maaser sheni* (tithe of produce) is to bring people to Jerusalem to see the service in the Temple, which would in turn inspire them to *Yiras Shamayim* and Torah study. Therefore, even after the destruction of the Temple, as long as people are learning Torah, this purpose is achieved because the learning will also bring them to fear of Heaven. The key purposes of the Temple are fulfilled, namely to provide a resting place in this world for the *Shechinah*, and to be an inspiration to serving Hashem.

To explain why the lack of Torah learning is the worst calamity for *Klal Yisrael*, Reb Aharon quotes a parable from Reb Chaim Volozhiner. He compares sin to a child who stumbles down a steep incline and is injured in the process. The anguish of the child's father is not caused by the pain of the specific wounds, but rather by the fall itself as the cause of the wounds. Similarly, says Reb Aharon, a lack of Torah learning is the root cause of sin and spiritual degeneration. Consequently the absence of Torah learning causes Hashem the most anguish, so to speak, even more so than the destruction of the Temple, which resulted from the decline of Torah study.

And that is why spreading Torah learning is an urgent and sacred duty. In his famous book, *Madreigas Ha'adam*, Rav Yoseph Y. Horowitz, the *Alter* of Novardok, elaborates at length and with great force about the vital importance of taking responsibility to teach and build Torah for the multitudes of the Jewish People. Quoting the verse: "cursed is the one who does not establish the words of this Torah,"[74] he cites the Talmud Yerushalmi's explanation: this refers to someone who has the power to strengthen and uphold Torah learning and values in the world and does not choose to do so. He cites the Gemara,[75] where the great Talmudic sage Rabbi Chiya explains how hard he worked to prevent Torah from being forgotten by the Jewish People:

---

73. *Mishnas Rabi Aharon*, p. 15 et seq.
74. Deuteronomy 27:26.
75. Bava Metzia 85b.

I planted [flax] bushes, and [when the flax grew] I made nets;
trapped deer [fed their meat to orphans] and prepared parchment
scrolls from their hides; wrote the five books of the Chumash on
the scrolls; and went up to the city [where there were no teachers of Torah] and taught five children [each one a different book
of] the five books of the Chumash; taught six children the six
sedarim of the Mishnah [each child a different *seder*] and I said
to them: '[From now] until I return, teach each other Chumash,
teach each other Mishnah.' And this is how I ensured that Torah
was not forgotten from Israel.

From here we see how devoted one should be to spreading Torah,
concludes the *Alter*. Rabbi Chiya was one of the great Talmudic sages.
He edited the *braisos* and thus made a major contribution to the establishment of the Talmud itself. He was one of the brilliant scholars of
the time, and yet he was devoted to spreading Torah by teaching young
children Chumash and Mishnah. And he set aside of his own honor
and dignity in order to do so, even becoming personally and physically
involved in the most mundane and practical preparations, such as manu-
facturing the parchments. The *Alter* notes that one can speculate as to
why he couldn't ask others to do these simple tasks. It's possible that
there weren't others to help or that Rabbi Chiya wanted to ensure that
none of the teaching materials would be morally tainted (coming from
stolen property, for instance.) Whatever the reason, what stands out is
that a leader of his greatness and stature devoted himself personally to
the Torah education of children.

The *Alter* also focuses on the method that Rabbi Chiya employed
to spread Torah. He didn't just teach as many people as he could find. He
created teachers. He trained five different children, and then instructed
them to teach each other. Each one had to teach what he knew. Each
one was both a pupil and a teacher. This approach demonstrated a far-
sighted vision. The *Alter* points out that one of the purposes behind
this method was to create people who themselves would be devoted to
spreading Torah to the *klal*. He wanted to create students who would
be filled with that value of responsibility for teaching others.

The *Alter* extrapolates the importance of taking responsibility for the *klal*. He writes that a person should not say that he will wait until he is much older to devote himself to the service of the community. This approach is flawed because ultimately, he will never do it; in addition, he will lose what he could have achieved during his youth.

The selfless devotion to teaching Torah displayed by Rabbi Chiya is also exemplified by the Talmudic sage Rabbi Preida. The *Alter* cites the Gemara[76] that Rabbi Preida had a student to whom he would teach the same material four hundred times. That, in itself, shows tremendous patience and complete self-sacrifice for the sake of teaching Torah. Rabbi Prieda was an outstanding scholar with a great intellect and yet was prepared to repeat the material so many times. On one occasion, the Gemara relates, Rabbi Preida had to go off to do a particular *mitzvah*. After teaching his student four hundred times, he could see that the student still did not understand. He asked him why not, and the student said because he could see that his teacher needed to go off to do a *mitzvah*, and he wasn't concentrating properly. Rabbi Preida taught it to him another four hundred times. After that, the student understood everything. The Gemara relates that a voice came from Heaven and offered Rabbi Preida the following choice of rewards for his efforts: "I will add to your life four hundred years, or you and your generation will merit going into Olam Haba." Rabbi Preida said, "I wish that I and my generation will enter into Olam Haba." God instructed that in the merit of making the right choice, Rabbi Prieda would be granted both blessings. The *Alter* notes that such self-sacrificing devotion can come only from a pure heart that is completely devoted to the cause.

The great merit of teaching Torah to children in particular is borne out by the Gemara[77] (mentioned by the *Alter* of Novardok), which tells about the great Talmudic sage Rav, who came to a place where there was famine, and no rain. He decreed a fast so that people would pray for the rain. A particular man went up as the *shliach tzibbur* (representative of the community), led the community in prayer, and the rains came immediately. Rav said to him, "What is your occupation?" He answered, "I teach children; and I teach the children of poor people in exactly the

---

76. Eruvin 54b.
77. Ta'anis 24a.

same way as I teach the children of the rich. And if someone is unable [to pay], I do not take anything from him. I have fish [delicacies] which I give to whoever has sinned, to entice them to come and learn Chumash."

The *Alter* stresses that the sacred duty of spreading Torah to the Jewish people cannot be fulfilled by remaining in one place. He cites the Midrash,[78] which severely criticizes the leaders of the Sanhedrin during a particular period of history who failed in this duty. The Midrash says that they should have gone from place to place throughout the cities of Israel "one day to Lachish, one day to Chevron, one day to Beit El, one day to Yerushalayim and so to all the places of Israel and teach Israel one thing in an hour, or two, or three in order that the name of the Holy One, Blessed Be He, should become great and sanctified."

But instead of taking on this responsibility, "they entered, each one to his vineyard, saying 'let tranquility come on my soul, so that I need not expend great effort.'" Their neglect of this important duty led to the terrible tragedy of Givat Binyamin, where 70,000 men died because they had not been taught Torah and *derech eretz*, says the Midrash. The Sanhedrin that was responsible was the one after Moshe, Yehoshua, and Pinchas.

The *Alter* likens the dire situation of neglect of Torah to a large boat in which there are many rooms. A person may be in his particular room where everything in fine, yet he is aware that in other rooms people are drilling holes in the floor, which will lead to the entire boat sinking. In such a situation, how could anyone say "My room is fine; what is going on elsewhere on the ship doesn't matter"? In such a situation, a person should go from room to room, warning people about the holes in the floor to prevent the boat from sinking! So too, we have a responsibility to spread Torah in a world where the Torah has been forgotten on such a large scale. We should, he says, have a sense of *pikuach nefesh* of the *klal*.

The Life-Giving Power of Torah Learning in Times of Turbulence
Rabbi Chaim Ozer Grodzenski published the first volume of his famous responsa, *Achiezer*, in 1922. It was a time of agony for European Jewry due to the suffering and dislocation of communities during the First

---

78. *Tanna Devei Eliyahu*, chap. 11.

World War. In the introduction to his book, he grapples with the apparent inappropriateness of publishing a new book with its attendant joy and excitement at a time of such pain. His passionate words of faith in the power of Torah learning ring out:[79]

> For They [the words of Torah] are our Life and the Length of our Days.
>
> Turbulent thoughts pound within one's heart – is this dire hour appropriate for publishing *sefarim*? Will not people wonder: 'The nation of Israel is drowning in a sea of tears and you are singing *shirah*? Our enemies from within and without are attempting to undermine the foundations of Torah…the sanctuary of Hashem is ablaze, the flames are consuming the *Aron Hakodesh*, the tablets and parchments are afire – and you occupy yourself with adornments?'
>
> However, this is the power of ancient Israel, in every generation and epoch, for the sake of Hashem and His Torah. Even when the sword was at his neck, the Torah was the Jew's delight throughout the day. Even during the *Churban*, when the nation's very existence was threatened and the heretics were gaining strength, the faithful never diverted their minds for a moment from Torah…. From the day that Israel was exiled from its land, the everlasting and unbroken chain of *Gaonim, Rishonim* and *Acharonim* was never broken. In the days of religious persecution, decrees, oppression and wanderings, they toiled with self-sacrifice to prepare a dwelling place for Torah. And so, the ancient edifice of *Toras Yisrael* was erected through them. Place was left for others to come along and offer their contribution, the giants of old allowed the dwarfs in later generations to climb on their shoulders and strengthen this exalted edifice, glorified in holiness, that any vessel fashioned near it would not cease from producing purity.
>
> To those that merited it, the study of Torah was always a life potion; to plumb the depths of Torah is a source of never-ending spring…. The spreading of Torah study is a shield in the

---

79. *Igros Reb Chaim Ozer* 1:7. Translation from ArtScroll's *Reb Chaim Ozer*, pp. 90–92.

face of retribution, a defense against those who stray and cause others to stray; the Torah and the light within will eventually return them to the good path and it is Torah that has stood by us to this day, strengthening us so that we do not become lost among the nations.

And then in 1939, when he was suffering from serious illness and the world around him was beginning to fall apart in death and destruction, Reb Chaim Ozer published another volume of *Achiezer*. There, he refers to the following verse:[80]

Were it not for Your Torah, which is my delight, I would have been lost in my affliction.

I must relate the kindness of Hashem, Who gives strength to the weary, that even at a time when I became surrounded by personal and communal tribulations – particularly during my illness – I was able to say, 'Were it not for Your Torah, which is my delight, I would have been lost in my affliction.' I have prepared for publication the third section of *Achiezer*, containing *chiddushei Torah* and responsa which were in manuscript form, including essays and letters that were written and arranged in my early youth and which I now scrutinized, clarified and arranged anew....

In truth, now is a time to accomplish for Hashem – they have nullified Your Torah! How great is the duty of the hour, so fraught with responsibility, upon anyone with the ability to accomplish. How frightful is the plight of our people! Even in the Middle Ages it was not like today, when the entire Diaspora is like one flaming torch. Synagogues and Torah scrolls are being burnt on every street corner; our enemies are continuously enacting decrees aimed at driving us to desecrate our religion; great and prominent Jewish communities are being uprooted while the gates of other countries are bolted before them. They are tossed about among the sea's waves, while tens of thousands of

---

80. *Igros Reb Chaim Ozer* 1:39. Translation mostly from ArtScroll's *Reb Chaim Ozer*, pp. 219–221.

other families are tossed about on dry land amidst the waves of hatred which flood and storm with full force. We are scorned and shamed, disgraced and trampled upon. Also, the light which has shone to us from the east, from our beloved Holy Land, may it soon be rebuilt, has become clouded over with a thick cloud; one knows not what the next day will bring. Great tribulations have surrounded us, murders, expulsions, wanderings – the entire Jewish nation, oppressed and crushed is drowning in a sea of blood and tears. Oh, what has become of us!

Now in earlier times, such as the Middle Ages and during the decrees of 5408 (1648), when our brethren were firm in their faith of Hashem and His Torah and knew that Hashem would not reject nor forsake His people, their faith gave them the strength and fortitude to withstand the terrors wrought by the tyrants; moreover, it gave them the ability to build new centers of Torah and Judaism, as is stated: 'Wherever they were exiled, the Divine Presence accompanied them' [Megillah 29a].

However, today, due to our many iniquities, there has been a weakening of faith. It has been a few generations since the Reform took root in the Western nations; through it, many have come to complete assimilation and intermingling [among the gentiles], literally. From these very countries, the evil has now come forth to pursue them in fury, to destroy them and drive them from their land. Their poisonous hatred of our people has spread to other countries as well.

In Eastern European countries, there are also many who have strayed and caused others to stray; devoid of faith, they have persevered in turning the multitudes away from the Torah's path. Moreover, a portion of the nation now publicly desecrates that which is sacred – they have failed to withstand the tests and have breached the sanctity of Shabbos, which is the foundation of the entire Torah; they have defiled their souls by eating forbidden foods…regarding which it is written: 'Be unto Me a holy people; do not eat flesh torn off in the field' [Exodus 22:30]…. Also, with regard to the holiness of the Jewish family, there has also been an increase of breaches and perpetrators.

Yet, our people have still not come to recognize the real source of its persecution; the nation has been smitten with blindness, all hearts have melted, all hands have grown weak; it has become difficult to tolerate the yoke of exile, the tribulations which increase from hour to hour in anger, fury and powerful wrath. Each day's curse is greater than that of the previous day.

Despite all this, we dare not despair. We must return to Hashem with all our hearts, as is written, 'When you are straitened…then you will return to Hashem, your God' [Deuteronomy 4:30]. We must encourage and strengthen ourselves and give strength to our brethren through action and deeds. We must console the persecuted and exiled and give them strength with comforting words and lift their depressed spirits. The great men of Torah and faith, the rare and elevated, must be on watch in all matters relating to fundamentals of Torah. They must lend strength to those whose hands are failing, so that they will withstand the tests and trust in Hashem that out of travail will come relief and deliverance.

One should know that the root of the malady is in the education of the young; it is an open disgrace that the generation is being educated in secular schools devoid of Torah and faith…. It is a sacred obligation to found religious schools in every community…that will be staffed with expert, Torah-observant teachers…. We must give special attention towards strengthening the yeshivas, large and small; they are the bastions of our faith, the time-honored institutions from which come forth Torah and light to the Diaspora and which dispel the darkness of the exile.

The light and wisdom of God's Torah dispel darkness – the darkness of exile and oppression, the darkness of suffering and affliction, the darkness of ignorance and superficiality, and the darkness of chaos and confusion. The light and wisdom of God's Torah, His eternal word, connects His people to Him as its Author.

Chapter Seven
The Yeshiva Movement

Rabbi Berel Wein

Lodged in a land of few natural resources or commercial opportunities, most of Lithuania's Jews lived in a perpetual state of poverty. Yet despite their harsh physical existence, learning Torah gave them a feeling of serenity and wellbeing, of achievement and accomplishment. In the modern era, Torah study faced complex challenges and the Lithuanian rabbis were forced to reinvent the way it was taught, in order to ensure that it would retain its supreme position as the defining value of Jewish life. That they were able to do so and succeeded against overwhelming odds is testimony to the eternity of Torah and to the love that the Jewish people have for it.[1]

The eighteenth century marked enormous changes in European life. The secular Age of the Enlightenment gave rise to a parallel "Enlightenment" known as *Haskalah* in the Jewish world. And like the worldwide secular Enlightenment, it questioned traditional beliefs and institutions,

---

1. For a hauntingly beautiful description of Lithuanian Jewish life see Avraham Kariv's *Lita Makurasi*, Jerusalem, 1960.

penetrating deeply into the Jewish world. Even though the *Haskalah* preached and practiced intellectual pursuit and wide-ranging knowledge, it removed the emphasis on Torah study – especially the study of Talmud – from its central place in Jewish life. In Germany and France, the rise of Reform, assimilation, and even conversion to Christianity followed hard on the heels of the introduction of the *Haskalah* into Jewish communal life. Torah study was considered a secondary activity at best, if not altogether unnecessary for Jewish youth.

Haskalah found a firm foothold in Lita. It became apparent that the old traditional structures of Torah study practiced in Lithuania for centuries were no longer adequate to the new challenges facing traditional Jewish society. It fell to the lot of Litvishe Jewish leadership to create a bastion of Torah study in the emerging modern era by implementing values, institutions, and methodologies that would revitalize Torah study.

The re-emergence and ascendancy of Torah learning as a distinctive phenomenon in the modern Jewish world began with the Gaon of Vilna, Rabbi Eliyahu Kramer. A genius and scholar of unprecedented proportions whose mastery of every facet of Torah knowledge was phenomenal, he placed Torah study back in the center of the communal agenda. However, the Gaon held no official position in the community, nor did he create any institutions; his vast Torah works were published posthumously by his sons. Yet the ideas and values that he represented permeated the Litvishe community and they would come to practical fruition in the early nineteenth century through the initiatives of his "disciples."[2] Though privileged to join him in Torah study at certain times of the year, his disciples cannot be considered his students in the classical educational meaning of the term.

Foremost among the Gaon's students was Rabbi Chaim Rabinowitz, who served as the rabbi of a small Lithuanian/Belarus community in the village of Volozhin. Rabbi Rabinowitz was deemed by his peers to be the ultimate rabbinic authority and leader of Lithuanian Jewry

---

2. The concepts of the modern yeshiva, the study of *Mussar*, and the drive to immigrate to the Land of Israel are all attributed to him and his disciples.

due to his vast knowledge of Torah and his preeminence as the main disciple of the Vilna Gaon.

Wrestling with the challenge of revitalizing Torah study, he sought to create a new type of educational institution, which became, in fact, the forerunner of the modern yeshiva of intensive Torah study. His goal was to restore *talmidei chachamim* to their previous, rightly-held, lofty status in Jewish society. In 1803 he sent a letter to all of the rabbis of Lithuania and Belarus stating:

> There are those who wish to study [Torah] and have no financial means to do so. And there are those who wish to study and are financially able to do so, but have no teacher to guide them in the true path of analytical Torah study... and they are therefore like sheep without a shepherd... and even though I am unworthy of a crown that does not truly fit me... nevertheless [I foresee] a time not far distant when the Jewish people will be without leaders... and the doors of the house of study will be locked. Therefore I do call upon my beloved brethren to hear the truth... to repair the breach in our wall and to support God's Torah [through the establishment of this new yeshiva] with all of our might, whether by supplying proper students or by providing the necessary financial support.[3]

The response to his poignant appeal enabled the Yeshiva Etz Chaim in Volozhin to open; and it operated successfully from 1803 until 1892, when it was closed by the Czarist authorities. With its curriculum of intensive study of the Talmud and its commentaries, the yeshiva became "the creative factory of the Jewish people." Ironically, that term was coined by the Zionist "poet laureate" of modern Hebrew language, Chaim Nachman Bialik (1873–1934), himself a former student of the yeshiva in Volozhin.

An eyewitness account of the times was written in 1864 by Rabbi Moshe Joseph, the rabbi of Krinak, Lithuania, describing in detail the

---

3. Moshe Sinowitz, *Etz Chaim*, Tel Aviv 1972, p. 16.

condition of Torah study in Lithuania when Rabbi Rabinowitz founded the yeshiva in Volozhin:

> I am seventy-eight years old today and when the holy rabbi [Chaim of Volozhin] founded the yeshiva [Etz Chaim in Volozhin] I was fifteen or sixteen years old. I was an intelligent youth and very observing of the ways of the world around me. Before the house of God [the yeshiva] was founded by him [Rabbi Rabinowitz] the [spiritual] world [of Lithuanian Jewry] had become desolate, empty and formless, for no one knew even of the name – yeshiva – and what was its purpose and way of life. No longer was there any fame of scholars or popularity for Talmudic scholarship, for the world had [suddenly] become devoid of intensive Torah [study.] Even the holy books, such as copies of the Talmud, were not to be found anywhere, except in the possession of certain exceptional people who were wealthy. Even in the synagogues of large communities there was not a complete set of the Talmud to be found, nor did the [populace] find such [books] necessary, because they were not used.[4]

Rabbi Joseph's report may have been bleaker than the actual reality because there were still illustrious *talmidei chachamim* present and active in Lita in the early nineteenth century. However the danger of the demise of intensive Torah study was real and very threatening. The new yeshiva in Volozhin was a school of great intellectual prowess and innovative creativity in both the methodology and curriculum of Torah study. As it had great appeal to the minds and hearts of the brilliant young men of Europe, it served as a potent counterforce to the secularization of the Jews advocated by the supporters of *Haskalah* values over Jewish tradition.

The yeshiva proved to be the mother of all later yeshivas, until the present day, as well. It pioneered in numerous ways, each meeting a specific need. The Yeshiva of Volozhin innovated:

---

4. Ibid., p. 15.

1. a fixed curriculum of study: the entire Talmud was covered in seven and a half years;

2. daily lectures by the heads of the yeshiva: there was a *Rosh Yeshiva* and an associate *Rosh Yeshiva* who alternated in delivering the daily lectures;

3. a fixed stipend paid by the yeshiva to its students for their support, room, and board: students from wealthy families were not entitled to such aid; and

4. the division of long hours of study into three units of time daily.

When Rav Chaim Rabinowitz passed away, he was succeeded as the head of the yeshiva by his son, Rav Yitzchak Rabinowitz, known lovingly by Litvishe Jewry as Reb Itzele Volozhiner (died 1849). Eventually in 1857, Rabbi Yitzchak's son-in-law, Rabbi Naftali Tzvi Yehudah Berlin, known by his acronym Netziv, became the head of the yeshiva.

The Netziv's associate from 1880 onwards was the husband of his granddaughter, Rabbi Chaim Soloveitchik. The Netziv's method of Talmud study was traditional, based primarily upon wide-ranging knowledge of all of the scholarly sources that had an impact on the subject under discussion. Rabbi Soloveitchik was the architect of a different and innovative style of studying Talmud: it was based on intensive analysis of the terminology and norms of the Talmud and its commentators, and an attempt to reveal the under-structure of the Talmudic debate. Though this type of Talmud study originally had its fierce critics in the rabbinic world,[5] this approach and methodology nevertheless became the accepted analytical norm of study in the Lithuanian yeshiva world; and with modifications, it continues to be so even today. The family dynasty of Rabbi Chaim Rabinowitz was known in Lithuanian Jewry as the *Beis Harav* – the "House of the Great Rabbi" of Israel.[6] It has many descendants in world Jewry today.

In 1815, a dozen years after the founding of the Yeshiva of Volozhin,

---

5. For a scathing critique of this "new way" of studying Talmud see the introduction to *Responsa* of Beis Ridvaz, Jerusalem, 1905.

6. See *From Volozhin to Jerusalem* by Rabbi Meir Bar-Ilan (Berlin), Jerusalem 1948, for an eyewitness familial view of the *Beis Harav*.

another yeshiva of its type was founded in the village of Mir. By 1840, the yeshiva in Mir numbered over one hundred students. When Volozhin was closed by the Czarist authorities in 1892,[7] the yeshiva in Mir was miraculously still allowed to continue operations normally. The Lord always protects the continuity of Torah study among the people of Israel.

Under the direction of Rabbi Eliyahu Baruch Kamai, the rabbi of Mir, the yeshiva grew and prospered. Rabbi Kamai's style of study – deeply analytical, yet constantly illuminated with flashes of pilpulistic brilliance – proved attractive to prospective students, as did his noble personality and friendly, soft attitude toward the students of the yeshiva. Rabbi Eliezer Yehudah Finkel, the son-in-law of Rabbi Kamai, arrived in Mir early in the twentieth century, and by 1907, he was taking an active role in the administration of the institution.

The son of the *Rosh Yeshiva* in Slabodka (Rabbi Nosson Tzvi Finkel, whose life and yeshiva will be discussed below), Rabbi Eliezer Yehudah Finkel was an outstanding scholar, as well as an efficient administrator and gifted fund raiser. When the yeshiva building, together with the entire town of Mir, was consumed by fire in 1911, Rabbi Finkel spearheaded the rebuilding of the yeshiva building. Mir became the primary yeshiva of Lita under Rabbi Finkel's impetus. But the stability of the yeshiva, and in fact of all Lithuanian Jewry, would soon be threatened by the gathering clouds of war.

During the First World War, the yeshiva in Mir was forced to flee eastward, deep into Russia, in 1916. Rabbi Kamai passed away in 1917 and his son, Rabbi Avraham Tzvi Kamai succeeded his father as the rabbi of Mir and as the associate *Rosh Yeshiva* with Rabbi Finkel. By 1921, the yeshiva was able to return and reestablish itself in Mir, now part of Poland. Rabbi Finkel, himself a follower of the *Mussar* Movement, brought to the yeshiva Rabbi Yerucham Levovitz, one of the *Mussar* luminaries of the age, to serve as its *Mashgiach*.

---

7. Sinowitz, p. 333, Rabbi Bar-Ilan (Berlin) and Rabbi Baruch Halevi Epstein in his *Mekor Baruch*, New York, 1903, p. 2026, all describe the struggle over the Russian government's insistence on introducing secular studies into the yeshiva curriculum and restricting the hours of Talmud study, as well as the eventual closure of the yeshiva by the Russian authorities. See the long article on the topic by the Netziv himself in *Meishiv Davar*, Warsaw 1893, section 1, chap. 44.

The *Mashgiach* in a Livishe yeshiva had a special role. He looked after the spiritual and emotional growth of the students and was their counselor and mentor. He also delivered regular lectures on *Mussar* and *hashkafah* as part of the yeshiva's learning schedule. Though there had originally been much controversy about the introduction of *Mussar* studies (works of ethics, philosophy, and self-improvement) into the yeshiva curriculum (as it would dilute the emphasis on pure Talmud study), by the 1920s almost all of the Lithuanian yeshivas were *Mussar* oriented. Mir was famous for this orientation. After World War I, young men streamed to study in Mir from many countries including Germany, the United States, South Africa, Switzerland, Czechoslovakia, Belgium, England, Romania, Hungary, and even Australia. Mir became the first truly international yeshiva of modern times.

The 1940 escape of the Mirrer Yeshiva to Shanghai, China, is well known. Through the efforts of Sempo Sugihara, the Japanese Consul in Kovno (at the behest of Dr. Zerah Warhaftig of the Jewish Agency), visas were obtained for Jews trying to escape Lithuania. Some 1,600 visas were issued, enabling their holders to travel through the Soviet Union to Japan, and then on to Shanghai. Among these were the students and faculty of the Mir Yeshiva, who were grateful to survive, despite considerable hardships. (It should be noted that after a frantic month of issuing visas, Sugihara was abruptly transferred to another consulate by Japan, an ally of Germany. Upon his return to Japan, he was dismissed from the Foreign Service for his act of defiance.) Throughout the war, rescue funds were being raised in the United States by Rabbi Avraham Kalmanowitz, who had come to the US to garner support for Lithuanian yeshivas. Through his intervention in obtaining visas and the sums he raised, many were able to seek refuge beyond the cauldron of Europe.

The fortitude of the Mir yeshiva faculty and students and their devotion to the value of Torah study – despite all odds – quickly came to the fore. While Torah Jewry and its institutions were being brutally obliterated in Europe, Torah learning in China took on a sense of mission and purpose as never before. A telling incident occurred in May 1942, when the first volume of the Mir Talmud (*Torah Ohr*) had just been printed in China, through outstanding devotion. Though the war with Japan was going on outside, the yeshiva held a grand feast to celebrate the publication, and was joined by the beloved Rabbi Shlomo Kalish, the Amshenover Rebbe. Even as bombs fell, the Rebbe, the Mir students, and their *rebbeim* danced in a lively circle. A non-Jewish, Polish journalist who observed this strange juxtaposition of courage and ecstasy wrote: "Those who did not witness the Amshenover Rebbe and yeshiva students dance at receiving this marvelous gift have never seen true Jewish joy and felt the secret of the Jew's eternity."[8]

After World War II, the yeshiva divided into two groups and locations. Today, one Yeshivas Mir is located in Brooklyn, New York (reestablished by Rav Kalmanowitz, mentioned above), and the second is Yeshivas Mir in Jerusalem. The Jerusalem Mir currently is one of the largest, if not *the* largest, institution of Torah study in the world, attracting students from around the globe. With more than 5,000 students, it is the hub of Torah study in the Holy City. Its leaders are descendants of the great Lithuanian rabbis who headed the yeshiva in pre-World War II Lithuania.[9]

It is interesting to note that while Torah was studied wherever Jews lived in Europe, the Land of Israel, America, and the rest of the Diaspora, Litvishe yeshivas informed the standard of intensive Torah study by which all others were measured. When Rabbi Meir Shapiro founded his great yeshiva in Lublin, Poland, in the 1920s,[10] he first toured Lithuania to study the methodology, curriculum, and way of life in the yeshivas there. He adapted many of their ideas and ways to fit his mainly Chasidic student body and their traditional way of studying Torah.

That he wanted to do so attests to the maturity of the Litvishe yeshivas of his day, an outgrowth of the responsiveness of *Roshei Yeshiva* to valid criticism. In early 1862, the great Chasidic master, Rabbi Chaim Halberstam of Sanz in Galicia, wrote[11] to Rabbi Aaron David Deutsch in Hungary strongly defending the Chasidic movement against the attacks

8. Quoted by Dr. Vera Schwarcz in *Bridge Across Broken Time: Chinese and Jewish Cultural Memory* (Yale University Press, 1998).
9. For a review of the yeshiva in Mir see the article in *Mosdos Torah B'Europa*, edited by Samuel Mirsky, New York 1956, p. 87. Also see *Yahadus Lita* published by The Association of The Lithuanian Jews, Tel Aviv 1959, vol. 1, p. 217.
10. See Mirsky, p. 393 for a review of this unique yeshiva.
11. Responsa, *Divrei Chaim*, vol. 2, Yoreh De'ah, Section 47.

of many Hungarian rabbis who were against it. One of the main points of that opposition was that Chasidus did not emphasize Torah study as the primary value in Jewish life. At that time, there was a large network of yeshivas in Hungary, though these yeshivas were not fashioned on the Lithuanian model of Volozhin and Mir. Nevertheless, they were the central places of Torah study in Slovakia, Romania, and Hungary, producing all of the rabbinic leaders of the time for those Jewish communities. Rabbi Halberstam maintained that there were other ways and methods to study Torah intensively. He said, "Yeshivas are not to be found in our areas [Galicia and Poland]. There are many positive and correct reasons for this, as I myself heard from my father-in-law, of blessed memory."

Though he did not enumerate the "positive and correct reasons," they can be surmised.[12] Criticisms of the mid-nineteenth century yeshivas would include:

1. the influence of *Haskalah* that penetrated the Lithuanian yeshivas;
2. yeshivas stifled creativity in their students because of the undue influence of the *Roshei Yeshiva*: their Talmud lectures were delivered in a distinctive style (*derech halimud*) that almost demanded exclusivity and slavish imitation by their students;
3. yeshivas encouraged intellectual prowess over piety of behavior and prayer; they were therefore overly elitist and bred arrogance and hubris in their students.

Like their Chasidic counterparts, Lithuanian yeshivas also produced rabbinic leaders, but they did not see that as their main function. They were out to produce *talmidei chachamim*. Many – but certainly not all – of the students would eventually become rabbis, but many of the greatest Lithuanian *talmidei chachamim* never held rabbinic positions.[13]

The uniqueness of the Lithuanian yeshiva movement was that it recognized those implied criticisms of Rabbi Halberstam as valid and dealt with them, especially in the latter part of the nineteenth century.

---

12. See Michael Silver's article in *Ma'aglei Chasidim*, Mosad Bialik, Jerusalem.
13. A prime example of this is Rabbi Avraham Yehoshua Karelitz (Chazon Ish).

Though it was definitely true that ideas of *Haskalah* had infiltrated the Lithuanian yeshivas, the yeshivas nevertheless became the main line of defense and rebuttal against those ideas. And the yeshivas fought the *Haskalah* with its own weapons – knowledge of Hebrew, Tanach, and philosophic ideas. The Lithuanian yeshivas co-opted these elements of *Haskalah* and built a society that eventually defeated the worst elements of the *Haskalah* program.

The Lithuanian yeshiva movement produced thinking, intelligent people who were loyal to Torah and unafraid of the ideas and storms of the turbulent nineteenth century. The great biblical commentaries of Rabbi Naftali Tzvi Yehudah Berlin,[14] Rabbi Yaakov Meklenberg,[15] Rabbi Meir Simchah Cohen,[16] Rabbi Baruch Halevi Epstein,[17] and Rabbi Yaakov Kaminetzky[18] are all examples of this method of defeating the Haskalah's approach to the Tanach and traditional Judaism by using many of the tools of *Haskalah* scholarship against it.

This attitude was adopted outside of Lithuanian Jewry as well, in the commentaries of such luminaries as Rabbi Samson Raphael Hirsch and Rabbi David Tzvi Hoffman in Germany, and Rabbi Meir Leibush Malbim in Romania. The uniqueness of Lithuanian Jewry's scholars was that they were unafraid of the *Haskalah*; they were secure in their faith that the study of Torah would provide all necessary answers and defenses for the truth of Torah and the continuance of vital and creative Jewish life and faith.

Though the Lithuanian yeshivas did develop rigorous and characteristic methodology in the study of Talmud, this methodology varied from yeshiva to yeshiva. The typical Lithuanian yeshiva student would hear lectures from many different *talmidei chachamim* during his formative years, and frequently at three or four different yeshivas. Therefore, he was open to various ways of approaching the study of Talmud and Torah. Many times, such as in Volozhin itself, varying methodologies

14. *Haamek Davar.*
15. *Haksav V'Hakabalah.*
16. *Meshech Chochmah.*
17. *Torah Temimah.*
18. *Emes L'Yaakov.*

were available within the same yeshiva. The lectures and methodologies of Talmudic analysis of the Netziv were radically different from those of Rabbi Chaim Soloveitchik, though they both taught on alternate days in the same yeshiva of Volozhin. Creativity and newness (*chidush*) were the goals in Torah study in all of the Lithuanian yeshivas and such great Torah teachers as Rabbi Shimon Shkop, Rabbi Moshe Mordecai Epstein, Rabbi Isser Zalman Meltzer, Rabbi Naftali Trop, Rabbi Chaim Rabinowitz, Rabbi Elchanan Wasserman, and Rabbi Baruch Ber Leibowitz all brought their own unique method of Torah study and Talmudic analysis to their students and to their written works.

In addition, it was quite common in Lithuania for young men to study independently with great rabbinic scholars and community rabbis, or even on their own and thus develop independently as great *talmidei chachamim* without ever attending any of the Lithuanian yeshivas. Because of this availability of options, the yeshivas themselves were less likely to impose rigid methodology of study on their students. The yeshiva was a beehive of different personalities, ideas, methods, and approaches to Torah knowledge and study – and this gave the Lithuanian yeshiva its true stamp of uniqueness and greatness.

The arrival of the *Mussar* Movement and its resultant conquest of the Lithuanian yeshivas brought with it a greater emphasis on prayer, ritual piety, emphasis on humility, and sensitivity in dealing with all other humans. As discussed in Chapter Four (on *Mussar*), the *talmid chacham* was thus transformed into a role model of Jewish probity and Torah holiness. Though the emphasis on intellectual rigor and study was never fully relaxed, there was now a definite and recognizable focus on correct human interpersonal behavior and meticulous observance of ritual and devotional prayer.

Thus the criticisms of the yeshivas inherent in Rabbi Halberstam's letter of the 1860s were largely dissipated by the end of the nineteenth century. The determined ability of Litvishe leadership to deal with their own problems and to be realistic in their proposed solutions – a pragmatic approach to life and challenges – is one of their great contributions to the Jewish world.

Of interest to Rabbi Shapiro, of Lublin, Poland, and others who sought to emulate Litvishe Torah study, was a yeshiva of great influence located in Slabodka, a suburb of Kaunas (Kovno). For a period of time there were two competing yeshivas in Slabodka: Knesses Beis Yisrael, which included *Mussar* in its curriculum, and Knesses Beis Yitzchak, which did not. The non-*Mussar* yeshiva eventually relocated to Kaminets-Podolsk, and Slabodka became synonymous with the *Mussar* yeshiva of Knesses Beis Yisrael headed by the gifted and saintly Rabbi Nosson Tzvi Finkel. Slabodka produced many of the great rabbis and educators of the Jewish world in the twentieth century. Its faculty, headed by Rabbi Moshe Mordecai Epstein, was world renowned and its student body saw itself as the elite vanguard of Torah study and ethical teachings in Jewish society.

It is no exaggeration to state that the Litvishe outlook on Torah study, human life, and Jewish values was spread throughout the United States, South Africa, England, and Israel mainly by the students of the yeshiva in Slabodka and students of other yeshivas who were strongly influenced by Slabodka. It was the catalyst for the cross-pollination of all the different nuances of Lithuanian Torah study into what came to be known as the Lithuanian way of Torah study and *hashkafah*.

In 1923 the yeshiva in Slabodka divided in two: one group, headed by Rabbi Nosson Tzvi Finkel, left Lithuania and settled in Jerusalem; the remaining students in Slabodka were under the leadership of Rabbi Isaac Scher. The yeshiva in Jerusalem soon moved to Chevron, where it was victimized by the infamous Arab pogrom of 1929. After a number of its students were massacred by Arabs, the yeshiva returned to Jerusalem, now calling itself the Chevron Yeshiva. In its Litvishe tradition, the Chevron yeshiva produced many of the leading rabbinic and educational leaders of the Land of Israel. It continues in its unique way to serve the cause of Torah study and the needs of Israeli society until this very day.

After World War II, Rabbi Scher and his son-in-law, Rabbi Mordecai Shulman, reestablished his branch of Slabodka in Bnei Brak, again continuing the methodology of Torah study and values that were the core components of the yeshiva in pre-war Lithuania.[19]

All of the yeshivas of Lita were products of several men of ingenuity, genius, tenacity, and commitment to the preservation of intensive

---

19. See Mirsky, p. 133 for a review of the yeshiva in Slabodka.

Torah study. More than most, however, the yeshiva in Radin was identified with one man: Rabbi Yisrael Meir Kagan, known as the Chofetz
Chaim. In 1869, he arrived in the small hamlet of Radin (in Vilna prov-
ince) and gathered around him young men to study Torah. From this
small core of committed disciples, the yeshiva developed and grew.

Larger than life, Rabbi Kagan integrated seemingly opposing
traits in one harmonious individual. A strong personality who took deci-
sive stands on the issues of the day, he was yet recognized by all for his
sincere piety; a gregarious person who never spoke a forbidden word;
an everyday Jew who was a scholarly genius of enormous rabbinic lit-
erary production; a humble, self-effacing person who nevertheless was
the effective leader of traditional Jewry.

In 1904 Rabbi Naftali Trop became the educational head of the
yeshiva and within the next decade the yeshiva grew to over three hundred students. Destroyed and exiled in World War I, the yeshiva returned
to Radin in 1921 and again prospered and grew.[20] Some of the outstanding
leaders of Lithuanian Jewry such as Rabbi Yosef Shlomo Kahaneman,
Rabbi Elchanan Wasserman, Rabbi Dovid Leibowits, Rabbi Mendel
Zaks, Rabbi Shmuel Belkin, and Rabbi Eliezer Levin had been students
at the yeshiva in Radin. In early 1942, the entire yeshiva – its luminous
faculty and gifted students – were annihilated by the Germans.

But their legacy of deep devotion to Torah study was not lost.
There are a number of successor yeshivas to Radin in the United States
and Israel today, headed in many instances by descendants of the faculty members of the original yeshiva in Radin. The rabbis of the Talmud
taught us that the Torah always attempts to return to its original homes
that were hospitable to it. It is no wonder that in spite of seemingly insur-
mountable odds, the Lithuanian yeshivas have reestablished themselves
as the premier houses of Torah study in today's Jewish world.

Another important institution of Torah study in Lithuania was
located in the city of Telshe.[21] This city was close to the Prussian bor-
der, on the crossroads between Germany, Western Europe, Russia, and
Eastern Europe. The yeshiva was founded in 1875, but only in 1881 with

20. Mirsky, p. 189.
21. The review of the Telshe Yeshiva is found in Mirsky, p. 169.

the arrival of Rabbi Eliezer Gordon – a student at Volozhin and a disciple of Rabbi Yisrael Lipkin of Salant – as rabbi of Telshe did it begin to grow and prosper. Telshe was the most "progressive" of all of the Litvishe yeshivas. It had an organized educational philosophy, a set curriculum and an academic structure. Eventually, it included a preparatory division (*mechinah*) for younger students, a teachers' institute for training religious educators, and a Hebrew gymnasium (high school) for women – the first institution of its type in Lithuanian Orthodox society.

The driving force behind the growth of the yeshiva in Telshe was Rabbi Yosef Yehudah Lev Bloch, who succeeded his father-in-law, Rabbi Eliezer Gordon, as the rabbi of Telshe and the head of its yeshiva. A dynamic personality with a most aristocratic bearing and demeanor, Rabbi Bloch weathered many internal and external storms in developing the yeshiva into a major force in Lithuanian Jewish life. He persevered and emerged triumphant in molding the yeshiva and influencing Lithuanian Jewish society. Rabbi Bloch died in 1929 and was succeeded by his son, Rabbi Avraham Yitzchak Bloch. As befell many other glorious institutions, the faculty and students of the yeshiva were destroyed by the Germans and their Lithuanian collaborators in the summer of 1942.

Yet Divine providence did not abandon the Telshe Yeshiva. Rabbi Avraham Yitzchak's younger brother, Rabbi Eliyahu Meir Bloch, and his brother-in-law, Rabbi Mordechai Katz, had gone to America to fundraise for the yeshiva. Upon learning that their beloved Telshe Yeshiva had been destroyed, they resolved to reestablish it. Overcoming their personal grief, they built the "new" Telshe Yeshiva with great tenacity in Cleveland, Ohio. (Their story is told in greater detail in Chapter Nine of this book.) There are a number of other significant and successful yeshivas in the United States and Israel that are under the aegis of the Telshe Yeshiva. Its students have played an important role in the shaping of South African Jewry as well.

The largest yeshiva in the United States today can trace its origins to a yeshiva located in the small village of Slutzk in Lithuanian Russia, founded in the early 1890s. Its head was the famous Talmudic genius, Rabbi Dovid Willowski, known by the acronym Ridvaz. In 1897, Rav Nosson Tzvi Finkel sent a group of young students from his yeshiva in Slabodka to help strengthen the yeshiva in Slutzk. One of them was Rabbi

Isser Zalman Meltzer who eventually became the leader and unofficial head of the yeshiva in Slutzk. When Rav Willowski left Slutzk in 1903 to immigrate to America (and eventually to the Land of Israel), Rabbi Meltzer became the official rabbi and recognized head of the yeshiva of Slutzk. The yeshiva was forced to close during the upheavals of World War I and the subsequent Bolshevik Revolution. Rabbi Meltzer was still in Soviet Russia in 1921 when the yeshiva reestablished itself in the Polish-Lithuanian town of Kletzk under the leadership of his son-in-law, Rabbi Aharon Kotler, a premier student of Slabodka.[22] In 1925, Rabbi Meltzer left Slutzk to become head of Yeshivas Etz Chaim in Jerusalem, and Rabbi Kotler then guided the yeshiva alone. At the eve of World War II, the yeshiva had a student body of two hundred sixty.

At the beginning of the war, Rabbi Kotler escaped to America and there founded a yeshiva now called Beis Medrash Govoha in Lakewood, New Jersey. It is currently the largest institution of intensive Torah study of its type in the United States. Rabbi Kotler pioneered the idea of truly exclusive and intensive Torah study in America on a grand scale, and his students became the educators and leaders of much of American Orthodoxy for the next generations. Though other distinguished leaders of the early twentieth century certainly contributed greatly to Torah growth in America, Rav Kotler is often credited with successfully transplanting the Litvishe style of Torah study to American soil.

And what, precisely, did that model represent? Common to all yeshivas in Lita was emphasis on strict adherence to the text; rational and logical understanding of the issues under discussion; constant review of the subjects taught; and intellectual creativity based upon an honest appraisal of the complexities revealed in the differing opinions of the classic Talmudic commentators. It was this rigorous challenge of ferreting out the true underlying structures of the Talmudic give-and-take debate, and always remaining loyal to the meaning of the text itself, that became the hallmark of Lithuanian Torah study and scholarship. The creation and development of the modern-day yeshiva as an institution, coupled with its emphasis on ethics and human interaction, are the lasting legacy of Lithuanian Jewish leadership – their gift to the entire Jewish people.

---

22. The review of the Slabodka Yeshiva is found in Mirsky, p. 229.

Despite the physical annihilation of Jewish Lithuania, its heroic devotion to knowledge and spirit arose again after the war and is the mainstay of Jewish life throughout the Jewish world. It is a worthy tribute to the strength and purity of *limud Torah* (Torah learning) in prewar Lithuanian yeshivas that Torah study and Lita remain synonymous terms – even today, so many years after its great halls of learning were tragically silenced.

Chapter Eight

The Klal Mensch

Rabbi Warren Goldstein

To be a *klal mensch*[1] is a complex and multi-layered concept. Literally translated as "a community-minded or inclusive person," it goes to the heart of the Torah worldview.

On a very basic level, the term *klal mensch* refers to a person who has respect for the halachic authority of the designated communal rabbinic leadership. A classic example of the Torah approach to these matters can be found in a letter of Rabbi Yitzchak Elchanan Spektor, the Kovno Rav,[2] who wrote in response to the news that a breakaway *beis din* and *kashrus* authority had been established in a major European capital – in opposition to the established local *beis din*:

> I was very, very shocked, astounded and distressed about the bad news that one group from Russia and Poland called *Machazikei HaDas* in the holy congregation of…wishes to separate and

---

1. I had heard this phrase from Rav Shmuel Kamanetsky, *shlita*.
2. *Igros Reb Yitzchak Elchanan* 1:337–338.

become a special community to appoint a rav, *shochet, bodek* and special butchers and to become their own congregation against the will and agreement of the Rav, the famous Gaon…of the holy congregation of… and the country and his Beis Din Tzedek. I feel that this will disturb peace and unity, and it will increase dissension and baseless hatred, which is equal [in severity] to all the serious sins, may God have mercy…. This despicable event is very bad to me.

Further in the letter, Reb Yitzchak Elchanan distinguishes between having many teachers, schools, charity collections – which is positive – and establishing a separate halachic infrastructure on matters such as *kashrus*, marriage, and divorce, which he says is forbidden by "the law of our holy Torah." Such initiatives "should never be done in Israel. To do so is to be brazen; and to, God forbid, breach the fences and decrees that the holy community established many years ago."

He supported the ruling of the incumbent *Av Beis Din* and his court forbidding this attempt at separation, and he concludes:

And woe to us that this has happened in our days, because this is clearly the operation of the evil inclination due to the multitude of our sins (may God have mercy); I am in great pain and very heartbroken. But my consolation is that the remnant of Israel will not do injustice and will not transgress on this very serious prohibition, and only peace and unity and love will prevail among us and all Israel.

TZURAS HAKEHILLAH

Factionalism causes *machlokes* (dissension), one of the very worst social ills from a Torah perspective. It also destroys the very notion of what a *tzibbur* and a *klal* mean. An important term in this context is *tzuras hakehillah*. Literally translated, it means "structure of the community," but it is a much wider concept. This expression was used by Rabbi Mordechai Gifter, the Telzer *Rosh Yeshiva*, in a letter to his *talmid muvhak*, Rabbi Azriel Chaim Goldfein, my *rebbi*. At the time, Rabbi Goldfein was teaching in the Torah school of St. Louis. Rav Menachem Tzvi Eichenstein was the *rav* of the city. His *va'ad ha'ir* (city counsel) – held the halachic authority of the city and oversaw, among other things, the *kashrus*, *gittin* (divorce), and *kiddushin* (betrothal). There was a group of people who were dissatisfied with the *kashrus* standards of the city and brought in meat from New York. The school was uncertain how to deal with the issue because there were some students whose families accepted the *kashrus* of the city's *rav* and others who did not. Rav Goldfein wrote to his *rebbi*, Rav Gifter, to ask for direction. The following is an extract from Rav Gifter's letter, dated March 3, 1968:

> St. Louis is possibly the only *kehillah* in America that has a "*tzuras hakehillah*" (the form of an organized *kehillah*) …. Therefore, one should guard this very, very much.

Rav Gifter wrote that even if the standard of *kashrus* is regarded as less than ideal by some, "if it's under the jurisdiction of the *rav* of the city, *shlita*, it is forbidden to speak negatively about the [butcher] shop; and [if I were the *rav*] I would also object [to those who would question anything under my supervision]."

Rav Gifter wrote further that if a person would like to be stringent, he may do so but "he has to be stringent on himself ['himself' was underlined in the letter] and not on others. And he is not allowed to do this publicly." Rav Gifter acknowledges the authority of the *rav* of the city to impose an *issur* on meat brought in from outside his jurisdiction and says that if the *rav* has not done so, someone would be allowed to bring in meat from the outside. But he says, in order not to undermine the authority of the *rabbonus* (rabbinate), "anyone bringing in meat from the outside, even in the way that he is allowed to, must do so secretly and for himself only." Rav Gifter also addressed the question that was asked as to how the teachers in the school should deal with this matter in regard to their students. Rav Gifter wrote that teachers should not mention the *chumros* to the students: "Are they obliged to expound before them [the students] the *chumros* [stringencies] of the individual?! And whoever [undermines the city *rav* and] teaches these stringencies to the students or to the *bala batim* [members of the congregation] will in the future have to give an account [before God for such actions]."

The value of *tzuras hakehillah* means to strengthen *kehillah* institutions in such a way that those institutions can include as many people as possible, not to divide and not to create segmented, narrow *kehillos*, albeit with more stringent standards in *shechitah* and other issues. In both examples above, the *tzuras hakehillah* was at stake and both rabbis were expressing reverence for the principle in the context of an entire city *kehillah*. The same principle applies within a particular *shul*. The *halachah* accords special status to the presiding rabbi of the *shul* or of the city, who is referred to as the *mara de'asra*.

One threat to the institution of *mara de'asra* is when another *rav* rules on a halachic matter that is within the jurisdiction of the local *rav*. Rav Chaim Ozer Grodzenski exemplifies this classic approach in a response to a halachic question sent to him by someone from a distant community.[3] He explained that he did not rule on *halachah* from afar except on very serious issues, such as those relating to an *agunah*. He added that in the particular case in question, he would definitely not issue a ruling because another *rav* had already done so. This reaction significantly demonstrated his respect for the local *rav* ruling on his own *sheilos*, deciding his own local questions. The reasons for this approach are clear. Very often in a halachic question, the local and human circumstances are halachically relevant; obviously those who are closest to the situation are best positioned to make a ruling. A careful investigation of the facts of a case is an absolute prerequisite to rendering a *psak*. Furthermore, if a distant rabbi rules, the authority of the *mara de'asra* and, thereby, the *tzuras hakehillah* is severely undermined, which leads to division, and even fragmentation.

MACHLOKES DESTROYS THE KLAL

Keeping a *kehillah* coherent and unified requires vigilance in avoiding dissension. This value is rooted in many Torah concepts – for example, the prohibition of *lo tisgodedu*.[4] According to the Gemara, one meaning of this expression is derived from the word *agudos* – groups, and refers

---

3. *Igros Reb Chaim Ozer* 1:14.
4. Deuteronomy 14:1.

to the prohibition of dividing into conflicting groups.[5] The exact practical dimensions of this *mitzvah* are debated in the Gemara, the Rishonim, and the Acharonim. In broad terms, this *mitzvah* reflects the importance of communal unity and cohesion. The Rambam writes:[6] "Included in this prohibition is that there should not be two *batei din* in one city, each one following a different custom, because this leads to *machlokes* [dissension]." The philosophical foundation of this *mitzvah* is to avoid *machlokes* and promote peace and harmony in the community.

Machlokes is very destructive to a person's *middos tovos* because, as the Vilna Gaon points out, peace is the foundation of all *middos*:[7]

> And peace is the all-encompassing utensil that contains all the *middos*, and it is the clothing for all the *middos*... and *middos* are the all-encompassing principle of the *mitzvos*. And He blessed them with peace so that they should be able to receive the Torah.

Many of the most serious sins, such as *lashon hara*, slander, anger, baseless hatred, revenge, bearing a grudge, insults, public embarrassment, and flattery derive from *machlokes*, declared the Chofetz Chaim. Moreover, it even can lead to *Chillul Hashem*, "a very great sin."[8] He explains that in anger – and in pursuit of victory in a dispute – the *yetzer hara* will entice a person to think that all of this sinful conduct is actually permitted; that, in his situation, it is a *mitzvah* to aggressively pursue and defeat the people with whom he is in conflict. The Chofetz Chaim reasons that the severity of the sin of *machlokes* is its capacity to be the gateway for many other sins. He includes it in his comprehensive list of

---

5. Yevamos 13b and 14a. It is an *issur mede'oraisa* as opposed to the law of "do not change because of *machlokes*" brought in the Gemara Pesachim 50b which is *mede'rabanan* (see *Igros Moshe* O.C. 4:34).
6. Rambam *Avodas Cochavim* 12:14. In this regard, the Rambam rules in accordance with Abaye in the Gemara, as opposed to Rovah, who holds more leniently that the prohibition applies only where there is a single *beis din* and does not apply where there are two separate *batei din*, even if they are in the same city. Many others rule according to Rovah's opinion.
7. *Perush HaGra Megillas Esther* 10:3.
8. *Sefer Shmiras Halashon, Sha'ar Hazechirah* chap. 15.

all possible *mitzvos* that are transgressed in the course of speaking *lashon hara*.[9] A vicious cycle is created with *lashon hara* causing *machlokes* and *machlokes* causing *lashon hara*.[10]

The Chofetz Chaim cites many Talmudic sources about the extreme evil of *machlokes* and how severely it is regarded by Hashem. God will forgive the treachery of idol worship more easily than the sin of dissension, he argues. Relying on numerous sources, the Chofetz Chaim states that ultimately *machlokes* causes death, destruction, and disintegration of people, communities, and society as a whole.

This is especially so when it involves undermining the respect and authority of a *talmid chacham*, or certainly that of the *rav* of a city. Again citing numerous Talmudic sources,[11] the Chofetz Chaim says that to be disrespectful toward a *talmid chacham*, whether in his presence or not, is a terrible sin. (He defines a *talmid chacham* in this context as someone qualified to *pasken* and who exerts himself in the study of Torah.) One consequence is that a person guilty of such a transgression is regarded as one who "disparages the word of God" and he loses his portion in the world-to-come.[12] He is punishable in this world with excommunication.[13] The Chofetz Chaim asserts that this rule still applies today.

He writes: "It is easy for them to dispute with the *rav* and the *beis din* of the city and to disparage them; and they are not afraid of the great punishment that will come from this in the world-to-come, as we explained; and also in this world, they will not escape terrible judgments because of this."[14]

Such conduct is "astounding." How, asks the Chofetz Chaim, can people who are otherwise observant of *halachah* not restrain them-

---

9. Introduction to *Sefer Chofetz Chaim* Neg. 12, and *Be'er Mayim Chaim*, where he cites the Smag and Rabbeinu Yonah, as well the dissenting opinion of *Rambam Sefer Hamitzvos, Shoresh* 8.

10. According to the Smag and Rabbeinu Yonah, *machlokes* is an independent and separate sin.

11. *Sha'ar Hazechirah* chap. 16.

12. Talmud Sanhedrin 99b, *Shulchan Aruch* Y.D. 243:6.

13. *Shulchan Aruch* Y.D. 243:7, Y.D. 343 Shach 88.

14. The Chofetz Chaim seems to accord the *rav* and *beis din* of a city the status in halachah of *Rabo*, a category which requires even more respect than an ordinary *talmid chacham*.

selves in this area? We learn from Dasan and Aviram, who supported Korach, that the power of the *yetzer hara* knows no bounds when it comes to dispute with *talmidei chachamim*. It leads people to complete self-destruction. The case of Korach and his supporters is instructive because it is the classic example of challenging the authority and respect of the *rav* and *beis din* of the community.

The Sin of this Generation

The Chofetz Chaim[15] writes that these sins continue to have particular relevance. He refers to the Talmud's statement that the destruction of the Second Temple occurred because of the related sins of *machlokes*, *lashon hara*, and causeless hatred; moreover, in any generation in which the Temple is not rebuilt it is as if it is destroyed anew. Therefore, reasons the Chofetz Chaim, our generation also must be guilty of these sins – otherwise the Temple would have been rebuilt.

In a public letter,[16] the Chofetz Chaim expresses anguish over the appalling prevalence of *machlokes* at that time. He says that a new development in this ancient malady is that people are publishing attacks on groups of fellow Jews in letters and newspapers. He writes that people collect signatures of support for their cause and their attacks on others, and how each side fights to increase their number of signatures. He cries out that "the exile is a bonfire [of dispute]" and he goes on to say that he is "very distressed that even in our Holy Land the deeds of the evil inclination have been successful, and it too has fallen into the trap of *machlokes*."

He points out that people always try to justify their sins by proclaiming the justice of their cause against their adversaries, but that nothing can justify their actions, adding, "I do not know who permitted to them the sin of *lashon hara* and the sin of *machlokes*, which is a great and terrible sin." These sins are magnified by causing *Chillul Hashem*, for when *talmidei chachamim* are involved in public attacks against each other, the reputation of His Torah is brought into disrepute. He states

---

15. Introduction to *Sefer Chofetz Chaim*.
16. *Kol Kitvei HaChofetz Chaim*, vol. 4, pp. 85–87.

that even the students of Rabbi Akiva who "did not treat each other with honor" were punished mainly for the sin of *Chillul Hashem*.

The Chofetz Chaim expresses enormous fear for the future, given the fact that thousands are guilty of the sins of *lashon hara, machlokes,* and *Chillul Hashem,* and he asks, "Who knows what can come from this? May God have mercy!" He concludes with a heartfelt plea:

> And therefore, my brothers and friends, have mercy on yourselves and *Klal Yisrael,* and let everyone in his place extinguish the fire of *machlokes* so that His great Name should not be desecrated any more, and in this merit we will merit to hear the voice announcing peace in the world.
>
> [signed] A youth of the Kehunah who writes with a broken heart,
> Yisrael Meir Hakohen

A terrible dispute once broke out between two factions in the Chofetz Chaim's own yeshiva. His son reports that when the Chofetz Chaim heard about this, he was very dispirited. He called together the students of the yeshiva for a long lecture about the evils of *machlokes* and *lashon hara,* concluding with the shocking statement that it would be better for seventy yeshivas to be destroyed than for the Chofetz Chaim to join one of the disputing factions.[17]

POLITICS AND DISSENSION UNDERMINE TORAH

Rav Moshe Feinstein once received an interesting inquiry about a *shul.* American and Israeli flags had been placed in a prominent place, and some members of the congregation who opposed this action were ready to form a breakaway *minyan.* From a halachic point of view, he ruled that it is permissible to pray in the synagogue, adding that, technically speaking, there is no prohibition against the flags being in the *shul* because they are secular symbols and have no religious significance. However, it would be preferable not to put them in a *shul,* and if they can be removed *without causing dissension,* they should be. Rabbi Feinstein rebuked those who wanted to break away to form a new *minyan,* writing:

---

17. I heard this anecdote from my *Rosh Yeshiva.*

God forbid to cause dissension because of this. And therefore, those who want to make a new *minyan* in another place because of this – and think that they are doing a great thing – are not behaving properly. And it is just political, [deriving] from the *yetzer hara* and the forces of evil – which through the multitude of our sins dances among us – until Hashem will have mercy and send us the righteous redeemer, and [Hashem] will pour upon us a spirit from above to walk in the path of Torah and truth.[18]

How clearly Reb Moshe's response separates politics from *halachah*, and reflects the pre-eminence of the values of peace and unity. His significant point, that the zealots "think that they are doing a great thing," underscores how frequently people cause dissension because they believe with righteous passion that they are doing a noble act. Reb Moshe's view that the desire to form a new *minyan* was "just politics" was expressed in the Anglicized Hebrew word *politika*, a secular term, which, significantly, has no classical Hebrew equivalent.

"Like two Torahs"

Bringing politics into Torah decisions corrupts the essence of Torah and relates to the prohibition of not dividing into groups (*lo tisgodedu*, as mentioned above). Rashi notes that such activity "looks like they are practicing two Torahs."[19] Rashi explains that the concern is for the possible *Chillul Hashem* inherent in the impression that there is not one clear, coherent Torah, which could lead to ridicule. The Ritva adds that it may appear "as if there are two Torahs and two divinities,"[20] basing his explanation on the verse, "You are the children of the Lord your God; do not divide into separate groups." Since we are the children of the same Father, we should not be divided.

To divide the *klal* by having "different Torahs" seriously undermines the power and scope of Torah. There is one Torah for everyone because it is God's Torah, which formed the blueprint of the world.

18. *Igros Moshe* O.C. 1:46.
19. Rashi Yevamos 13b (s.v. *lo ta'asu*).
20. Ritva Yevamos 13b (s.v. *maiy*).

When factions claim sole ownership, excluding all those who do not follow their *derech*, they cause a *Chillul Hashem* because the authenticity of
the Torah as a God-given system of absolute truth is called into question.

"Turn it over and over for everything is in it," says the Mishnah.[21]
Commenting on this Mishnah, the Maharal of Prague explains that the
Torah's greatness is reflected in its all-encompassing nature. The fact that
the Torah was given to the *klal* at Mount Sinai means that it is above
any particular individuals, or even any group of individuals, who set
themselves apart from the nation as a whole. To be a *klal mensch* is to
live with the belief that the Torah belongs to the entire Jewish People.

Mutual Tolerance and Respect in Halachic Disputes

As stated above, one area of Jewish life that can lead to creating the
impression of "two Torahs" is that of halachic disputes. Interpreting
the *halachah* and applying it to new cases can lead great, loyal, and
dedicated *talmidei chachamim* to different results as, in fact, occurred in
innumerable cases recorded throughout the Mishnah and the Gemara
and in the writings of the Rishonim and the Acharonim. Yet, the Torah's
approach to *halachah* is that all discussion should be conducted with
mutual tolerance and respect.

These differences of opinion concern the most fundamental question in Torah: what is God's will? In some of these disputes, there was
a final decision on normative law that everyone accepts. For example,
after many years of debates and disagreements between the schools of
Hillel and Shammai, the law was finally decided in accordance with
the school of Hillel.[22] But many disputes, in particular those of the
Rishonim and the Acharonim, remained unresolved during their time
and through later generations as well.

According to the philosophy of *halachah* expressed by Rav Moshe
Feinstein in his introduction to *Igros Moshe* (discussed in Chapter Six
above), we do not view an opposing halachic opinion expressed by a
duly qualified *talmid chacham* as wrong, or violating the law. "Both are
the words of the living God," when each opinion in the debate has been

21. Pirkei Avos 5:25.
22. Eruvin 13b.

formulated by an authentic *talmid chacham* with integrity and fear of Heaven, and after the application of proper diligence.

A different and contrasting philosophy of *halachah* would be to view the process as one of discovering only one correct answer, in which case the opposing opinions in a halachic argument would have to be wrong. Historically, our great rabbinic leaders have not subscribed to this point of view.

Reb Moshe points out that the Sephardic communities who followed the Rambam and Beis Yosef, and the Ashkenazic communities who followed the Tosafos and the Rama, are all viewed as fulfilling "the words of the living God" even when they are in disagreement. The followers of one opinion do not view the followers of another conflicting opinion as committing a sin, even if the other opinion is more lenient in an area of the law where infringement entails severe consequences, such as the laws of Shabbos.

As support for this explanation, Reb Moshe further cites the following Talmudic example:[23] Rabbi Eliezer held that when a circumcision takes place on Shabbos, all the necessary preparations for the *bris* may be done, including secondary preparations such as cutting down trees to make coals which will generate the heat required to manufacture a knife needed to cut the foreskin. But his was a minority opinion, and the *halachah* was decided in accordance with the majority opinion that permitted only those preparations for the *bris* that could not be done before Shabbos. According to this opinion, cutting down trees, making a fire, and producing a knife would be regarded as multiple serious violations of the Shabbos laws. Yet, the Gemara records that there was a town in the Land of Israel that followed this lenient opinion of Rabbi Eliezer and was rewarded by God for doing so.[24] Reb Moshe concludes that even the rejected opinion of Rabbi Eliezer was treated by God as if

---

23. Talmud Shabbos 130a.
24. This was obviously done before there was a final universally accepted *psak* on the matter. Once the Sanhedrin, or later, the Talmud has finally ruled on a matter, an individual rabbi or community cannot diverge. So in this example it would be forbidden for anybody to rely on Rabbi Eliezer's opinion.

it were the truth, because it was the result of a proper process of application and interpretation of a great *talmid chacham.*

Legitimate differences of opinion of authentic *talmidei chachamim* should be conducted in an atmosphere of peace and tolerance. As support for this concept, Reb Moshe cites the halachic arguments of the schools of Hillel and Shammai, which are characterized by the Talmud[25] as expressive of the verse by the prophet Zechariah, "love truth and peace."[26] Truth and peace can co-exist. The Talmud[27] points out that the sons and daughters of the scholars of the schools of Hillel and Shammai married one another despite serious differences of halachic opinion. Differing legitimate approaches to Torah should not lead to a division into separate camps of opposing halachic or ideological views.

"THE HERITAGE OF KEHILLAS YAAKOV"

The importance of community to the enterprise of God's Torah is expressed very clearly through the famous verse: "The Torah was commanded to us by Moshe; it is the heritage of the *kehillah* of Yaakov."[28] In fact, when the Gemara[29] discusses which verse a child should learn first, as soon as he or she is able to speak, it asks the question: *"Torah mai heh?"* ("Torah, what is it?") It then cites the above verse to explain. From the wide way of phrasing the question "Torah, what is it?" this verse is actually defining a very important ideological principle of the Torah.[30] And that principle is that the Torah belongs to the entire *kehillah* of the Jewish people. "The Torah was commanded to us by Moshe; it is the heritage of the *kehillah* of Yaakov" is therefore the first verse a child should be taught, for it marks the beginning of a lifetime mission of Torah study.

Based on the Talmud,[31] the Rambam[32] writes that Hashem blessed the Jewish People with three crowns of glory: the crown of priest-

25. Yevamos 14b.
26. Zechariah 8:19.
27. Talmud Mishnah Yevamos 13b; Rashi (s.v. *lo*) Talmud Yevamos 14b.
28. Deuteronomy 33:4.
29. Sukkah 42a.
30. The Torah Temimah makes this point in his comments on this verse.
31. Yoma 72b.
32. *Hilchos Talmud Torah* 3:1.

hood, the crown of kingship, and the crown of Torah learning. The first two are limited to certain groups of people. The unique feature of the crown of Torah, he writes, is that it belongs to all, that it is accessible and available to anyone who wants to acquire it. As proof, he cites the verse: "The Torah was commanded to us by Moshe; it is the heritage of *Kehillas Yaakov.*"

The inclusive nature of the crown of Torah learning, as opposed to the crowns of priesthood and kingship, is a sign of the Torah's greatness, says the Maharal. The more exclusive something is, the more limited it is. The more inclusive, the more expansive and powerful it is. Furthermore, it is the widest possible definition of *kehillah*, which enhances the glory of God's Name in the world because "[i]n the multitudes of the people is the glory of the King." This verse establishes a well-known concept in *halachah:* the greatest *Kiddush Hashem* is achieved when *mitzvos* are done in the largest possible gathering. The very notion of community, of *Klal Yisrael*, is to carry Hashem's Name in the world, so the broader and more inclusive the structure, the more it is able to carry the Name of Hashem.

The Holy One, Blessed Is He, the Torah, and Yisrael Are One

The Dubno Maggid[33] says that unity of the Jewish People is crucial to the very existence of the Torah, for it can be fulfilled only as a communal initiative. He refers to the Talmud, which says that the only vessel that can contain blessing is that of peace. The "blessing," he explains, is the Torah, which can only have a place to exist in this world when the Jewish People live together with peace and unity. No single individual can fulfill all of the *mitzvos*, which are, in fact, a national collaborative project of *Klal Yisrael*.

The Ohr HaChaim points out that the Israelite nation as a whole was involved in the enterprise of building the *Mishkan* in the desert, citing this passage: "And all the work of the *Mishkan*, the tent of meeting, was completed. And the children of Israel did in accordance with everything that God had commanded Moses, so did they do."[34] While it

---

33. *Sefer Ohel Yaakov – parshas* Nasso (s.v. *od nuchal*).
34. Exodus 39:32.

may be argued that relatively few skilled people (Betzalel and the expert artisans) were involved in the construction, he answers that these select individuals were acting on behalf of the entire people.

He notes that this precedent is, in fact, the case with all of the commandments. The Talmud lists 613 commandments, 248 positive commandments and 365 negative ones, corresponding to the different parts of the human body. Yet there is no one Jew who can fulfill all 613 commandments. Some commandments apply only to *Kohanim*. Some apply only to *Levi'im*. Some apply only to men, some only to women, some only to the work of the Temple, some only to farmers involved in agriculture, some only to kings, and some only to those involved in the military. How, then, can a person achieve completeness of all 613 commandments? The answer, says the Ohr HaChaim, is that the keeping of all 613 commandments is a communal project of *Klal Yisrael*. All Jews are partners.

"And Israel encamped by the mountain"[35] prior to the giving of the Torah. The verb "encamped" refers to the entire nation. In doing so it conveys that the nation was united for the purpose of receiving the Torah "like one man with one heart."[36] The Talmud comments that "the Holy One, Blessed Is He, and the Torah and Yisrael [the Jewish People] are one."[37] Therefore, fragmentation of any one of those elements manifests in all three. That is why it was very important that, when the people encamped at Mount Sinai to receive the Torah, they had to be united in that purpose "with one heart." Disunity would have adversely affected the receiving of the Torah.[38] Division undermines the notion of *tzibbur*, undermining an important characteristic of the essence of Torah.

---

35. Exodus 19:2.
36. *Mechilta* – Rashi cites it on the verse.
37. Zohar *Parshas Achrei Mos* 73a.
38. I heard this explanation for "one man with one heart" from my *Rosh Yeshiva, zt"l*, based on the teachings of the Maharal.

ALL JEWS BELONG TO THE KLAL

Even sinners are part of *Klal Yisrael*. The classic source for this concept is the inclusion of the *chelbenah* in the *ketores* (the incense for the service in the Temple). A Gemara[39] cited by Rashi on the Chumash, says that the *chelbenah* had a bad smell and yet it was included in the *ketores* in order to teach us "any fast in which the sinners of Israel are not included is not a fast; for behold, the *chelbenah* whose smell is bad was counted by the Scripture among the spices of the *ketores*." Rashi uses the language, "It should not be unimportant in our eyes to include the sinners of Israel in our groups of fasting and prayer."

The Maharal[40] explains that when we beg God for mercy during a time of fasting or prayer, it is particularly the submission and the repentance of those who are furthest from Hashem that evoke Divine mercy. Another interpretation[41] refers to the great *Kiddush Hashem*, sanctification of God's Name, when sinners are included in the group and return in repentance. This is also the foundation of the Yom Kippur prayers, where in *Kol Nidrei*, we declare permission to include everybody within the community, even the transgressors. We define *tzibbur* in its wider sense at the start of the day of Yom Kippur. Verses are recited as part of the *Kol Nidrei* service that link God's forgiveness with the merit of the *tzibbur*: "May it be forgiven *for the entire congregation* of the Children of Israel and for the stranger who dwells among them, for the sin befell the entire nation through carelessness."[42] Emphasis is on the forgiveness, which is given to the entire nation. Similarly, this verse is also recited: "Please forgive the iniquity of this people according to the greatness of Your kindness, as You have forgiven this people since Egypt and to this point."[43]

The inclusive notion of *kehillah* is manifest in the concept of a *minyan*. The verse "And I will be sanctified amidst the Children of Israel"[44] refers to the *mitzvah* of *Kiddush Hashem*, of sanctifying God's Name.

---

39. Kereisos 6b.
40. *Gur Aryeh.*
41. *Sifsei Chachamim.*
42. Numbers 15:26.
43. Numbers 14:19.
44. Leviticus 22:32.

One of the ways that it is fulfilled is through saying *Kaddish, Kedushah, Barchu*, and through other public prayers.

All of this has always been true, but in modern times the approach to non-observant Jews can, in fact, be more inclusive than it had been in previous generations. This lenient approach has been operative in halachic decisions for the past century.[45] The Torah way of *darchei noam* – ways of pleasantness – provides an effective framework for positive relationships between religious and secular Jews.

This approach of openness and love comes through in the interaction between Reb Chaim Ozer Grodzenski and Dr. Samuel Schmidt, who was the editor of Cincinnati's weekly Jewish newspaper.[46] Dr. Schmidt was a secular Zionist-socialist. Through his contact with the Chief Rabbi of Cincinnati, Rabbi Eliezer Silver, he had come a little closer to Torah. What changed him completely was his meeting with Reb Chaim Ozer. In early 1940, Rabbi Silver sent Dr. Schmidt to Vilna as a representative

---

45. One example is the definition of people who regularly transgress the laws of Shabbos in public. The classic Talmudic approach is that they are regarded like idolaters because to desecrate Shabbos is an act of apostasy against Hashem, for Shabbos affirms the foundations of our faith in God's existence and in His creation of the world. Rav Yaakov Emden said, in the context of nineteenth-century Germany, that there was an argument for a more lenient approach. He pointed out that some Jews were making *Kiddush* – which is a declaration of faith in God and His creation of the world – and then going off to desecrate Shabbos. He argued that such a violation of the laws of Shabbos – although wrong – cannot necessarily be interpreted as an act of apostasy since the person also said *Kiddush*.

Reb Chaim Ozer included the opinion of Rabbi Yaakov Emden in a complex discussion to find a *heter* for an *agunah* situation that arose in South Africa. The question was written to him by his brother-in-law, Rav Yitzchak Kasowsky, who was the *Av Beis Din* in Johannesburg at the time. The two witnesses who had signed on the *get* openly transgressed some of the Shabbos laws. In terms of the classic Talmudic approach, they are considered invalid witnesses, thus rendering the *get* void. Reb Chaim Ozer ruled that the *get* could be relied upon. One of his main arguments referred to Rav Yaakov Emden's point that Shabbos transgressors of these times could not be viewed as severely as in previous generations.

The Chazon Ish (*Shechitah* 2:28, *Yibum* 118:6) also rules that the halachic status of a transgressor raised by non-observant parents is that a *tinok shenishba* – a baby captured at birth (by those who would not teach him Judaism), which means that their sins are considered as committed under duress.

46. Shimon Finkelman, *Reb Chaim Ozer*, ArtScroll/Mesorah 2002, p. 231.

of the Vaad Hatzala of the Agudas HaRabonim to get a first-hand assessment of what was going on in Vilna at the time. Dr. Schmidt describes his meeting with Reb Chaim Ozer:

> The Gaon sat smiling pleasantly, and the atmosphere was peaceful, for he was officially not seeing visitors at that hour. He began to ask me about myself and listened carefully to every detail I related from my history. I told him of my visit to Poland on behalf of the Joint in the early 1920s when I came as a medical expert specializing in immunizing the masses against various epidemics... and of my mission to Israel some years later on behalf of Hadassah.... Reb Chaim Ozer, the genius in Torah and other wisdom, then asked me very personal questions about myself. He listened with rapt attention, and then, with a look of true friendship said, 'Allow me, Dr. Schmidt, to address you in a familiar way, by your first name – Reb Shmuel.' His words touched my heart and my tears flowed freely. 'I am not worthy of this,' I protested. He replied, 'Heaven forbid! For a Jew living in the security of America, to undertake a dangerous mission and travel under wartime conditions to a faraway land in order to assist his fellow Jews and rescue the yeshivas – this is proof of his worth!' He continued to offer me encouragement. The next morning I donned a tallis and put on tefillin for the first time... and I became observant in Torah and mitzvahs, in all their fine details.

The warm, gentle, and respectful bearing of Reb Chaim Ozer won him over. His attitude is also reflected in a personal letter of thanks that Reb Chaim Ozer wrote to Dr. Schmidt:

> My esteemed friend, wholesome in knowledge, Dr. Shmuel Schmidt, may his light shine forth, honor has come on behalf of the Agudas HaRabonim.... Now that he is returning home after a successful mission, I find it incumbent to express my appreciation... for his self-sacrifice in traversing oceans.... Praiseworthy is he for having merited to be this kind of emissary... I ask that he convey thanks in my name to his esteemed wife for having consented to his undertaking such a journey.

The letter was signed at the bottom with characteristic humility, "one who blesses him, Chaim Ozer Grodzenski."[47]

The Chazon Ish came from Vilna, where he had been close to Reb Chaim Ozer, and he maintained contact with him even after the Chazon Ish arrived in Israel. The Chazon Ish[48] asserts that it is forbidden to hate any sinner today; in fact, one is required to love him because the *mitzvah* of rebuke no longer applies. This is because no one is qualified to rebuke properly – in such a way that others will listen and take heed. Precedent for this reasoning had already been set by Rabbi Chaim of Volozhin, who said that the only way to influence people is through soft and gentle interaction, not with anger and harshness.[49]

The Chazon Ish[50] also taught that keeping good relations with Jews who are not halachically observant is so important that the Talmud even allows for halachic leniencies to prevent tension. For example, the Talmud rules that it is permissible to sell certain farming implements to people who are suspected of using them for infringing the laws of the *Shemittah* (Sabbatical) year. Selling the tools also could involve infringement of the Torah prohibition, "Do not place a stumbling block in front of the blind," i.e., not to cause or facilitate another person's sinning. One would expect that in a situation of doubtful infringement of Torah prohibitions, it would be forbidden to sell the implements. But the Chazon Ish explains:

> If we are stringent with doubts, we will create another stumbling block: that kindness and "ways of life and peace" will be prevented between us and them. They are only ignorant and we are obligated to sustain them and be good to them. And how much more [important is it] not to increase hatred and tension between us and them. For then, we also would transgress the prohibition

---

47. Ibid., pp. 232–233.
48. Chazon Ish *Shechitah* 2:28, *Yibum* 118:6. He cites from many sources including Talmud Arachin 16a; *Teshuvos Maharam MiLublin* 13 and other sources.
49. It was his opinion that a person who is not able to rebuke with kindness and gentleness, but becomes angry with transgressors, is actually exempt from the *mitzvah* of rebuke (see notes at the back of new printing *Nefesh Hachaim*, para. 114).
50. Chazon Ish *Shevi'is* 12:9.

'do not hate' and many other negative commandments, whose prohibition is no less severe than the one from which we are trying to save ourselves.

In the spirit of these words, one of today's most pressing strategic and moral callings is to hold *Klal Yisrael* together in an atmosphere of dignity, peace, and kindness between secular and religious Jews, and between the various ideological camps within the Torah communities. This calling is one of our greatest challenges – but also one of our greatest opportunities to find merit before Hashem for the bringing of the Final Redemption.

Chapter Nine

Mission and Destiny

Rabbi Warren Goldstein

Connecting to *Klal Yisrael* is such a fundamental principle that the Rambam[1] (based on the Talmud[2]) writes: "One who separates from the paths of the community – even though he has not transgressed any sins except dividing from the Congregation of Israel, and does not do *mitzvos* with them, and does not enter in their troubles and does not fast in their fasts – but rather goes in his path like a member of the nations of the world as if he is not one of them [the Jewish People] – has no portion in the world-to-come."

This terrible fate is reserved for transgressors of a few select categories, such as those who do not believe in God or in the Divine origin of the Torah. Separation from the *klal* is defined by the Rambam as a similarly grave sin. Attachment to the *klal* means, among other things, to "enter in their troubles." This includes praying for the welfare of the *klal*; and that is why virtually all our official prayers are phrased in the

---

1. Rambam *Hilchos Teshuvah* 3:11.
2. Talmud Rosh Hashanah 17a, based on the Rif, not Rashi.

plural. It includes helping the *klal* and its members with practical acts of giving and kindness. In its broadest sense, it means taking responsibility for the welfare of *Klal Yisrael* in every aspect, from its physical to its spiritual needs.[3]

These values are captured in the term *klal mensch*. This role is part of a broader life mission of every Jew to become a giver and to accept responsibility for the *klal*, to give to and to help others in all areas of life. In his famous essay, "*Kuntres Hachesed*," Rabbi Eliyahu Dessler explains that there are two kinds of people: givers and takers, and that the ultimate goal of living a Torah life is to become a giver.

PERSONAL GROWTH THROUGH KLAL WORK

The Torah says, "And the boy grew up…and Moshe grew up and went out to his brothers and saw their suffering."[4] The Maharal explains the repetition of "grew up." The first time refers to physical growth and the second time to moral and spiritual growth. The Hebrew word for "grew up" in this passage is *vayigdal*, literally translated as becoming big, to become a *gadol*. Going out of his way to see the suffering of his brothers was an act of greatness for Moshe, who could have remained in the privileged and protected environment of the palace; yet he gave it all up because of his concern for the *klal*.

Many contributions to the *klal* are at the price of personal sacrifice. Conventional wisdom views commitment to one's own needs and to those of the *klal* to be in conflict. In contrast to this attitude, Rav Yosef Horwitz, known as the *Alter* of Novardok,[5] says that it is *only* through contributing to the community that a person can refine his *middos*. A person who is involved only with his own needs has no arena in which to become a great person. When working for the betterment of the *klal*, one must use all of his character traits for the sake of Heaven; he can achieve what needs to be done only if he has complete mastery over

3. One of the central values emphasized by my *rebbi*, Rabbi Goldfein, *zt"l*, was that of responsibility, which he said was emphasized by the Telzer *Roshei Yeshiva*.
4. Exodus 2:10–11.
5. All of the references to the writings of the *Alter* of Novardok in this chapter come from his essay "*Mezakeh Harabim*," published in his book *Madreigas Ha'adam*.

himself. The *Alter* writes that doing communal work is complicated, requiring one to refine one's *middos* and to galvanize all of one's potential strength of character and wise discernment:

> Sometimes the matter requires that a person behave with pride, and sometimes with submissiveness, sometimes with cruelty, and sometimes with compassion…sometimes with modesty and sometimes with publicity, sometimes to teach new things, sometimes to protect old things, sometimes to speak close to the natural inclination and sometimes far from it, sometimes with new, sometimes with old, sometimes with someone who wants, and sometimes where it is against that person's will. Sometimes it is spiritual work and sometimes it is physical work. Sometimes to speak and sometimes to be silent, everything for the benefit of the thing that is required.

As many people may protest that they do not have such wisdom, or the stamina to take on *klal* responsibilities, the *Alter* counters that once a person begins the work, help comes to him from Heaven. That help materializes, however, only if the person is truly devoted and carries out his task. The more that a person accepts, the easier it becomes, for he merits the help of Hashem that is given "for the sake of the many – to save them from tests, whether physical or in the spirit, whether in strength or in intellect." The very embracing of responsibility brings with it the merit and the support of Hashem sufficient to carry it out.

Initially, it may well appear that the task is too heavy, but once the responsibility is accepted, great blessing and support come from Hashem. The *Alter* writes: "One who accepts upon himself responsibility – although in the beginning it will be bitter – in the end it will be sweet; for he will merit to influence others also seeking to perfect their lives. He can rely on help from Heaven at all times and in all places and at all hours."

Rav Shlomo Wolbe explains that one's soul comes into this world filled with potential greatness that must be actualized by living in accordance with Torah principles through life's events. That potential is actualized in direct proportion to the degree that a person becomes a *klal mensch*.

In practical terms, Rav Wolbe explains that becoming a *klal mensch* is achieved by taking on more and more responsibilities throughout life. Marriage is an important part of this journey, for one has to expand oneself to make space and be responsible for a spouse. Raising children forces a person to assume even greater responsibility, expanding one's identity to become more of a *klal mensch*. Rav Wolbe says that the next stage of expansion is to assume communal responsibility. "A *talmid chacham* who is in the city – all matters of the city are placed on him,"[6] whether he has an official position or not. Rav Wolbe elaborates at length that to be a *klal mensch* means taking responsibility for *Klal Yisrael*, *Eretz Yisrael*, and eventually even the entire world.

The Expansion of Self-Identity: Who Is Included in "I"?

Rav Shimon Shkop[7] says that love of self is a natural force in every human being; but the task of every person is to expand the definition of self-identity to include as many other people as possible. A lowly, coarse person sees himself as only a physical body. Someone slightly more elevated includes his soul as part of his self-identity. At a higher level, one includes his or her spouse; and on the next level, one's children are included in the definition of self-identity. And so it goes. The more spiritually elevated a person is, the more people are included in his sense of "I." A greater person will go beyond immediate family to local members of his *shul*, school, or community. A truly great person, says Reb Shimon, will include all of *Klal Yisrael* and even the entire world, in his sense of "I." From such a lofty perspective, there is no conflict between the needs of self and those of the *klal*. It is our task, therefore, to become holy people who harness the natural force of self-love, expand the concept of self to include the *klal*, and use it to benefit others.

In fact, according to Reb Shimon, the definition of *kedushah* (holiness) is to give to others. In so doing, we emulate God, Who does everything for the benefit of His creations. "Our purpose should always be to dedicate our physical and spiritual capabilities for the good of the many...and in my opinion this entire matter is included in Hashem's

---

6. Talmud Mo'ed Katan 6a.
7. Introduction to *Sha'arei Yosher*.

commandment, 'You shall be holy'.... Included in this *mitzvah* is the foundation and root of the ultimate purpose of our lives – that all of our work and toil should always be dedicated to the good of the *klal*."[8]

The reason we should dedicate all our abilities to the good of the *klal*, Reb Shimon continues, is that, in reality, all gifts and blessings given by Hashem to an individual are actually intended for *Klal Yisrael*. They are given to the individuals in the *klal* as custodians who are duty-bound to share these gifts with the *klal*, in accordance with the needs of others. He says that this applies to material gifts, such as wealth, and spiritual gifts, such as a brilliant intellect. The former must be distributed to the poor and the latter must be properly utilized: one who is so gifted must learn and teach so that Torah can be spread far and wide. When a person who has received gifts from God uses them for the benefit of the *klal*, he is rewarded with more of that gift. This principle is illustrated in the teachings of the Talmud: one who gives *tzedakah* generously will be rewarded with wealth. Reb Shimon explains that if a "custodian" fulfills his mandate well, he will be given more things to look after.

In keeping with this thought, Reb Shimon explains a statement in the Talmud that says: "one learns most from one's students." He says that (in addition to the obvious explanation that students add to the insight of their teachers) it means that God rewards the teacher with more insight and knowledge, for he has properly discharged his obligation as a custodian of the knowledge and intellect with which he had been blessed.

The practical application of this principle on a communal level is the obligation of spreading of Torah through establishing educational institutions, i.e., the sharing of Torah knowledge on a broad level. All people with sufficient Torah knowledge are required to share it with the *klal*, not to sit and learn merely for their own spiritual benefit in splendid isolation from the world.

Of course, different people will make different contributions, depending on their talents and desires. Some become school teachers, others become lecturers at yeshivas, others become community rabbis, and a select few can become *roshei* yeshivas, *dayanim*, and *poskim*. The

---

8. Ibid.

common denominator is the burning passion to spread Torah for the good of the *klal*.

It should not be assumed that these obligations fall only upon professional appointees and designated leaders. Every Jew can and should reach out to spread Hashem's Torah and *mitzvos* in whatever way possible. The *Alter* of Novardok shows how one private citizen made a major contribution: Elkanah lived during the era of the Tanach when the *Mishkan* (the Tabernacle) was in Shilo, and in his time, attendance at the *Mishkan* during festivals was quite low, as many Jews opted to stay home. The Midrash says that on their pilgrimage to the *Mishkan*, Elkanah and his family would make it a point to sleep in the streets of the towns they passed through, in order to draw attention. People would ask, "Why are you sleeping here?" They would answer that they were going up to Shilo in order to fulfil the *mitzvah*, and then invite the questioners to join them on the pilgrimage. Slowly, but surely, they began to build up a following. In the first year, five households joined them; in the second year, ten; increasing all the time. Ultimately, Elkanah restored the practice of going to Shilo to the Jewish People. The Midrash concludes: "The Holy One, Blessed Be He, said to Elkanah, 'You have tipped the scales of merit for My People and educated them in *mitzvos*, and you have brought merit to the multitudes. I will therefore bring out a son from you who will bring merit to the multitudes of Israel and educate them in *mitzvos*.'" That son was the prophet Shmuel.

The *Alter* points out that the *mitzvah* of going up at the times of the festival is one that goes against human nature: it requires families, including those with young children, to move with great effort and trouble. Yet Elkanah and his family had dedication and commitment, and through their personal example, they were able to inspire so many people to do this. The *Alter* emphasizes that we must never underestimate the power of a few individuals to influence many people.

THE VERTICAL KLAL

The Mishnah recounts: "Rabbi Yochanan Hasandlar said, 'Any community dedicated to Heaven will endure forever.'"[9] *Avos De'rabi Nosson*

---

9. Pirkei Avos 4:14.

explains that the community referenced is *Knesses Yisrael*, the community of Israel at Sinai. Accordingly, the community "dedicated to Heaven" that will endure forever spans more than 3,300 years – from Mount Sinai to the present. We can term *Knesses Yisrael* a vertical community, rooted in Sinai. All the generations from Sinai until now form one community. To identify fully with the *klal* means identifying with Jews in the world today as well as with previous generations.

When we learn Torah, we rely on the Oral Tradition and power of accumulated learning of generations of *talmidei chachamim*. This is indicated in the foundational verse: "Torah was commanded to us by Moshe; it is the heritage of *Kehillas Yaakov*." The "*kehillah* of Yaakov" includes all generations of Jews from the beginning. The *Torah Temimah* says that this verse entrenches the fact that the *mesorah* we received from Moshe Rabbeinu, handed down for generations, is the entirety of what the Torah is about. When we teach a child this verse, we are telling him that the only way to understand what the Torah says is via this community.

Rav Moshe Feinstein[10] notes that from the context in which it appears, the verse refers especially during times of exile, when some people may try to reinterpret the Torah according to their own whims. Especially during such times of turbulence, we must rely on the interpretation as received and held fast by *Kehillas Yaakov*.

The Gemara says that the main covenant between Hashem and *Klal Yisrael* is through the *Torah She'baal Peh* (the Oral Law).[11] The mechanisms of interpretation of *Chazal* (Talmudic scholars of blessed memory) through the Sanhedrin – and the various other bodies of the Oral Tradition of the Talmud – all are the enterprise of *Klal Yisrael* as a whole. So it is not just for the commandments, but even the understanding of the Torah itself that we require the vertical *tzibbur*. Hillel, the famous Talmudic sage, pointed out to a potential convert that even the *alef-beis* cannot be understood without the Oral Tradition. Torah is like one long conversation among the generations, based on the Oral Tradition given by Hashem to Moshe Rabbeinu at Mount Sinai.

---

10. *Darash Moshe*, Deuteronomy 33:4.
11. Gittin 60b.

Anyone who studies Torah is in constant dialogue with voices coming from that cumulative community, voices that span thousands of years of our history. The Rambam traces 40 generations of scholars from Moshe Rabbeinu to Rav Ashi, the editor of the Talmud. They include Yehoshua, the Prophets, the Men of the Great Assembly, the Rabbis of the Mishnah, and the Rabbis of the Gemara. Through all of them, the enduring truth of the vision of Sinai was transmitted to the post-Talmud scholars, and then on to the Rishonim – the Rambam, Rashi, and many others. It is an eternal world of generations of *talmidei chachamim* in living conversation and debate across continents and historical eras.

This sense of living with our sages of old is expressed in a letter written in 1935 by Rav Chaim Ozer Grodzenski in response to a proposed commemoration of the 800th anniversary of the Rambam's birth, organized by the Spanish government. Many American Jewish organizations welcomed the initiative, but some within Agudas HaRabonim of America had concerns, which they addressed to Reb Chaim Ozer, who wrote in response:[12]

> In principle, the dissenters are correct, for such jubilee celebrations are foreign to us. We do not need to commemorate the Rambam's birth, for he lives on wherever teachers and students discuss his words; his teachings on which we meditate every day are his eternal remembrance. Only those who have abandoned the source of flowing waters and are distant from the Torah's wisdom seek such memorials. Who knows what sort of 'Maimonides Monument' their spirit will pursue?

Having expressed that view, Reb Chaim Ozer then favors participation so as not to alienate others:

> In our country [Lithuania], where, thank God, there is knowledge of Torah in great measure, and a significant segment of the Jewish population recognizes well the depth of Torah wisdom,

---

12. *Igros Reb Chaim Ozer* 1:306. Translation from *Reb Chaim Ozer*, ArtScroll/Mesorah, p. 214.

there has been no talk of any major organization planning anything in this regard…. However, in America, where superficialities and publicity seem to make their mark, it is not proper for the Orthodox to express opposition to this; under the circumstances, I am inclined to go along with those who would join it [the commemoration], so that the multitudes, who do not understand our reasoning, will not be filled with astonishment.

This is no slight to the honor of other Rishonim, of blessed memory, since the idea was conceived by the Spanish government [not by the Jews themselves] and it was Spain who called for the participation of our brethren. Thought should be given to how this opportunity can be used for the strengthening of Torah. My heart is not taken with the suggestion of publishing a collection of novella to Rambam. This has been an everyday occurrence for many generations – the wellsprings have not ceased to this day. May Hashem grant you proper counsel.

Note also, how – in classic style – Reb Chaim Ozer does not render a final decision and does not impose his opinion from a distant country, but rather leaves it up to the local rabbis who understand the situation first hand. And so, he says, "I am inclined to go along with…" and "May Hashem grant you wise counsel."

OUR RELATIONSHIP WITH PREVIOUS GENERATIONS

To be part of *Klal Yisrael* is to be part of the accumulated merit of the generations that have come before, and to humbly acknowledge and respect their merit on which we rely for everything. *Z'chus Avos* (the merit of our holy ancestors) is a pillar of Torah values and continuity and the strength of *Klal Yisrael*. When the Jewish People crossed over the Red Sea they sang, "This is my God and I will glorify Him; the God of my fathers, and I will exalt Him."[13] Rashi comments: "I am not the beginning of the *kedushah*; rather the *kedushah* and His Divinity has been established and stood with me from the days of my fathers." Being part of the destiny of *Klal Yisrael* is to humbly see our generation

---

13. Exodus 15:2.

as completely dependent on those who came before us; we are "not the beginning of the *kedushah*."

The Talmud relates that even a simple handmaiden at the splitting of the sea experienced a greater revelation of God's presence than the greatest prophets of later generations. Rav Elyah Meir Bloch explains that even at such a time of greatness, the Jewish people at the edge of the Red Sea had to humbly acknowledge that they were not the "beginning of the holiness," but a continuation of it, and that that everything that had been achieved was due to the foundations laid by the forefathers. Similarly, Reb Elyah Meir cites the Talmud[14] concerning the inauguration of the Temple by King Shlomo. Initially, the gates would not open, no matter how much he supplicated. The Talmud says that he offered up twenty-four different supplications and prayers, but God did not answer his prayers until he requested that it be done in the merit of his father, King David. Then, only in the merit of King David, did the gates open. Through building the Temple, King Shlomo reached a level that even his father, King David, had not reached. Nonetheless, at such a time, he was reminded that his achievements were based on the merit of his father.

There is a well-known halachic principle that reflects the respect we must demonstrate for previous generations: *shelo lehotzi la'az al harishonim* – not to slander the earlier generations, which means that a current halachic ruling should not cast aspersions on the halachic standards of previous generations. It often applies to the laws of divorce: nothing should be done that could, even indirectly, imply that *gittin* of the past were invalid, since this would mean that a woman who remarried based on such a *get* entered into an adulterous relationship, and her children halachically would be regarded as *mamzerim* (illegitimate). *La'az* in this area is regarded so seriously because of the disastrous nature of the consequences. But *la'az* also applies in other areas. For example, Rabbi Yosef Eliyahu Henkin said, regarding those who wished to impose new *chumros* on an old *mikveh* in Rochester, New York, "Anyone who wishes to change shall [do so] only for himself [privately], and should not [through a public *chumrah*] imply *la'az* on the old practice."[15]

---

14. Gemara Shabbos 30a.
15. *Kisvei HaGri Henkin*, vol. 2, p. 69.

This concept goes further than avoiding *chumros* that will cause *la'az* on the previous generations. It extends to resorting to very elaborate explanations to defend the practices of previous generations. A classic proponent of this approach was Rav Yechiel Michel HaLevi Epstein, the Aruch Hashulchan. One dramatic example of his approach is his discussion of how, during the summer months, flour becomes so infested with insects that even those who check it carefully will not find all of them.[16] Furthermore, the vast majority of the Jews of Eastern Europe did not inspect their flour at all and would only remove insects that were clearly visible. The seriousness of the prohibition of eating insects is well known, yet the Aruch Hashulchan searched for some possible halachic justification for what the people were doing. He writes: "God forbid to say that *Klal Yisrael* would stumble in a great prohibition such as this. It is not pleasing to their Master [God] that you should say such a thing about them. And [therefore] it is proper to search for merit [in what they are doing]."[17] He analyzes a number of explanations of revered halachic authorities who had also delved into finding merit in the popular practice, and adds a halachic justification of his own. The purpose of the Aruch Hashulchan's analysis was not to *pasken* for what we should do in practice, but rather to justify the *halachic* conduct of generations of Jews.

In another example, the Aruch Hashulchan goes to great lengths to defend the accepted *leniency* in Lithuania of eating *chodosh*.[18] At first reading, there seems to be no justification for the leniency. The Aruch Hashulchan cites, and rejects as unconvincing, other explanations that seek to justify the generations-old *leniency*. He reasons that, given the timing of the agricultural season in Russia and Lithuania, the prohibition of *chodosh* would impose unbearable hardship on the community. Eventually, with deep respect for previous generations, the Aruch Hashulchan joyously announced a basis for justifying the long-standing lenient practice.[19] He argues that in the case of *chodosh*, any halachic

16. *Aruch Hashulchan* Y.D. 100:13–18.
17. *Aruch Hashulchan* Y.D. 100:13.
18. *Aruch Hashulchan* Y.D. 293:18–21.
19. *Aruch Hashulchan* Y.D. 293:19. See in that paragraph the joyous poetic play on the language of a verse from Psalms.

explanation must take into consideration that "for generations they [an established observant Jewish community] have conducted themselves like this [in a lenient way]."[20]

Deep respect for *minhag* (custom) is rooted in respect for *Klal Yisrael*. Rav Shlomo Zalman Auerbach[21] often quoted with affection the words of Rabbi Shlomo Kluger (known as the Maggid of Brody), who writes:[22] "About my custom [concerning the time for *Kabbolas Shabbos*], know that I do not conduct myself in accordance with any *chumrah* [stringency] more than the lowest of the nation and the simplest of the simple; if only my portion in *Olam Haba* should be with one *am ha'aretz* [ignorant person] who walks simply and lowly."

Reb Shlomo Zalman also lived by this philosophy. For example, the *Mishnah Berurah* says that – strictly speaking – at least nine men must be concentrating on the repetition of the *Amidah*; if not, the blessings recited by the *shliach tzibbur* are considered to be in vain. Therefore, if the *shliach tzibbur* is concerned that there are insufficient numbers concentrating, he should have in mind that the *Amidah* is a *nedavah* (freewill offering). This ensures that even if the *Amidah* is invalid, it nevertheless will not create a further sin of taking God's name in vain, as we do have the discretion to bring a voluntary offering before Hashem. Reb Shlomo Zalman was asked if he follows the instruction of the *Mishnah Berurah*. He answered that in his youth he did; but in later years, he stopped. He explained, "Whatever will happen to *Klal Yisrael* who are not careful with making a condition like this will happen to me as well."

THE DESTINY OF KLAL YISRAEL

To be a *klal mensch* is to identify not only with the history of *Klal Yisrael*, but also its future and its destiny. The destiny of *Klal Yisrael* is connected to God's grand vision for the Redemption of *Klal Yisrael* and, indeed, of all mankind. As the Mishnah quoted above states: "Rabbi Yochanan Hasandlar said, 'Any community dedicated to Heaven will endure for-

20. *Aruch Hashulchan* Y.D. 293:21.
21. *Halichos Shlomo*, vol 1, p. 121 note 13. Also see there the reference to Rav Shlomo Kluger and all information contained in this paragraph and the next.
22. *Sefer Ha'alef Lecha Shlomo, Orach Chaim, siman* 112.

ever.'" Rabbi Yochanan Hasandlar, a direct descendant of King David, was a student of the famous Rabbi Akiva, and lived during the Roman military occupation in the immediate aftermath of the destruction of the Second Temple – an era in which calamitous events ultimately led to the exile of the Jewish People from the Land of Israel. The Sforno points out that at the time Rabbi Yochanan spoke, the future outlook of the Jewish People seemed bleak. His own mentor, Rabbi Akiva, was executed for teaching Torah in defiance of tyrannical Roman decrees; and so to claim that the Jewish People, if they were dedicated to Heaven, would "endure forever" must have seemed quite unrealistic. The mighty Roman Empire with its elaborate civilization must have had a much greater prospect of survival than the small and beleaguered Jewish nation. But the Roman Empire is no more. Its values, its legal system, its political system, and now even its language, have vanished from the daily lives of all humanity. And yet we, the spiritual heirs and descendants of Rabbi Yochanan Hasandlar and Rabbi Akiva, are still here today, and we share their values, their ideals, and their laws as contained in our Torah.

In the introduction to his siddur, Rabbi Yaakov Emden famously wrote that the miracles performed by God to ensure the survival of the Jewish People throughout the many years of exile are even greater than the awe-inspiring miracles of the Exodus from Egypt – the ten plagues, the splitting of the sea, the manna falling from Heaven and the Clouds of Glory. Jewish destiny defies the normal laws of history. By any logical and rational assessment, we should not exist as a separate, identifiable people after almost two thousand years of exile, dispersion, and persecution.

This eternal destiny of *Klal Yisrael* carrying the Torah forever is contained in the words of the prophet Yishayahu:

> 'And as for Me, this is My covenant with them,' said Hashem. 'My spirit that is upon you and My words that I have placed in your mouth shall not be withdrawn from your mouth, nor from the mouth of your offspring,' said Hashem, 'from this moment and forever.'[23]

---

23. Isaiah 59:21.

To be a *klal mensch* is to believe in the future and the destiny of *Klal Yisrael* as it is connected to the Torah. This passion drove one of the most courageous eras of recent Jewish history. After the Holocaust, much had been destroyed, yet the many stories of heroism of the rebuilding of yeshivas and Torah communities that emerged during and after the war declared the eternal connection between the Torah and the future of *Klal Yisrael*. These stories speak of the indestructible fervor for the destiny of *Klal Yisrael* rooted in Torah, and symbolize everything there is to say about being a *klal mensch*. Here is one such story that I heard from my *Rosh Yeshiva*, who was a devoted disciple of these heroes:

Prior to the German invasion of Lithuania in June of 1941, Rav Elyah Meir Bloch and Rav Mordechai (Mottel) Katz were sent by their colleagues and families to the United States to secure funding and visas for the community of the Telz Yeshiva. They had realized that trouble was coming, but no one, of course, realized the extent of the horror of the impending disaster. Reb Elyah Meir and Reb Mottel were smuggled out of Europe, heading east, and eventually reached the United States via Siberia and Japan.

Soon after they arrived in America, they heard the devastating news that the Germans had destroyed the entire town of Telshe on 20 Tammuz 5701 (July 15, 1941) and that their colleagues and families – including Reb Elyah Meir's brothers, Rav Avraham Yitzchak Bloch and Rav Zalman Bloch – had been murdered. Reb Elyah Meir's wife and all of his children, except for one daughter, had also perished. Reb Mottel learned of the murder of his wife and his ten children. The pain was excruciating, unbearable.

There was no one to bring to America; everyone was dead. The two shattered Telzers were left stranded, bereft of family, in a strange country whose language they could not speak. The Telz Yeshiva was no more. There were almost no Jews left in Telshe and there was almost nothing left of the Jewish Lithuania they had known.

Instead of succumbing to despair, Reb Elyah Meir and Reb Mottel resolved that a new Telz Yeshiva had to be established in America as quickly as possible. With superhuman effort and dedication, the Telz Yeshiva of Cleveland arose in 1942, carrying on the Torah legacy while Europe was still burning. How did they find the courage and fortitude to start again after such devastation? How could they rebuild so soon after such horrific loss?

"DIVINE MISSION"

Rav Mordechai Gifter, a student of Rav Avraham Yitzchak Bloch, joined Reb Elyah Meir and Reb Mottel in building and developing the Telz Yeshiva in America, and many years later he recalled the strength of Reb Elyah Meir's determination to rebuild. I quote from Rav Gifter's words, which he wrote years later:

> There was a specific characteristic which permeated the work and efforts of the *Rosh Yeshiva* [Reb Elyah Meir]. Upon his arrival in this country by way of Siberia and Japan, he met with a group of friends at the Broadway Central Hotel in New York. I recall the gist of what he then spoke…. The *Rosh Yeshiva, zt"l,* was motivated by a deep sense of Divine mission, sent to America by a message couched in the persecution and destruction of European Jewry. It was this sense of mission which brought forth all his endless efforts in the building of Torah in this country…. It was this sense of mission which motivated him in all his indefatigable work for the *Klal Yisrael*…. This sense of mission grows from a realization that life has a purpose and a deep awareness of that purpose…. When one's life is permeated with this consciousness, then all is part of the plan of Divine Providence – all situations and conditions in life represent the various forms in which one must perform the mission for which he has been sent into *Olam Hazeh* – this world. This was the nature of the *Rosh Yeshiva's* life.

We can infer from Rav Gifter's observations that a person's mission is to be found in "all situations and conditions in life." Clearly, there is no one mission for all people. Everyone has a different set of circumstances given by God, and consequently, a different mission for which he or she was sent into this world. This is a philosophy of life that sees every last detail as "part of the plan of Divine Providence" and that every moment and every aspect of life is meant to be lived with a "sense of mission." There are many missions that a person fulfills throughout life.

A grand vision is fulfilled through a detailed, practical on-the-ground approach.

A lofty and broad vision, though essential, is fulfilled only through the day-to-day practicalities and not through excessive focus on the macro-forces of history. The Telzer *Rosh Yeshiva*, Reb Elyah Meir's father, Rav Yosef Yehudah Lev Bloch, explains a puzzling passage in the Talmud: "The son of David [the Messiah] will not come until they [the Jewish People] have despaired of the Redemption."[24] How can it be, he asks, that on the one hand we are commanded to long for the Redemption and expect its imminent arrival; and yet, on the other hand, the Redemption will come only when we have despaired of the *Mashiach* arriving? He explains that the Talmud means that the Redemption will not come until we have despaired of bringing it *ourselves*. The Final Redemption for *Klal Yisrael* and for the world is solely in hands of God, and His calculations are beyond human comprehension. He will bring about the end of history, and the salvation of the Jewish People and all mankind, at a time that is in accordance with His judgment. Any attempt to interfere with the process of the Final Redemption leads to calamity.

History in "Small" Events

Rav Elyah Meir Bloch makes clear that the way we write ourselves into eternity is not through grandiose actions that would influence the mega-forces of history; rather, it is often the smallest things that gain eternal and historic significance. A person does not always realize when he is making history. Reb Elyah Meir cites this Midrash:[25]

> If Reuven had known that the Holy One, Blessed Be He, was writing about him – 'and Reuven heard and saved him [Yosef from the brothers] from their hands' – he would have carried him on his shoulders back to his father. And had Aharon known that God was writing about him – 'behold, he [Aharon] is coming towards you [Moses] and he will see you with joy in his heart' – he would have gone out to him with cymbals and tambourines.

---

24. Sanhedrin 97a.
25. *Midrash Rabah Numbers, parshah* 34.

And had Boaz known that the Holy One, Blessed Be He, was writing about him – 'and he handed her [Ruth] parched grain, and she ate and was satisfied, and had some left over' – he would have fed her fattened cows.

Reb Elyah Meir explains that only the events that are of eternal and historic significance in the unfolding drama of the ultimate Redemption of all humankind were written in the Torah and Tanach. For example, the fact that Moshe was the king of Kush for many years was not recorded in the Torah because it did not have eternal significance. But the actions of these three great people – Reuven, Aharon, and Boaz – did have lasting importance, though they did not realize at that time that they were making history.

According to Reb Elyah Meir, the Midrash means that Reuven did not realize that his attempt to save Yosef from the brothers was so important that it was deemed worthy by Hashem of being recorded in the Torah. Aharon did not realize that his generosity of spirit toward his brother, Moshe, was going to ensure that Moshe would accept the mission and be the instrument through which God would liberate His people. Boaz did not know that his kindness to Ruth was laying the foundations for the family that would eventually give birth to King David, and ultimately to the *Melech Hamashiach* (the Messiah).

The Midrash goes on to say that although the books of the Torah have been finalized, there is a spiritual *Sefer Torah* being written in the Heavens on an ongoing basis, as the prophet Malachi[26] states, "Then those who fear Hashem spoke to one another, and Hashem listened and heard, and a *book of remembrance* was written before Him for those who fear Hashem and those who give thought to His name."

This "book of remembrance" is the Heavenly "*Sefer Torah*": it is the unfolding story of the development of *Klal Yisrael* and the entire world, a continuation of the story that began and is recorded in the *Sefer Torah* that was given to us at Mount Sinai. Only what we do to advance *Klal Yisrael*, and indeed all human beings, toward the ultimate goal of the Final Redemption is being recorded. Written by Eliyahu the

---

26. Malachi 3:16.

prophet, the record of our deeds is signed by the *Melech Hamashiach* and Hashem Himself.

On the one hand, we are unwittingly participating in an immense cosmic drama of God's plans for the ultimate Redemption of the world. On the other hand, the way that this vision is fulfilled is through the fine details of the *halachah*, i.e., living a good life in accordance with the will of Hashem. It is in these "small" things – such as generosity of spirit, help of one brother to another, and kindness to a convert and a widow – that actually turn the course of history.

"THE WORLD WAS CREATED FOR ME"

The Midrash states: "Just as the faces of all people are different, so too are their souls different."[27]

A well-known Mishnah[28] says that to destroy one life is to destroy an entire world, and to save a life is to save an entire world. Moreover, "a person is obliged to say: 'the world was created for me.'" Rav Chaim Shmulevitz maintains that believing "the world was created for me" is the foundation of superlative behavior because it inspires people to live up to the unique potential that God has placed within them. This emphasis on the importance of each individual does not run counter to the concept of the *klal*. It is, in fact, necessary for the good of the *klal*, for a single individual to have the power to make a unique and significant contribution to the whole community. Commenting on the biblical passage recording that Yaakov left Be'er Sheva, Rashi[29] quotes the Talmud, which says that when a *tzaddik* leaves a place, glory, light, and beauty leave with him.

The Gemara mandates that if someone is present at the time of another person's death, he has a duty to tear his clothes because it is like witnessing a Torah scroll being burnt.[30] Rav Yosef Dov Soloveitchik explains the analogy to the burnt *Sefer Torah*: One of the laws of the writing of a *Sefer Torah* is that it requires the unique handwriting of

---

27. *Midrash Tanchuma Pinchas*, section 10.
28. Sanhedrin 36a.
29. Genesis 28:10.
30. Shabbos 105b.

each scribe. For example, if one scribe wrote in red ink, and another one wrote over it with black ink, it would not be considered a valid Torah scroll; though for the purposes of the laws of Shabbos, it would be considered the *melachah* (forbidden Shabbos labor) of writing. Based on the analysis of the Rishonim, Rav Soloveitchik explains that a unique handwriting is required for a Torah scroll; but for Shabbos, writing is defined as a *melachah* even if it is not unique handwriting. Thus, every *Sefer Torah* is unique because it is written in the unique handwriting of its scribe, giving rise to the comparison between the burning of a Torah scroll to the death of a human being. Although other people continue to exist, that special, particular person can never be replaced.

INDIVIDUALITY AND THE COMMUNITY

Paradoxically, to be a *klal mensch* is to nurture one's individuality. The importance of *Klal Yisrael* is directly linked to the distinctiveness of every single individual within it. The combined value of the community and the individual is beautifully expressed in the *mitzvah* of the half-shekel contribution and counting. Everyone gave an equal amount toward the greater good. Through the equal contribution of a half-shekel, the equal value of every individual was emphasized. Rav Moshe Feinstein[31] explains that this is an uplifting realization: the Hebrew word for "count" comes from the root "to lift up." When a person realizes that Hashem wants his or her contribution as much as that of the greatest leader, he will substantially improve his deeds.

Rav Mordechai Gifter[32] approaches the message of the half-shekel in yet another way: the *klal* can never be successful without the contribution of each individual. The *klal* has a tremendous power, of course, that an individual does not have; yet the *klal* is only as strong as the potential of each individual. The more diverse and rich are the talents of all its component parts, the greater the potential of the *klal* to make an impact on the world.

Rav Chaim Volozhiner states that the Mishnah: "Do not separate yourself from the community" applies to the study of Torah as well as

---

31. *Darash Moshe* 30:12.
32. *Pirkei Torah*, Exodus 30:11 and 30:15.

to building society. He cites the famous statement of Rabbi Yehudah Hanasi ("Rebbi"), "I have received a lot from my teachers, even more from my colleagues, and the most from my pupils." One who is part of a community of learners benefits from many different people, with their different talents and their different roles. Their combined efforts increase knowledge and wisdom, so that both the individual and the community are enriched by the joint enterprise.

In all areas of life, individuals have unique contributions to make. To separate from the community weakens both the community and the people who separate themselves.

WHAT UNIFIES THE DIFFERENT COMPONENTS OF THE KLAL?

The values of community and individuality complement each other when both are harnessed for the sake of Heaven. In the Torah, we see the combination of individuality and community expressed through the different tribes of Israel possessing specific characteristics represented by their different encampments and flags in the desert. Rabbi Yaakov Kaminetzky explains that the different colors and symbols of each flag represented the unique contribution each tribe would make. This situation had the potential to be enormously divisive. What would hold all of these tribes together, if each had a unique characteristic? Reb Yaakov points out that the flags were given to the Jewish People only after they received the Torah, for then they shared a common purpose. The *Mishkan*, which contained the tablets, symbolized the common unifying mission of the Torah. They all encamped around the *Mishkan*, which held the entire enterprise together. The common goal of furthering Torah in the world held together the differing tribes, as well as the individuals within each tribe.

"The Torah was commanded to us by Moshe, it is the heritage of the *kehillah* of Yaakov." Rav Elyah Meir Bloch writes that "the heritage of the *kehillah* of Yaakov" means that whatever *Klal Yisrael* achieves as a whole belongs to every individual member, even if that individual was involved in another aspect of the mission. He cites the classic example of the partnership between the financial resources and business acumen of Yissachar and the Torah scholarship of Zevulun. The tribe of

Yissachar shared equally in the merit of the Torah learning of Zevulun. Comparing different life roles to going into battle, he notes that some people are on the frontlines and others have different tasks within the army, but everyone is a partner in it.

The *Alter* of Slabodka explains how each person is given a unique set of circumstances by Hashem that are distinctly appropriate for his personal mission in this world. He writes that "the soul of every single person is sent from on high" with a unique Divine mission that pertains to the *klal* (the community and society as a whole) – and also to that person as a *prat* (as a single, separate entity) with its own potential that needs to be fulfilled.[33]

The *Alter* draws an analogy between the Heavenly kingdom and the earthly one: Just as each person has a specific role in an earthly kingdom or country, so too each person has a different role to play in the workings of God's kingdom. In this analogy, some people are ministers and princes – those who are blessed with wealth and power – and they carry the heavy responsibility for ensuring that the needs of the general population are met. They are meant to use their powers in support of another group of influential people: the sages.

The sages (*talmidei chachamim*) must teach the rest of the nation the correct way to live in all aspects of human existence – matters between man and man, as well as those between man and God. The vast majority of people carry the responsibility of building society (*yishuv ha'olam*), working the land, building houses, and engaging in commerce. The Hebrew term *yishuv ha'olam* includes anything that furthers human civilization on earth. Everyone who is able to make some contribution to society is expected to do so. This is clear from the Gemara, which explains that the reason a professional gambler is disqualified as a kosher witness is that such a person is not involved with *yishuv ha'olam*.[34]

It is obvious from the *Alter* that the majority of the nation was never intended to be involved in full-time learning and teaching. That

---

33. The *Alter*'s notes to Rabbi Yisrael Salanter's essay *Eitz Pri* as published in the *sefer Ohr Yisrael* with the notes of Rabbi Reuven Leuchter, pp. 19-20.
34. Talmud Sanhedrin 24b, according to one opinion that is brought by the Rambam and *Shulchan Aruch*.

was always meant to be the preserve of the select few with exceptional intellectual ability and the appropriate personality. He also makes clear that the main duty of *talmidei chachamim* is to spread the wisdom and guidance of Torah to the rest of the people, and not to remain isolated, merely learning for themselves.

What about people who are not able to be involved with the building of society due to their physical suffering or poverty? The *Alter* answers that they, too, have a Divine mission: to carry their affliction with dignity, fortitude, and faith in Hashem. The Ramchal explains the concept of *"mazal"* by saying that the life circumstances of all people are part of a greater plan of God that stretches from the beginning of time until the end. Thus, when Rabbi Elazar ben Pedas[35] begs Hashem to end his poverty, Hashem answers that He could certainly do that, but it would involve changing the configuration of human history from Adam until that point.

Accepting the assignment given by God, and not longing for someone else's circumstances, is a basic value. Rav Naftali Amsterdam once remarked to his *rebbi*, Rav Yisrael Salanter, "Rebbi, if I had the head of the author of the *Shaagas Aryeh*, and the heart of the author of the *Yesod Veshoresh Ha'avodah*, and the *middos* of the Master [Rav Yisrael Salanter], then I would be able to be a true servant of Hashem." Rav Yisrael Salanter answered him, "Naftali, with *your* head, and with *your* heart, and with *your middos*, you are able to be a true servant of Hashem."

Rav Shlomo Wolbe relates this story in explaining the approach of his *rebbi*, Reb Yerucham of Mir, who emphasized the importance of the individual and the greatness that each individual could reach. An aspect of this philosophy is based on a Midrash,[36] which describes the greatness of Yaakov as being *levado* (alone). Being alone, set apart, is a Divine characteristic. That singular experience of aloneness encapsulates the calling of each individual to reach the unique greatness that only he or she can reach.

Rav Moshe Feinstein[37] explains that in the eyes of Hashem, every

35. Gemara Ta'anis 25a.
36. *Genesis Rabah* 77:1.
37. *Darash Moshe*, Exodus 6:26.

mission is of equal value, even though, to us, one may seem less important than another. The classic example he cites is the Talmudic statement that Moshe and Aharon were equal before Hashem in terms of their greatness. He questions this: since we know that the Torah says there has never been anyone as great as Moshe, how could Aharon be equally great? He answers that when a person achieves what he is meant to do on this earth, fulfilling his God-given mission with his God-given potential, he has reached the highest level he can, and he stands in equal value to anyone else, in the eyes of Hashem. Objectively speaking, Aharon was not as great as Moshe; but since he achieved his unique mission, and Moshe achieved his, the two are equal in the eyes of Hashem.

There is a fascinating Gemara[38] that illuminates this point, and it is cited by Rabbi Moshe Feinstein. It tells of Rabbi Yosef, the son of Rabbi Yehoshua, who passed away, saw the next world, and came back to live in this world again. Asked what he saw, he responded, "I saw an upside-down world…. Those on top were below and those below were on top." His father said to him, "You saw a clear world." The conventional understanding of this Gemara is that he saw that the criteria of success in this world and the next world are different. He saw an inversion of status from this world to the next.

Rav Moshe Feinstein rejects this interpretation because it does not adequately explain Rabbi Yosef's surprise. He was, after all, one of the great Talmudic sages: why would he have expected the criteria of status and success in the next world to be the same as in this world? Therefore, Reb Moshe concludes, Rabbi Yosef was surprised to see even people who had achieved more in Torah terms below other people who had, objectively speaking, achieved less in Torah terms. Those who reached higher levels in the next world had fulfilled the mission and potential that God had given them and, subjectively, they achieved more than others, who objectively had achieved more. Each person is judged in terms of the unique talents and potential given to him by God to fulfill his Divine mission.

38. Bava Basra 10b.

A KLAL MENSCH BUILDS HASHEM'S WORLD

In his *sefer, Eitz Pri,* Rav Yisrael Salanter explains some of the complex spiritual and philosophical principles concerning blessing and suffering in his world. He acknowledges that, on a practical level, it is impossible to know whether one's blessings in this world causes one's reward in the next world to be reduced; nor can one discern whether one's suffering in this world is atonement for sins to reduce punishment in the next world or not. He says that the only way to ensure a positive outcome (that one's blessings in this world are not deducted from one's reward in the next world and that the suffering one endures in this world is considered atonement) is through devoting oneself to the service of Hashem. We must allow ourselves to become His instrument for the building of this world. If everything that we do in this world is for the sake of Hashem, we are here on His "business" and all of the "expenses," the blessings, and all the suffering are on His "account," and not on ours. We must "be here" solely for God, which Reb Yisrael defines as being completely dedicated to fulfilling His commandments.

To be involved with "the business of Hashem"[39] is not just about doing good deeds and *mitzvos;* it is about building a world in which good deeds and *mitzvos* are part of the infrastructure and the very reality of existence. So too, when it comes to learning Torah, it is not merely about one's own personal study of the material. It is about the work of supporting and contributing to the building of Torah institutions and a Torah culture within *Klal Yisrael,* thereby ensuring the continuity of Torah from generation to generation.

Reb Elyah Meir's partner in rebuilding Telz, Rav Mordechai Katz, would often tell his new American students about what kept him going. He said to them (in Yiddish) on many occasions,[40] "*Noch aza churban, yeder ainer darft zitzen un lernen, veren grois in Torah, un gayen umetum de gantze velt tzu shaffen Torah un Yiddishkeit.*" (After such destruction, everyone must sit and learn, become great in Torah, and go around the whole world to build Torah and Judaism.)

Note that his vision was not only to teach Torah, but to "build"

---

39. This term is used by Rabbi Leuchter.
40. I heard this from my *Rosh Yeshiva, zt"l.*

it; and not only to build Torah in certain places, but to "go around the whole world." His was a burning passion to ensure that Torah not be forgotten. *Klal Yisrael* has been given the Torah as a precious gift from Hashem, and it would be a betrayal of our most sacred mission to "lose it" through neglect and forgetting, God forbid.

The concept of building the world is what Torah is all about. As the Gemara says: "What does it mean, 'builders'? Says Rabbi Yochanan, 'These are the *talmidei chachamim* who are involved in the building of the world all the days of their lives.'"[41] That is what it means to be a builder, to build the world. We are required not only to teach Torah and to learn Torah, but to build it; not only to do *mitzvos* but to "build" them.

Building is something more profound than simply learning or teaching.[42] It is about creating a world where Torah values are given practical expression through the establishment of schools, yeshivas, and welfare institutions, and constructing the societal infrastructure that gives expression to all the values of the Torah. Anything that an individual does to contribute to building such a world is part of being in the service of Hashem. He is a true *klal mensch*, belonging completely to Hashem.

This is the burning mission of a *klal mensch:* total devotion to the destiny of *Klal Yisrael* and to the Redemption of the world, to writing a chapter in the great Heavenly Torah that unfolds the destiny of mankind through *Klal Yisrael*, from Mount Sinai to the Final Redemption, culminating in the prophetic vision of a future world, which will one day become reality: "The wolf shall dwell with the lamb and the leopard shall lie down with the kid, and a little child shall lead them[43]…they shall not hurt nor destroy in all My holy mountain, for the earth shall be full of the knowledge of the Lord as the waters cover the sea[44]…and they shall beat their swords into plowshares and their spears into pruning hooks. Nation shall not lift up sword against nation; neither shall they learn war anymore."[45]

---

41. Shabbos 114a.
42. I heard this idea about the difference between learning and building from my *Rosh Yeshiva.*
43. Isaiah 11:6.
44. Isaiah 11:9.
45. Isaiah 2:4.

Appendix

Historical Context

Rabbi Berel Wein

No worldview can be properly understood without some knowledge of the circumstances in which it arose and flourished. It is instructive to look at the history and life experiences of the Lithuanian Jewish community to understand the context of the values discussed in this book.

The Jews arrived in Lithuania in the fourteenth century from Germany and Central Europe; migrations there later included refugees from the traumatic Expulsion from Spain. Lithuania-Poland was then a minor empire in Eastern Europe; it incorporated much of the Kingdom of Poland known as Congress Poland, parts of Belarus and Latvia, as well as all of present day Lithuania. Eventually, by the end of the eighteenth century, there was a substantial Jewish population there (estimated at approximately 250,000), with over 300 Jewish communities, mainly concentrated in a number of large cities – Vilnias (Vilna), Kaunas (Kovno), Panevezhys (Ponivezh), Siosulai, (Shavil), Ukmerge (Vilkomir), and Brest-Litovsk (Brisk). Many Lithuanian cities had populations of over 20,000 Jews, and there were hundreds of small towns and villages with significant numbers of Jews scattered throughout the country. By the nineteenth century, the Jews were the largest national minority in Lithuania. But even though they eventually had representation in the Lithuanian parliament in the 1920s, they remained a distinct and unassimilated minority within that country.

Lithuania was a poor country with limited natural resources and a very harsh, dank climate. The mass of the Lithuanian population consisted of unlettered peasants who lived a very coarse life, with many given over to alcoholism. A strongly Roman Catholic country, Lithuania harbored latent anti-Semitism in all levels of society. The Jews who had contact with the local population in various occupations – contractors, innkeepers, craftsmen, porters, merchants – felt, justifiably, intellectually and morally superior. So there was no overwhelming temptation to assimilate into Lithuanian life or even to learn its language. Since it was a poor country, the Lithuanian Jews, unlike those of Poland and Central Europe, had no dreams of wealth or power.

They developed their own dialect of Yiddish, concentrated their lives on family and community – and above all, on Torah study. These factors – the poverty of the country, the conditions and way of life of its non-Jewish population, the inhospitable climate – all combined to place a particular stamp on Lithuanian Jewry's life and society.

In the eighteenth century, the towering figure of the Gaon of Vilna dominated the Lithuanian and broader Jewish world. His emphasis on Torah study above all else was the hallmark of Lithuanian Jewry. The Gaon's concentration on this basic value of Jewish life was put into practice by his disciple Rabbi Chaim Rabinowitz, who, at the beginning of the nineteenth century, founded and headed the great Yeshivah of Volozhin, the "mother" of all later educational institutions of its type. Volozhin was the wellspring that produced rabbinic, religious, and general leadership for decades, and its influence is still felt today. The shadow of the Vilna Gaon is omnipresent in the great yeshivas of our generation all over the Jewish world, for many are cast in the Lithuanian mold, even if they are Sephardic, Chasidic, American, English, South African, or Israeli in orientation, faculty, and student body.

Through the disciples of the Vilna Gaon, Lithuanian Jews spearheaded the return of Eastern European Jews to the Land of Israel at the dawn of the nineteenth century, long before Zionism as a movement was even on the horizon. The basic foundation of the *Yishuv Hayashan* (the old, original Jewish settlement of the Land of Israel) was laid by Lithuanian Jewry.

Another disciple of the Gaon, Rabbi Yosef Zundel of Salant, became the mentor and inspiration of Rabbi Yisrael Lipkin of Salant, the founder of the nineteenth-century Lithuanian *Mussar* Movement. Its emphasis on sincere inner piety and moral, ethical behavior among Jews in all areas of their lives also became a hallmark of Lithuanian Jewish life.

The late eighteenth and early nineteenth centuries saw the rise of the *Haskalah* (Jewish "Enlightenment") movement, which included many famous Lithuanian poets, writers, and activists of that period. The *Haskalah* was strongly and openly opposed by the rabbis and traditional Jewish society because it rejected the Divinity, eternal relevance, and authority of the Torah. However, the dispute never took on the bitterness and violence that marked this struggle in other Jewish societies. In fact, contrary to the situation that existed in other Jewish enclaves, the Lithuanian *maskil* ("enlightened one") was less anti-religious than his Polish, Galician, and Hungarian counterparts and many remained observant Jews. Traditional Lithuanian Jewry fought *Haskalah* with intellect, writings, and open debate – but not with fists and widespread bans. Eventually, *Haskalah* disappeared as a movement in Lithuania and metamorphosed into the secular Zionist movements, Socialist and Communist activism, and into the Jewish labor union, commonly known as the Bund.

Though relatively small – the Lithuanian Jewish community numbered somewhat fewer than 300,000 souls in 1939 – it was a thriving civilization. It was destroyed in a few short years of the 1940s by the murderous forces of Hitler and Stalin. Perhaps only two or three percent of Lithuanian Jewry survived these two onslaughts.

However, the miniscule remnant of Lithuanian Jewry was able to continue the teachings and values of Lithuanian Jewish life and Torah to a new generation of students. The great post-war hero of Lithuanian Jewry, Rabbi Shlomo Yosef Kahaneman, the Ponivezher Rav, declared that he intended to rebuild Torah in the Land of Israel by re-establishing the eighteen leading yeshivas of pre-war Lithuania. He also held out bright prospects for Torah Jewry in America and South Africa. The vast majority of Lithuanian Jews who left Europe in the first half of the twentieth century, and had escaped the Holocaust, migrated to South Africa.

We have not kept count, but we certainly can hazard an opinion that there are many more than eighteen Lithuanian-influenced yeshivas functioning successfully today in the Land of Israel. Among all of the unexpected and almost miraculous developments in Jewish life since the end of World War II, the rebirth of these Torah institutions is certainly one of its major events.

Lithuanian Jewry is no more – but even in its death, just as it was in its life – its influence, disproportionate to its numbers and social power, remains a beacon of Torah light and instruction for all who seek it.

Books of the Tanach

Torah/Five Books of Moses

Bereshis – Genesis
Shmos – Exodus
Vayikra – Leviticus
Bamidbar – Numbers
Devarim – Deuteronomy

Nevi'im/Prophets

Yehoshua – Joshua
Shoftim – Judges
Shmuel – Samuel
Melochim – Kings
Yishayahu – Isaiah
Yirmiyahu – Jeremiah
Yechezkel – Ezekiel

Trei Asar/The Twelve Prophets

Hoshea – Hosea
Yoel – Joel
Amos – Amos
Ovadiah – Obadiah
Yonah – Jonah
Michah – Micah
Nachum – Nahum
Chavakuk – Habakkuk
Tzephaniah – Zephaniah

The Legacy

Chaggai – Haggai
Zechariah – Zechariah
Malachi – Malachi

Kesuvim/Writings
Tehillim – Psalms
Mishlei – Proverbs
Iyov – Job
Shir Hashirim – The Song of Songs
Rus – Ruth
Eichah – Lamentations
Koheles – Ecclesiastes
Esther – Esther
Daniel – Daniel
Ezra/Nechemiah – Ezra/Nehemiah
Divrei Hayamim – Chronicles

Glossary

A

Acharonim: The latter rabbinic scholars from the sixteenth century onwards

aggadah: The non-legal moral, historical, and philosophical teachings of the Talmud

aggadic: Deriving from aggadah

agunah, agunos (pl.): A woman whose husband has disappeared. She cannot remarry unless his death is ascertained; in today's usage, a woman who cannot remarry because of the husband's refusal to grant her a divorce.

alef-beis: The Hebrew alphabet, so called by its first two letters

aliyah: The honor of going up to the Torah to recite blessings for the public reading of the weekly parshah (see below)

Alter: Literally, the elderly man; a term of respect and endearment for certain sages of great wisdom and renown

am ha'aretz: Literally, the people of the land; it connotes an unlearned person

Amidah: The prayer recited thrice daily while standing – nineteen blessings long during the weekdays, seven blessings on Shabbos and holidays

Amora, Amoraim (pl.): A scholar during the period of the composition of the Talmud

arel: An uncircumcised man

Ashkenazic: Referring to Jews of German and Eastern European descent and their customs

assur: Forbidden

Av Beis Bin: Chief Justice of a rabbinical court

B

bein adam le'atzmo: Relationship to one's self

bein adam lechaveiro: Relationships between human beings

bein adam leMakom: Relationship between humans and God

bein hazmanim: Vacation period between semesters in the yeshiva schedules

beis din, batei din (pl.): Rabbinic court

beis midrash: Literally, house of study; study hall

bench, benching: Grace after Meals; blessing someone

bimah: A raised platform; the table from which the Torah is read; a euphemism for high honor or position

bodek: An examiner

braisa, braisos (pl.): Talmudic teachings that were codified after the completion of the Mishnah

b'tzelem Elokim: Literally, in the form or image of the Creator; a phrase used to denote the intrinsic worth of human beings who were created in the "image" of the Creator

C

Cave of Machpelah: The burial place of Adam, Eve, Abraham, Sarah, Isaac, Rebecca, Jacob, and Leah; located near Hebron in the Land of Israel

chai: Creatures that have life: animals, birds, fish, reptiles, humans, etc.

chametz: Leavened grain products, which are forbidden on Pesach

chanifah: A fawning compliment, corruption of others

Chasid, Chasidim (pl.): One who adheres to the traditions of Chasidism, a religious movement that began in 1730 in Eastern Europe; usually involves the spiritual leadership of a Rebbe

Chasidic: Pertaining to Chasidim

Chasidus: The philosophy and behavior patterns of Chasidim

chelbenah: One of the spices used to create the incense in the Temple service; by itself, it is foul-smelling

chesed: Goodness, kindness; charitable deeds.

chidushim: Novel interpretations of Torah and Talmudic subjects

Chillul Hashem: A desecration of Torah values and of God's name

chochmas hatorah: The wisdom of the Torah

chodosh: Literally, new; a newly harvested grain crop that is not to be eaten in the Land of Israel until after the first day of Passover

Chumash: The Pentateuch; the Five Books of Moses

chumrah, chumros (pl.): Stringency of Jewish behavior over and above behavior mandated by the basic legal rulings; extra piety

Cusi, Cusim (pl.): Samaritans (in Talmudic times); in general usage, refers to those of Jewish origin who deviate from Jewish tradition; non-Jews

D

da'as: Knowledge, good sense

daf: A folio, a page

darchei noam: Ways of pleasantness

daven: Pray

dayan, dayanim (pl.): A judge

de'oraisa: Of biblical, Torah origin

de'rabanan: Of rabbinic, Talmudic origin

derech: Path, way, direction in life

derech eretz: Moral behavior; societal courtesies and norms; general studies

derech halimud: Methodology of study

din: Law

dina demalchusa dina: Translated as: the law of a state is also the law for Jews who live in that state

domem: Inanimate objects

dveikus: An intimacy with holiness and a striving to connect to the Creator

E

edus: Testimony, proof

eirlich: Straight, trustworthy, loyal, principled

Eretz Yisrael: The Land of Israel

Erev Pesach: Passover eve

F

Four Species: The four species of vegetation used in the rituals of the holiday of Sukkos – citron, palm branch, myrtle leaves, and willow branches

frum: Pious, observant
frumkeit: Pious behavior; sometimes used to mean overly pious behavior

G

Gadol, Gedolim (pl.): Literally, large; a leading Torah scholar or *talmid chacham*
Gedolei Yisrael: The leading Torah scholars (or *talmidei chachamim*) of the Jewish People
Gehinom: Hell
Gemara: Talmud
geneivas da'as: The purposeful misleading of others; deceit; false appearances
get, gittin (pl.): A document of divorce
glatt (kosher): Literally, smooth; unquestionably kosher; a stringent definition of what is kosher

H

halachah, halachos (pl.): Torah law
halachic: Pertaining to Torah law
Hashem: A common reference to God; literally, the Name of God
hashkafah: Literally, a view; an ideology; a way of viewing life and the world; worldview
Haskalah: Enlightenment, a movement in eighteenth and nineteenth centuries devoted to substituting Jewish culture for Torah philosophy and observance as a basis for Jewish life
hefker: Literally, devoid of ownership; without responsibility or discipline
heter: A lenient halachic decision, a dispensation
hin: A liquid measurement

I

issur: A prohibition

K

Kabbolas Shabbos: Welcoming Shabbos, the prayer service on Friday evening before Shabbos evening service
Kareis: A severe Heavenly punishment for sin that affects longevity and/or immortality; literally, being cut off from life

kashrus, kosher: Describes the acceptability of foods to be eaten; more broadly, the permissibility of certain behavior or halachic acceptability

kavod habriyos: Honor, dignity, and sensitivity due to other human beings

kavod harabbonus: Honor, dignity, and sensitivity due to rabbis

kedushah: Holiness, sanctity

kehillah: The community; the community of Jews

Kehillas Yaakov: The community of Jacob; the Jewish People as a whole

Kehunah: The priesthood of the descendants of Aaron

ketores: The incense offering in the Holy Temple in Jerusalem

Kiddush: The ritual blessing over wine that ushers in Shabbos or a holiday

Kiddush Hashem: The sanctifying of God's name; exemplary pietistic behavior; martyrdom

kiddushin: Betrothal, marriage

klal mensch: A person who feels responsible for the community's welfare

Klal Yisrael: The Jewish People as a whole entity

kli mefoar: A glorious or beautiful vessel or utensil

kodshim: Sacrificial meat

Kohanim: The priestly descendants of Aaron

kol hamisga'eh: A display of arrogance or hubris toward others

kollel: An institution of advanced Torah studies for married men

Kol Nidrei: The prayer of disavowal of unintended vows that begins the Yom Kippur service

krias Shma: The recitation of the *Shma* prayer (which is, "Hear O Israel, the Lord is our God, the Lord is One" and subsequent paragraphs)

L

lashon hara: Evil speech, slander, gossip

l'shem Shamayim: For the sake of Heaven; selfless behavior

levado: He, alone

Levi'im: Descendants of the tribe of Levi

lishmah (*Torah lishmah*): For no ulterior motive; for the sake of Torah study alone; no personal gain involved

Lita: Lithuania

Litvaks: Lithuanian Jews

Litvishe: Lithuanian

Levirate marriage: the marriage of a childless widow to her brother-in-law

lo tisgodedu: Generally, a warning against forming separate groups within a synagogue or community; literally, not to cut one's skin in grief

M

Maariv: The prayer service recited at night

maaser sheni: The tithe of produce that was to be brought to Jerusalem and consumed there

machlokes: Dispute; dissension; the splitting of a family or community

mamzer, mamzerim (pl.): An illegitimate child

Maseches Derech Eretz: One of the so-called minor tractates added to the Talmud concerned with proper interactions between people

Mashgiach (of a yeshiva): Spiritual adviser

Mashiach: The Messiah

maskil: An "enlightened" one; a member of the movement that wished to "modernize" Judaism in nineteenth-century Lithuania

mazal: Fortune, luck

Mechilta: A halachic Midrash text commentary to the Book of Exodus

mechinah: A preparatory school or class for younger students before attendance at a yeshiva

mechusrei emunah: Those who are lacking in faith and integrity

mede'oraisa: Derived directly from the text of the Torah

mede'rabanan: Of rabbinic Talmudic origin

Megillas Esther: The Book of Esther

mekiz dam: Bloodletting

melachah: There were 39 *melachos* (labors) involved in building the *Mishkan* (see below). These labors, and their derivatives, constitute forbidden work on Shabbos; often translated as "work" or "task."

Melech Hamoshiach: The King Messiah

mensch: Literally, a person; generally, a good and moral person

menschlichkeit: Good and moral behavior

mesorah: Jewish tradition; laws and customs handed down from generation to generation

meurav bein habriyos: A congenial person who is accepted by others

middah, middos (pl.): A measure; a character trait

middos tovos: Good character traits

Midrash: The homiletic and aggadic commentary to the Tanach based on the Oral Tradition

mikol ha'adam: Distinguished from all other humans

mikveh: A ritual purification pool

Minchah: The afternoon prayer service

minyan: A required quorum of ten men for public prayer services

Mishkan: The Tabernacle of Moses built in the Sinai desert

Mishnah: The Oral Law of Sinai committed to writing under the editorship of Rabbi Judah the Prince (Rabbi Yehudah Hanasi) c.200 CE

Mishnayos (pl.): Segments of the Mishnah

Misnagdim: the opponents of the Chasidic movement, mainly centered in Lithuania

mitzvah, mitzvos (pl.): Commandment

mitzvah de'rabanan: A decree of rabbinic (not Torah) origin

mara de'asra: Literally, the owner of the place; generally, an alternate term for the rabbi of the community or synagogue

Moshe Rabbeinu: Moses our teacher

Mussar: Ethics, self-criticism, self-improvement

mussar mashgiach: A member of a yeshiva faculty, an adviser affiliated with the *Mussar* Movement; a spiritual adviser concentrating on matters of ethical behavior and self-improvement

Mussar Movement: The nineteenth-century movement in Lithuania devoted to the ethical improvement of Jewish society

N

negaim: Plagues, punishments

negi'ah: Literally, touching; generally, a prejudice or self-serving bias

neshamah: Soul

Nesiv Derech Eretz: The path of proper behavior toward other human beings and the world, generally

Nevi'im: Prophets

Noahide (Noahide laws): The seven laws given to the sons of Noah forbidding paganism, blasphemy, stealing, murder, sexual immorality, eating from the flesh of an animal while that animal still lives, and mandating the establishment of courts of justice

o

ohel mo'ed: The tent of assembly in the desert during the time of Moses; the Tabernacle/*Mishkan*

Olam Haba: The spiritual world to come; the immortality of the soul; the perfect world that will arise after the Messianic era (see world-to-come)

Olam Hazeh: This world; the material world in which we live

Oral Torah: Given by God to Moses and the Jewish People at Sinai and summarized in the Mishnah and Talmud

Oral Tradition: Teachings of Judaism given by God at Mount Sinai and passed down orally through the generations

p

parshah: A chapter of the Torah; the weekly portion of the Torah read in the synagogue on Shabbos

parush meahavah: A pious person who separates himself from normal life out of love for God

parush meyirah: A pious person who separates himself from normal life out of fear of God.

pasken: Deciding a halachic issue or question

passuk: A biblical verse

perushim: Originally, the Pharisees of Second Temple times; later, scholars in Lithuania who devoted themselves completely to study and piety, separating themselves from family and community; ascetics

pikuach nefesh: In the interest of saving a life; a matter of life and death

pilpulistic: A method of Talmudic study that emphasizes extreme creativity, and that doesn't focus on the meaning of the text

pinkas, pinkas ha'ir: Literally, a notebook or record; the official book of records of a family, community, or city

posek, poskim (pl.): A decider of Jewish law; one who rules on cases of halachah

psak: A definitive decision on a matter of halachah

R

Rabbinic prohibition: A series of edicts instituted by the rabbis of the Mishnah/Talmud to prevent erosion of Torah law

rabbonus: The rabbinate as an institution or profession

rasha: An evil person

rav: Rabbi, master or teacher

Rebbe: A Chasidic spiritual leader

rebbi, rebbeim (pl.): Teacher, mentor

Responsa: The rabbinic correspondence regarding questions of Torah law

Rishonim: The classical Talmudic commentators of the medieval era (c. 900–1500)

S

Second Temple: The Holy Temple founded in Jerusalem by Ezra after the Babylonian exile; destroyed in 70 CE

Sephardic: Spanish; referring to Jews and customs originally from Spain, in contradistinction to Ashkenazic Jews and customs

Seudah: A festive meal, particularly for Shabbos or a holiday

Shas: The Talmud. The term is an acronym of *Shishah Sedarim*, alluding to the Six Orders (sections) of the Mishnah

Shechinah: The Spirit of God; God's presence

shechitah: The ritual slaughter of poultry and animals

sheilah, sheilos (pl.): A question, query, or problem posed in Jewish law

shiva: The week-long period of mourning for a deceased relative

shleimus: Perfection, wholeness

shliach tzibbur: The cantor who leads the prayer services; literally, the agent of the community

shlita: Acronym of the Hebrew words that mean "may he live for many more good years," usually expressed after mentioning or writing the name of a distinguished living rabbi

Shma: Literally, hear; the term used to describe the main Hebrew prayer "Hear O Israel, the Lord is Our God, the Lord is One"

shochet: A ritual slaughterer of poultry and animals

shoresh: Literally the root; the basis

Shevi'is: Pertaining to the Sabbatical year

Shul: Synagogue

sidrah: The portion of the Torah reading of the week; the institution of Talmudic learning in ancient Babylonia

sifrei mussar: Books of *Mussar*, of ethics, philosophy, and moral behavior and standards

sinas chinam: Baseless hatred

T

tallis: A prayer shawl

talmid, talmidim (pl.): A student or disciple

talmid chacham, talmidei chachamim (pl.): A Torah scholar; one of the sages of old

talmid muvhak: The chosen, closest student of the mentor; the ultimate transmitter of the mentor's teachings and methodology

Talmud: The compendium of the Oral Law completed in sixth-century Babylonia and in the Land of Israel; it includes the Mishnah which was codified c. 200 C.E. and the Gemara, which is an elucidation of the Mishnah

tamei tzara'as: A physical affliction that indicates a spiritual affliction, as described in the Tanach

Tanach: The twenty-four books of the canon of the Hebrew Bible: The Five Books of Moses, the books of the prophets and the other holy books known as "Writings," such as Proverbs, Psalms, etc.

Tannaim: The master teachers and authors of the Mishnah

Targum: Onkelos the Aramaic translation of the Hebrew text of the Torah, written by Onkelos, a Greco-Roman second-century convert to Judaism, and which was based on the Oral Tradition

tefillin: Phylacteries worn by men during daily morning prayers

Telzer: Someone from the town or yeshiva of Telz in Lithuania

Telzer Rosh Yeshiva: The head of the yeshiva of Telz

Temple: The Holy Temple in Jerusalem; refers to both the First and the Second Temples

tiferes: Glory, beauty, nobility; one of the seven kabbalistic spheres of holiness tinok shenishba: Literally, a baby who was kidnapped and not raised in a Jewish manner; generally, anyone who has never received a basic Jewish education

Torah Temimah: A work of biblical commentary authored by Rabbi Baruch Epstein, nineteenth and twentieth centuries, Lithuania

Tosafos: A medieval detailed analytical series of glosses to the Talmud

Torah She'baal Peh: The Oral Law

treif: Non-kosher

Tur: A compilation of Jewish law authored by Rabbi Yaakov ben Aher, fourteenth century Spain

tzaddekes: A righteous, pious woman

tzaddik, tzaddikim (pl.): A righteous, pious man

tzedakah: Charity; proper, righteous deeds

"tzelem kop": Literally, "a cross in his head," a pejorative comment about Lithuanian Jews. It described the supposed lack of spiritual enthusiasm by Lithuanian Jews and their focus on study and intellectual analysis above all else. As usual with brief Yiddish expressions, it is impossible to convey the full flavor of the term in English.

tzibbur: The community; a congregation

tzitzis: The fringes worn by Jewish males on a four-cornered garment such as a *tallis*

tzomeach: Something that grows from the earth; vegetation (as a group)

tzuras hakehillah: The form and makeup of a community

w

world-to-come: Life after death, immortality; the eventual utopian perfection of this world

Written Torah: The Five Books of Moses

Y

Yaakov Avinu: Our father Jacob

Yad Hachazakah: The magnum opus of Maimonides (Rambam), twelfth century Spain, Morocco, and Egypt. It is a complete codification of all of Torah law, as found in the Talmud

yashrus: Straight, moral, honest behavior and thought

yeshiva, yeshivas (pl.): Schools of intensive Torah study

yeshivishe: Referring to the mores, customs, and lifestyles of yeshiva students

yetzer hara: Literally, evil inclination; improper desires and passions

Yishuv Hayashan: The original Jewish settlers in the Land of Israel in the eighteenth and nineteenth centuries, predating Zionism

Yissachar and Zevulun: Two sons of Jacob. The relationship of these two tribes of Israel is often used to describe a patron/scholar financial arrangement. Zevulun, the merchant, supports Yissachar, the *talmid chacham* – and they share equally in the great spiritual reward of the Torah learned

Yomim Noraim: The High Holidays – Rosh Hashanah and Yom Kippur

Yuharah: Arrogance, hubris

Z

zt"l: Acronym of "the memory of the righteous is a blessing"; a respectful phrase used after naming a deceased distinguished, pious person

Rabbinic Personalities: A Chronology

PERSONALITY	BIRTH	DEATH
Raban Yochanan ben Zakkai	5 BCE?	115?
Shammai	10 BCE	60 CE
Rabbi Akiva	15	135
Raban Shimon ben Gamliel	35?	110?
Rabbi Yehoshua ben Korchah	100?	175?
Rabbi Yehudah ben Kenusiah	120?	195?
Rabbi Yehudah Hanasi	140?	210?
Bar Kapara	155?	215?
Rabbi Chiya	160?	225?
Rabbi Yochanan Hasandlar	200	300
Rav Asi	230?	295?
Mar Ukva	235?	315?
Rav Safra	260?	325?
Rabah bar Nachmani	270	320
Rav Ashi	352	427
Rabbeinu Gershom	920?	985?
Rabbi Bachya ibn Pekuda	990?	1035?
Rashi	1040	1105
Rabbeinu Tam	1100	1171
Rambam	1135	1204
Ramban	1194	1270

The Legacy

PERSONALITY	BIRTH	DEATH
Rabbeinu Yonah ibn Gerundi	1210	1263
Smag – Rabbi Moshe of Coucy	1210?	1275?
Rabbeinu Bachya	1250?	1320?
Maharal – Rabbi Yehudah Loew	1520	1609
Maharsha – Rabbi Shmuel Eliezer Edels	1555	1631
Ramchal – Rabbi Moshe Chaim Luzzatto	1707	1746
Vilna Gaon – Rabbi Eliyahu Kramer	1720	1797
Dubno Maggid – Rabbi Yaakov Krantz	1741	1804
Rabbi Avraham Danzig	1748	1821
Rabbi Chaim Rabinowitz of Volozhin	1749	1821
Rabbi Shlomo Eiger	1760?	1830?
Rabbi Itzele Volozhiner	1780	1849
Rabbi Shlomo Kluger	1783	1869
Rabbi Yaakov Meklenberg	1785	1865
Rabbi Yosef Zundel of Salant	1786	1866
Rabbi Chaim Halberstam	1793	1876
Rabbi Yitzchak Meir	1799	1866
Rabbi Seligman Baer Bamburger	1807	1878
Rabbi Samson Raphael Hirsch	1808	1888
Rabbi Meir Leibush Malbim	1809	1879
Rabbi Yisrael Salanter (Rabbi Yisrael Lipkin)	1810	1883
Rabbi Aaron David Deutsch	1812	1878
Amshenover Rebbe – Rabbi Yaakov Kalish	1814	1878

PERSONALITY	BIRTH	DEATH
Netziv – Rabbi Naftali Tzvi Yehudah Berlin	1817	1893
Rabbi Yitzchak Elchanan Spektor	1817	1896
Rabbi Azriel Hildesheimer	1820	1899
Rabbi Simchah Zissel Ziev	1824	1898
Rabbi Yechiel Michel HaLevi Epstein	1829	1908
Rabbi Naftali Amsterdam	1832	1916
Rabbi Yitzchak Blazer	1837	1907
Rabbi Yisrael Meir Kagan	1838	1933
Rabbi Avraham Bornsztain	1838	1910
Rabbi Tzvi Hirsh Broida	1840	1913
Rabbi Eliezer Gordon	1840	1910
Rabbi Jacob Joseph	1843	1902
Rabbi Meir Simchah Cohen of Dvinsk	1843	1926
Rabbi David Tzvi Hoffman	1843	1921
Rabbi Dovid Willowski	1845	1914
Yom Tov Lipman Lipkin	1846	1875?
Rabbi Yoseph Y. Horowitz	1848?	1921?
Rabbi Eliyahu Baruch Kamai	1849	1917
Rabbi Nosson Tzvi Finkel	1849	1927
Rabbi Chaim Soloveitchik	1853	1918
Rabbi Chaim Rabinowitz	1856	1931
Rabbi Shimon Shkop	1860	1939
Rabbi Yosef Yehudah Lev Bloch	1860	1930
Rabbi Baruch Halevi Epstein	1860	1941
Rabbi Shimon Shkop	1860	1939
Rabbi Chaim Ozer Grodzensky	1863	1940
Rabbi Baruch Ber Leibowitz	1864	1939
Rabbi Moshe Mordechai Epstein	1866	1934
Rabbi Isser Zalman Meltzer	1870	1953
Rabbi Naftali Trop	1871	1928

PERSONALITY	BIRTH	DEATH
Rabbi Chaim Zvi Rubenstein	1872	1944
Rabbi Yerucham Levovitz	1873	1936
Rabbi Elchanan Wasserman	1875	1941
Chazon Ish – Rabbi Avraham Y. Karelitz	1878	1953
Rabbi Eliezer Yehudah Finkel	1879	1965
Rabbi Yosef Eliyahu Henkin	1881	1973
Rabbi Avraham Grodzensky	1883	1944
Rabbi Yosef Shlomo Kahaneman	1886	1969
Rabbi Dovid Leibowitz	1889	1941
Rabbi Yechezkel Sarna	1890	1969
Rabbi Aharon Kotler	1891	1962
Rabbi Avraham Yitzchak Bloch	1891	1941
Rabbi Yaakov Kaminetzky	1891	1986
Rabbi Avraham Kalmanowitz	1891	1965
Rabbi Eliyahu Dessler	1892	1953
Rabbi Mordechai Katz	1894	1964
Rabbi Elyah Meir Bloch	1894	1955
Rabbi Yechezkel Levenstein	1895	1974
Rabbi Moshe Feinstein	1895	1986
Rabbi Eliezer Menachem Mann Shach	1895	2001
Rabbi Eliezer Levin	1896	1992
Rabbi Mendel Zaks	1898	1974
Rabbi Mordechai Rogow	1901?	1957
Rabbi Menachem Mendel Schneerson	1902	1994
Rabbi Chaim Shmulevitz	1902	1979
Rabbi Yosef Dov Soloveitchik	1903	1993
Rabbi Zev Wein	1903	2006
Rabbi Menachem Tzvi Eichenstein	1910	1981
Rabbi Shmuel Belkin	1911	1976
Rabbi Yisrael Mendel Kaplan	1913	1985

PERSONALITY	BIRTH	DEATH
Rabbi Shlomo Wolbe	1914	2005
Rabbi Mordechai Gifter	1915	2001
Rabbi Chaim Kreisworth	1918	2001
Rabbi Azriel Chaim Goldfein	1935	2007

RABBI BEREL WEIN is the founder and director of the Destiny Foundation. For over twenty-five years, he has been identified as one of the foremost Orthodox historians in the world. Rabbi Wein is a recipient of the Torah Prize Award from Machon HaRav Frank in Jerusalem for his achievements in teaching Torah and spreading Judaism throughout the world. Rabbi Wein is a regular columnist for the  *Jerusalem Post*, and the author of many books, including *Vision & Valor: An Illustrated History of the Talmud*, also available from Maggid Books. He lives in Jerusalem.

RABBI WARREN GOLDSTEIN has been the Chief Rabbi of South Africa since January 2005. As a national leader, the Chief Rabbi drives Torah, humanitarian, and educational initiatives across South Africa. A qualified Dayan, Rabbi Goldstein's other published books include *Sefer Mishpat Tzedek*, on the *halachah* of business competition, and *Defending the Human Spirit*, which presents the  greatness of Torah law in areas of government, morality, and society. The Chief Rabbi has a PhD in human rights and constitutional law and is a regular columnist for the *Jerusalem Post*. www.chiefrabbi.co.za.

The fonts used in this book are from the Arno family

Maggid Books
The best of contemporary Jewish thought from
Koren Publishers Jerusalem